Lecture Notes in Computer Science 9016

Commenced Publication in 1973
Founding and Former Series Editors:
Gerhard Goos, Juris Hartmanis, and Jan van Leeuwen

More information about this series at http://www.springer.com/series/7412

Alain Trémeau · Raimondo Schettini
Shoji Tominaga (Eds.)

Computational
Color Imaging

5th International Workshop, CCIW 2015
Saint Etienne, France, March 24–26, 2015
Proceedings

 Springer

Editors
Alain Trémeau
University Jean Monnet
Saint-Etienne
France

Shoji Tominaga
Chiba University
Chiba
Japan

Raimondo Schettini
Dipartimento di Informatica Sistemistica
  e Comunicazione
Università degli Studi di Milano-Bicocca
Milano
Italy

ISSN 0302-9743
Lecture Notes in Computer Science
ISBN 978-3-319-15978-2
DOI 10.1007/978-3-319-15979-9

ISSN 1611-3349   (electronic)

ISBN 978-3-319-15979-9   (eBook)

Library of Congress Control Number: 2015933159

LNCS Sublibrary: SL 6 – Image Processing, Computer Vision, Pattern Recognition, and Graphics

Springer Cham Heidelberg New York Dordrecht London

Printed on acid-free paper

Springer International Publishing AG Switzerland is part of Springer Science+Business Media
(www.springer.com)

Preface

We welcome you to the proceedings of CCIW 2015, the Computational Color Imaging Workshop, held in Saint-Étienne, France, during March 24–26, 2015.

This fifth CCIW was organized by University Jean Monnet, Saint-Etienne, with the endorsement of the International Association for Pattern Recognition (IAPR), the *Association Française pour la Reconnaissance et l'Interprétation des Formes* (AFRIF) affiliated with IAPR, and the *Groupe Français de l'Imagerie Numérique Couleur* (GFNIC).

The aim of the workshop was to bring together engineers and scientists of various imaging companies and research laboratories from all over the world, to discuss diverse aspects of their latest work, ranging from theoretical developments to practical applications in the field of color imaging, as well as color image processing and analysis.

Since the first Computational Color Imaging Workshop organized in 2007 in Modena, Italy, CCIW has been an inspiration for researches and practitioners in the fields of digital imaging, multimedia, visual communications, computer vision, and consumer electronics, who are interested in the fundamentals of color image processing and its emerging applications.

For CCIW 2015 there were many excellent submissions of high scientific level. Each paper was peer reviewed by at least two reviewers. Only the best 17 papers were selected for presentation at the workshop. The final decision for the papers selection was based on the criticisms and recommendations of the reviewers, and the content relevance of papers to the goals of the workshop. In addition to the submitted papers, six distinguished researchers were invited to this fifth CCIW to present keynote speeches.

In this 5th Computational Color Imaging Workshop, challenging issues and open problems not sufficiently addressed in the state of the art were addressed. In the following, we summarize issues and problems that were covered by the papers accepted in CCIW 2015 or invited speeches, and put in perspective these papers relative to the other papers published recent in the state of the art.

The 5th Computational Color Imaging Workshop (CCIW 2015) was started on March 24, 2015 with a keynote presentation by Mathieu Hébert on *Color and Spectral Mixings in Printed Surfaces*. Meanwhile, many studies addressed issues related to color mixing, but very few studies were carried out on spectral mixing within the visible range. In his presentation, Mathieu Hébert presented different computational mixing models (additive, non linear additive, multiplicative, non linear multiplicative, etc.,) of spectra data for modeling of heterogeneous surfaces (e.g., textured materials, goniochromatic surfaces, printed samples, etc.,). Recently, spectral variability within an image has raised more attention in the field of hyperspectral images and some techniques have been proposed to address this issue, e.g., spectral bundles [33], but most of these techniques have been developed for spectral data outside the visible range.

In the Color reproduction session, Dmitry Kuzovkin et al. proposed an automatic method for example-based image colorization and a robust color artifact regularization method [15]. This paper proposed new improvements for color mapping which were not .

covered by the recent survey on color mapping written by H.S Faridul et al. [9]. In the next presentation, G.M. Atiqur Rahaman et al. proposed to extend the Murray–Davies reflectance model used for modeling spectral halftone images and to improve the efficiency prediction of this model to changes in reflectance by a power function [27]. Lastly, Ryosuke Nakahata et al. proposed a dynamic relighting method for moving planar objects with unknown reflectance [25]. By acquiring the surface spectral reflectance of moving objects, this method is able to reproduce accurate colors on a display device. This research topic is still largely unexplored. Most of the solutions using a projector-camera system were published recently in the state-of-the-art address issues related to photometric compensation but not to color compensation. Moreover, most of these papers deal with static surfaces and not with moving surfaces. However, wide range of applications such as augmented reality, education, cultural heritage, and interactive art installations could benefit from progress in this field.

Another challenging issue in computational color imaging is related to the color rendering of color reproduction. Some authors tried to improve this issue by improving first the color acquisition. In his invited speech, titled *The good, the bad and the ugly: the color we would like, the color we have, its appearance and dynamic range*, Alessandro Rizzi discussed some "hidden" issues, often not taken into account, related to color acquisition that can introduce severe errors in the color information [22]. Among these issues, he focused on the limits of accurate camera acquisition, the usable range of light of our vision system, and the role of accurate versus non-accurate luminance recording for the final appearance of a scene.

In the Color sensation and perception session, G.M. Atiqur Rahaman et al. investigated issues related to the acquisition and analysis of memory colors of objects found in natural scenes [28]. In the next presentation, João M.M. Linhares et al. investigated the effect on a display gamut of varying the optical density and the position of the maximum sensitivity of the cones spectra of anomalous trichromatic observers [16]. Lastly, Jorge L.A. Santos et al. investigated reaction times for normal color and dichromatic observers in a visual search experiment. [29]. These three papers addressed a wide range of problems related to vision science (i.e., to sensation and perception). As discussed by J.J. McCann in [23], the problems investigated in color image processing community are not only related to digital imaging disciplines but define an area of research on the frontier between vision science and image/display technology and must be addressed from several different perspectives/disciplines (physics, psychophysics, artificial intelligence, and fine arts). Thus, for example, according to J.J. McCann, the color appearance of a scene is not only correlated to the surfaces reflectance (which depend on the spectral distribution and the dynamic range of the illumination) and to the scene spatial content (e.g., a flat representation or a 3D scene), but also to the sensitivities of the human L, M, S cones.

The 5th Computational Color Imaging Workshop (CCIW 15) continued till March 25, 2015 with a presentation, by invited speaker, Joost Van de Weijer on *Color features in the era of big data*. The process of unsupervised feature learning (e.g., deep learning) has recently received a lot of attention in the field of computer vision. Meanwhile many studies were carried out only on color data, since recently few studies have been carried out on multimodal data (e.g., RGB and depth data [12] or RGD and temporal data [26]). However, several papers have demonstrated that machine learning plays an important role in bridging the gap between feature representations and decision making (e.g., for object/scene recognition, human pose estimation, and gesture/activity recognition) by learning useful information from a large set of RGB-D data [2]. In [2], Kai Berger discussed challenging issues related to the use of the publicly available datasets and suggested that in the following years there will still be challenges for multiple RGB-D sensors relying on the emission of light to be addressed by the community. One challenging issue of unsupervised feature learning is to benchmark dataset with ground truth (e.g., for video labelling). Unfortunately, very interesting datasets, such as the KITTI dataset, do not provide a semantic segmentation benchmark yet. In [32], Joost Van de Weijer et al. provided an overview of color name applications in computer vision, including image classification, object recognition, texture classification, visual tracking, and action recognition and demonstrated that in general color names outperform photometric invariants.

In the Color image processing session, Pablo Martinez-Canada et al. proposed a configurable simulation platform that reproduces the analog neural behavior of different models of the human visual system at the early stages [21]. Next, Yann Gavet et al. proposed to use the Color Logarithmic Image Processing (CoLIP) for white balance correction and color transfer [11]. Yann Gavet demonstrated that the CoLIP framework is correlated to the human visual perception system, as first, it follows the Weber/Fechner law with its logarithmic model and second, it is based on the opponent-process theory from Hering. Next, Gianluigi Ciocca et al. investigated the influence of color on the perception of image complexity. To this end they performed two different types of psychophysical experiments that they reported [6]. These three papers addressed a wide range of color image processing solutions related to vision science. Lastly, Andreas Kleefeld et al. proposed a new framework for color-valued median filters [14].

Another challenging issue in computational color imaging is related to the processing of spectral imaging data. In his invited speech, titled *Optics and Computational Methods for Hybrid Resolution Spectral Imaging*, Masahiro Yamaguchi introduced the concept of "Hybrid Resolution Spectral Imaging" (HRSI) and presented algorithms for reconstructing a spectral images [35]. The goal is to combine a high-resolution RGB image and a low-resolution spectral image in order to capture high resolution spectral video with a compact and handy camera system. Thanks to hybrid spectral imaging systems, it becomes possible to think of new applications and new developments in spectral imaging.

In the Spectral imaging session, Simone Bianco investigated if the performance of hyperspectral face recognition algorithms can be improved by considering 1D projections of the whole spectral data along the spectral dimension [3]. Feature band selection, dimensionality reduction, and feature extraction are challenging issues for face recognition task and also for other computer vision tasks. Even if, in the last ten years, many studies tried to solve these issues in the field of face recognition, several of them remain to be overcome. Similar issues remain to be overcome in other application fields. For example, Naveed Akhtar et al. proposed a sparse representation-based approach for hyperspectral image super-resolution [1]. They tested their approach using the hyper spectral images of objects, real-world indoor and outdoor scenes, and remotely sensed hyper-spectral images. In the next presentation, Hilda Deborah et al. proposed a spectral noise model using spectral database of uniform color/pigment patches, which answers the challenge of identifying spectral noise model [8]. Lastly, Xingbo Wang et al. investigated the colorimetric performance of CFA/MSFA-based image acquisition system [34]. Despite the number of studies dealing with spectral imaging, little attention has been given to the evaluation of the quality of spectral images and of spectral imaging systems. However, we can note that there is a general tendency to address this issue from several different perspectives (physics and psychophysics).

Next, in cooperation with the European COST action TD 1201, on March 26, 2015, a special session on Color in digital cultural heritage was organized.

The process of color digitization of 3D objects in cultural heritage has recently received much attention due to still improving quality and resolution of digital objects [19, 4, 5]. One tendency to improve color accuracy is to use a multispectral system. Thus, Jay Arre Toque et al. proposed to use a high-resolution multispectral scanning for mesoscopic investigation of discoloration of traditional Japanese pigments [30]. On the other hand, Ailin Chen et al. proposed to use a hyperspectral camera to visualize invisible information (i.e., outside the visible range) in paintings for restoration purpose [7].

Another tendency is to improve the performance of color-difference formulas [24] or to evaluate with these formulas if a color digitization system is accurate enough. Thus, Tatiana Vitorino et al. proposed to use the ColorChecker chart to assess the usefulness and comparability of data acquired with two hyper spectral systems [31]. On the other hand, Juan Martinez-Garcia et al. proposed to use a specular color chart to calibrate the color digitization of highly specular materials with a microscopic imaging system [20].

The process of 3D objects visualization in cultural heritage has also received much attention due to the development of color rendering and color correction algorithms. Some authors studied these issues from the observer's perspective (i.e., visual observation). Thus, Sergio Nascimento et al. investigated which color compositions observers prefer when they look at some paintings [17]. Other authors proposed to address these issues using photometry/spectrophotometry models. For example, Lindsay MacDonald in his invited speech, titled *Representation of Cultural Objects by Image Sets with Directional Illumination* addressed problems related to the modeling of the diffuse and specular reflectance of 3D objects and to the 3D surface reconstruction from photometric stereo [18]. Another approach consists of addressing these issues using computer vision models. For example, Zoltan Kato in his invited speech, titled *Relative Pose Estimation and Fusion of 2D Spectral and 3D Lidar Images* discussed problems related to the pose estimation without the use of any special calibration pattern or explicit point correspondence [13]. This paper addressed one of the most challenging issues in digital cultural heritage, which is the fusion of 2D RGB/spectral imagery with other 3D range sensing modalities (e.g., Lidar). On the other hand, Citlalli Gamez Serna et al.

proposed a semi automatic 2D-3D registration framework to produce accurate realistic results from a set of 2D uncalibrated images and a sparse 3D point cloud representation of an object digitized with laser scanning [10].

March 2015

Alain Trémea
Raimondo Schettini
Shoji Tominaga

Acknowledgments

Many organizations and people helped us in the planning of this meeting. Among them, we are pleased to acknowledge the generous support of the University Jean Monnet at Saint-Etienne, the Laboratoire Hubert Curien (UMR 5516) and Télécom Saint-Etienne, France, the University of Milano-Bicocca, Italy, and the Graduate School of Advanced Integration Science, Chiba University, Japan.

Special thanks to the COSCH action (COST action TD 1201) for the co-organization and co-funding of the special session on color in digital cultural heritage. The research laboratory hosting this workshop was supported by Saint-Etienne Métropole, the Région Rhone-Alpes (ARC 6, programme MONEITHS), and the PRES of Lyon (programme PALSE IRF).

Special thanks also go to all our colleagues on the Conference Committee for their dedication and hard work, without which this workshop would not have been possible.

References

1. Naveed Akhtar, Faisal Shafait, Ajmal Mian, Sparse Spatio-spectral Representation for Hyperspectral Image Super-resolution, Lecture Notes in Computer Science, Proceedings of ECCV Volume 8695, pp 63-78, 2014.
2. Kai Berger, A State of the Art Report on Multiple RGB-D Sensor Research and on Publicly Available RGB-D Datasets, Chapter 2, pp 27-44, Book titled Computer Vision and Machine Learning with RGB-D Sensors, Springer, 2014
3. Simone Bianco, Can linear data projection improve hyperspectral face recognition?, Proceedings of the 5th International Workshop CCIW'2015.
4. F. Boochs, A. Bentkowska, C. Degrigny, M. Karaszewski, A. Karmacharya, Z. Kato, M. Picollo, R. Sitnik and A. Trémeau, Colour and space in cultural heritage. Key questions in 3D optical documentation of material culture for conservation, study and preservation, Proceedings of the 5th International Conference EuroMed 2014, Best paper award, pp 11-14, Limassol, Cyprus, november 3-8, 2014.
5. F. Boochs, A. Trémeau, O. Murphy, M. Gerke, J.L. Lerma, A. Karmacharya, and M. Karaszewski. Towards a knowledge model bridging technologies and applications in cultural heritage documentation, Proceedings of the ISPRS Technical Commission V Symposium, pp 81-88, 23-25 June, Riva del Garda, Italy, 2014.
6. Gianluigi Ciocca, Silvia Corchs, Francesca Gasparini, Emanuela Bricolo, and Riccardo Tebano, Does color inuence image complexity perception? Proceedings of the 5th International Workshop CCIW'2015.

7. Ailin Chen, Colour Visualisation of Hyperspectral Images in Art Restoration. CIMET Master Thesis, Gjøvik University College, Norway.
8. Hilda Deborah, Noël Richard and Jon Yngve Hardeberg. Spectral Impulse Noise Model for Spectral Image Processing, Proceedings of the 5th International Workshop CCIW'2015.
9. H. S. Faridul, T. Pouli, C. Chamaret, J. Stauder, A. Tremeau, and E. Reinhard, A Survey of Color Mapping and its Applications, Eurographics 2014 - State of the Art Reports, pp. 43-67, 2014.
10. Citlalli Gamez Serna, Ruven Pillay, and Alain Trémeau, Data fusion of objects using techniques such as Laser Scanning, Structured Light and Photogrammetry for Cultural Heritage Applications, Proceedings of the 5th International Workshop CCIW'2015.
11. Yann Gavet, Johan Debayle, and Jean-Charles Pinoli, The Color Logarithmic Image Processing (CoLIP) antagonist space and chromaticity diagram, Proceedings of the 5th International Workshop CCIW'2015.
12. Md. Abul Hasnat, Olivier Alata and Alain Trémeau, Unsupervised RGB-D image segmentation using joint clustering and region merging, Oral presentation (7.7%) in the British Machine Vision Conference (BMVC), Nottingham, UK, Nottingham, Sept 2014.
13. Zoltan Kato, and Levente Tamas, Relative Pose Estimation and Fusion of 2D Spectral and 3D Lidar Images, Proceedings of the 5th International Workshop CCIW'2015.
14. Andreas Kleefeld, Michael Breub, Martin Welk, and Bernhard Burgeth, Adaptive Filters for Color Images: Median Filtering and its Extensions, Proceedings of the 5th International Workshop CCIW'2015.
15. Dmitry Kuzovkin, Christel Chamaret, and Tania Pouli, Descriptor-based Image Colorization and Regularization, Proceedings of the 5th International Workshop CCIW'2015.
16. João M.M. Linhares, Jorge L. A.Santos, Vasco M. N. de Almeida, Catarina A.R. João, and Sérgio M.C. Nascimento, The display gamut available to simulate colors perceived by anomalous trichromats, Proceedings of the 5th International Workshop CCIW'2015.
17. Sérgio M.C. Nascimento, João M.M. Linhares, Catarina A. R. João, Kinjiro Amano, Cristina Montagner, Maria J. Melo, Marcia Vilarigues, Estimating the colors of paintings, Proceedings of the 5th International Workshop CCIW'2015.
18. Lindsay MacDonald, Representation of Cultural Objects by Image Sets with Directional Illumination, Proceedings of the 5th International Workshop CCIW'2015.
19. Maciej Karaszewski1, Krzysztof Lech, Eryk Bunsch, Robert Sitnik, In the pursuit of perfect 3D digitization of surfaces of paintings : geometry and color optimization, Proceedings of the 5th International Conference EuroMed'2014, pp 25-34, Limassol, Cyprus, November 3-8, 2014.
20. Juan Martínez-García, Mathieu Hébert, and Alain Trémeau, Color calibration of an RGB digital camera for the microscopic observation of highly specular materials. Proceedings of the SPIE conference on Measuring, Modeling, and Reproducing Material Appearance, 9 - 10 February 2015.

21. Pablo Martinez-Canada, Christian Morillas, Juan Luis Nieves, Begona Pino,and Francisco Pelayo, First Stage of a Human Visual System Simulator: the Retina, Proceedings of the 5th International Workshop CCIW'2015.
22. John J. McCann and Alessandro Rizzi, The Art and Science of HDR Imaging, Wiley-IS&T Series in Imaging Science and Technology, ISBN: 978-0-470-66622-7, 416 pages, November 2011.
23. John J. McCann, Spatial imaging in color and HDR: Prometheus unchained, Proceedings of SPIE, Human Vision and Electronic Imaging XVIII, Vol. 8651, pp 865107, 2013.
24. Manuel Melgosa, Alain Trémeau, and Guihua Cui, Colour Difference Evaluation, Chapter 3, pp 59-79, Book title Advanced Color Image Processing and Analysis, C. Fernandez-Maloigne eds., 2013.
25. Ryosuke Nakahata, Keta Hirai, Takahiko Horiuchi, and Shoji Tominaga, Development of a Dynamic Relighting System for Moving Planar Objects with Unknown Reflectance, Proceedings of the 5th International Workshop CCIW'2015.
26. M. M. Nawaf, A. Trémeau, M.D. Abul Hasnat, D. D. Sidibé, Color and Flow Based Superpixels for 3D Geometry Respecting Meshing, Proceedings of the IEEE Winter Conference on Applications of Computer Vision (WACV 2014), Steamboat Springs, pp 147-154, march 24-26, 2014.
27. G M Atiqur Rahaman, Ole Norberg, and Per Edström, Experimental analysis for modeling color of halftone images, Proceedings of the 5th International Workshop CCIW'2015.
28. G M Atiqur Rahaman, and Md. Abul Hasnat, Collection, Analysis and Representation of Memory Color Information, Proceedings of the 5th International Worshop CCIW'2015.
29. Jorge L. A. Santos, Vasco M. N. de Almeida, Catarina A. R. Joa, Joao M. M. Linhares, and Sérgio M. C. Nascimento, Visual search for normal color and dichromatic observers using a unique distracter color, Proceedings of the 5th International Workshop CCIW'2015.
30. Jay Arre Toque, Pengchang Zhan, Peng Wang, and Ari Ide-Ektessabi, High-resolution multispectral scanning for mesoscopic investigation of discoloration of traditional Japanese pigments, Proceedings of the 5th International Workshop CCIW'2015.
31. Tatiana Vitorino, Andrea Casini, Costanza Cucci, Ana Gebejes, Jouni Hiltunen, Markku Hauta-Kasari, Marcello Picollo, and Lorenzo Stefani, Accuracy in colour reproduction: using a ColorChecker chart to assess the usefulness and comparability of data acquired with two hyper-spectral systems, Proceedings of the 5th International Workshop CCIW'2015.
32. Joost Van de Weijer and Hahad Khan, Color features in the era of big data, Proceedings of the 5th International Workshop CCIW'2015.
33. Miguel Angel Veganzones, Lucas Drumetz, Guillaume Tochon, Mauro Dalla Mura, Antonio Plaza, José M. Bioucas-Dias, and Jocelyn Chanussot, A New Extended Linear Mixing Model to Address Spectral Variability, Proceedings of the IEEE Workshop on Hyperspectral Image and Signal Processing: Evolution in Remote Sensing (WHISPERS 2014), Jun 2014, Lausanne, Switzerland.
34. Xingbo Wang, Phlip Green, Jean-Baptiste Thomas, Jon Hardeberg and Pierre Gouton. Evaluation of the colorimetric performance of single-sensor image acquisition

systems employing colour and multispectral filter array, Proceedings of the 5th International Workshop CCIW'2015.

35. Masahiro Yamaguchi, Optics and computational methods for hybrid resolution spectral imaging, Proceedings of the 5th International Workshop CCIW'2015.

Organization

CCIW 2015 was organized by University Jean Monnet, Saint-Etienne, France, in cooperation with the University of Milano-Bicocca, Italy and the Graduate School of Advanced Integration Science, Chiba University, Japan.

Executive Committee

Conference Chairs

Alain Trémeau   University Jean Monnet, Saint-Etienne, France
Raimondo Schettini   University of Milano-Bicocca, Italy
Shoji Tominaga   Chiba University, Japan

Program Committee

Ide-Ektessabi Ari, Japan
Sebastiano Battiato, Italy
Simone Bianco, Italy
Frank Boosch, Germany
Francesca Gasparini, Italy
Theo Gevers, The Netherlands
John Ynge Hardeberg, Norway
Markku Hauta Kasari, Finland
Mathieu Hébert, France
Javier Hernández-Andrés, Spain
Keigo Hirakawa, USA
Takahiko Horiuchi, Japan

Katsushi Ikeuchi, Japan
Hiroaki Kotera, Japan
Lindsay Macdonald, UK
Yoshitsugu Manabe, Japan
Damien Muselet, France
Sergio Nascimento, Portugal
Shigeki Nakauchi, Japan
Juan Luis Nieves, Spain
Jussi Parkkinen, Finland
Bogdan Smolka, Poland
Maria Vanrell, Spain
Joost van de Weijer, Spain

Local Arrangements Committee

Alain Trémeau   University Jean Monnet, Saint-Etienne, France
Eric Dinet   University Jean Monnet, Saint-Etienne, France
Mathieu Hébert   University Jean Monnet, Saint-Etienne, France
Juan Martinez   University Jean Monnet, Saint-Etienne, France
Damien Muselet   University Jean Monnet, Saint-Etienne, France
Olivier Alata   University Jean Monnet, Saint-Etienne, France

Keynote/Invited Talks

Alessandro Rizzi	Universitá degli Studi di Milano
Mathieu Hébert	University Jean Monnet, Saint-Etienne, France
Joost van de Weijer	Computer Vision Center, Barcelona, Spain
Masahiro Yamaguchi	Tokyo Institute of Technology, Tokyo, Japan
Zoltan Kato	Institute of Informatics, University of Szeged, Hungary
Lindsay McDonald	3DIMPact Research Group, University College London, UK

Sponsoring Institutions

University Jean Monnet, Saint-Etienne, France
University of Milano-Bicocca, Italy
Graduate School of Advanced Integration Science, Chiba University, Japan
International Association for Pattern Recognition (IAPR)
Groupe Français de l'Imagerie Numérique Couleur (GFINC), France
Association Française pour la Reconnaissance et l'Interprétation des Formes (AFRIF)
Laboratoire Hubert Curien (UMR 5516), Saint-Etienne, France
Télécom Saint-Étienne, France
COSCH action (COST action TD 1201), Germany
Saint-Étienne Métropole, France

Contents

Visual Search for Normal Color and Dichromatic Observers Using a Unique Distracter Color 111
Jorge L.A. Santos, Vasco M.N. de Almeida, Catarina A.R. João, João M.M. Linhares, and Sérgio M.C. Nascimento

First Stage of a Human Visual System Simulator: The Retina 118
Pablo Martínez-Cañada, Christian Morillas, Juan Luis Nieves, Begoña Pino, and Francisco Pelayo

Color Image Processing

The Color Logarithmic Image Processing (CoLIP) Antagonist Space and Chromaticity Diagram 131
Yann Gavet, Johan Debayle, and Jean-Charles Pinoli

Does Color Influence Image Complexity Perception? 139
Gianluigi Ciocca, Silvia Corchs, Francesca Gasparini, Emanuela Bricolo, and Riccardo Tebano

Adaptive Filters for Color Images: Median Filtering and Its Extensions 149
Andreas Kleefeld, Michael Breuß, Martin Welk, and Bernhard Burgeth

Spectral Imaging

Can Linear Data Projection Improve Hyperspectral Face Recognition? 161
Simone Bianco

Spectral Impulse Noise Model for Spectral Image Processing 171
Hilda Deborah, Noël Richard, and Jon Yngve Hardeberg

Evaluation of the Colorimetric Performance of Single-Sensor Image Acquisition Systems Employing Colour and Multispectral Filter Array 181
Xingbo Wang, Philip J. Green, Jean-Baptiste Thomas, Jon Y. Hardeberg, and Pierre Gouton

Color in Digital Cultural Heritage

High-Resolution Multispectral Scanning for Mesoscopic Investigation of Discoloration of Traditional Japanese Pigments 195
Jay Arre Toque, Pengchang Zhang, Peng Wang, and Ari Ide-Ektessabi

Data Fusion of Objects Using Techniques Such as Laser Scanning, Structured Light and Photogrammetry for Cultural Heritage Applications 208
Citlalli Gámez Serna, Ruven Pillay, and Alain Trémeau

Invited Talks

Color and Spectral Mixings in Printed Surfaces

Mathieu Hébert$^{(\boxtimes)}$, David Nebouy, and Serge Mazauric

CNRS UMR5516 Laboratoire Hubert Curien, Université de Lyon,
Université Jean Monnet de Saint-Etienne, 18 rue Benoît Lauras, F-42000 Saint-Etienne, France
mathieu.hebert@univ-st-etienne.fr

Abstract. The present paper discusses the concept of subtractive color mixing widely used in color hardcopy applications and shows that a more realistic concept would be "spectral mixing": the physical description of the coloration of light by printed surfaces comes from the mixing of light components selectively absorbed by inks or dyes during their patch within the printing materials. Some classical reflectance equations for continuous tone and halftone prints are reviewed and considered as spectral mixing laws. The challenge of extending these models to new inkless printing processes based on laser radiation is also addressed.

Keywords: Color mixing · Printing · Halftone colors · Spectral reflectance

1 Introduction

Color mixing is a key-concept in color reproduction, either by painting, printing, or displaying. It refers to the observation that a large panel of colors (the color gamut) can be achieved by varying the amount of a limited set of base colors, called primaries. With light emitting systems, the primaries are light sources, often with red, green and blue color, that are either superposed or juxtaposed with a shorter period than the visual acuity. Since the tristimulus values of the produced colors is a linear, additive combination of the tristimulus values of the three primaries, this type of color mixing has been called *additive color mixing*. This concept, based on Grassman's additivity law, enabled the color matching experiments at the basis of colorimetry [1]. In opposition to the light emitting systems, paintings and printed hardcopies selectively attenuate the incident white light in different proportions according to the wavelength. Layers of primaries, paints or inks, are coated on a reflecting support and play a role of spectral filtering of light. This type of color mixing is improperly called *subtractive color mixing* [2], by reference to the fact that part of the incident light is removed by filtering, but the tristimulus values of paint or ink mixtures cannot be obtained by combining the tristimulus values of the primaries; it is therefore not a color mixing in the sense of colorimetry.

However, the subtractive color mixing is also related to a physical experience, which consists in producing many colors by mixing nonscattering dyes, usually of cyan, magenta and yellow color. According to the Beer-Lambert-Bouguer law [1], the spectral absorption coefficient of the dye mixture, $K(\lambda)$, is a linear, additive

© Springer International Publishing Switzerland 2015
A. Trémeau et al. (Eds.): CCIW 2015, LNCS 9016, pp. 3–15, 2015.
DOI: 10.1007/978-3-319-15979-9_1

combination of the spectral absorption coefficients $K_j(\lambda)$ of the individual dyes. "Spectral mixing" would therefore be more exact than "color mixing". As the light is exponentially attenuated as a function of the traveled distance in the mixture layer, the *internal spectral transmittance* of a layer of mixture with thickness h is

$$t(\lambda) = e^{-K(\lambda)h} = \prod_j e^{-c_j K_j(\lambda)h} \tag{1}$$

where c_j denotes the relative concentration of each dye. By defining a reference concentration of each dye and a reference layer thickness, an internal transmittance $t_j(\lambda)$ can be attached to each primary, and the internal transmittance of the mixture can be written

$$t(\lambda) = \prod_j t_j^{\varepsilon_j}(\lambda) \tag{2}$$

where ε_j denotes the relative optical thickness of each dye, i.e. the product of its relative concentration and the layer thickness. Note that doubling the amounts of primaries or doubling the layer thickness yields same internal transmittance $t^2(\lambda)$, i.e. a double optical thickness. Mixing the dyes or coated them on top of each other would yields exactly the same color.

The Beer-Bouguer-Lambert law is an essential physical law to explain the colors achieved by painting and prints, but not sufficient because no object is a simple mixing or superposition of absorbing media. At least, the mixture has an interface with air whose optical effect cannot be neglected [3-4], and it is generally deposited on a support, specular or diffusing, whose internal reflectance has obviously capital impact of the final color. The refractive index of the layers may also have significant impact, as observed by stacking colored films on a white background with or without optical contact [5-7]. Lastly, the Beer-Bouguer-Lambert law is restricted to non-scattering media; extension to scattering media is possible but more difficult, except when scattering is sufficiently strong so that the Kubelka-Munk model applies [8-9].

Our intension in this paper is to review some spectral reflectance models developed for predicting the color of printed surfaces and present them as so many examples of *spectral mixing laws*. By recalling some of the main spectral mixing equations that have been physically validated on different types of printed surfaces [10-11], this study extends the recent study aiming at defining different color mixing systems for computer graphics applications [12]. For the sake of simplicity, we address only the case of printing on diffusing supports (paper, white polymer...) with inks assumed to be nonscattering. This already covers most classical printing systems such as woodcut, analog photography, offset, inkjet, laser jet, dye diffusion thermal transfer (D2T2) printing techniques [13]. We also address, in the last section, new inkless printing technologies being currently developed, which produce colors on laser-sensitive layers [14-15]. For the surfaces colored with these new processes, the classical concept of internal transmittance of primary, introduced above in the context of the Beer-Lambert-Bouguer law and used in most of the models reviewed here, needs to be revisited.

2   Spectral Mixing Laws for Contone Printing

Printing systems capable of depositing variable amounts of dyes on the support on each printable pixel, therefore able to produce uniformly colored surfaces as analog photographs, are called continuous tone, or "contone" printing systems. Thermal transfer and thermal diffusion printers belong to this category, especially dye diffusion thermal transfer (D2T2) printers used for proofing applications [13]. On an optical point of view, the structure of the print comprises: a diffusing support, a dye mixture layer, and the dye-air interface. The optical equation proposed in 1953 by Williams and Clapper for photograph prints [16], which have comparable structure, applies. Berns used a simplified version of this equation in 1993 to predict the spectral reflectance of D2T2 prints [17] by ignoring the diffuse or collimated angular distribution of light in the dye layer. The model is based on the spectral internal reflectance $\rho(\lambda)$ of the support and the spectral internal transmittance $t(\lambda)$ of the dye layer assumed to have same refractive index m (typically around 1.5). The reflectance and transmittance of the dye-air interface are computed on both faces according the angular distribution of the light and the measuring geometry: r_s denotes the specular reflectance of the interface (it is zero when the specular reflection is not viewed by the detector), $T_{in} = 0.95$ is the transmittance for incoming light at 45°, $T_{ex} = 0.96 / m^2$ is the transmittance for the exiting radiance at 0° (the term $1/m^2$ accounts for the effect of the refraction on the radiance [18]), and $r_i = 0.6$ is the reflectance at the dye side for the light diffuse by the support [18, 19]. The flux transfers between the support, the dye layer and the interface are presented in Fig. 1.

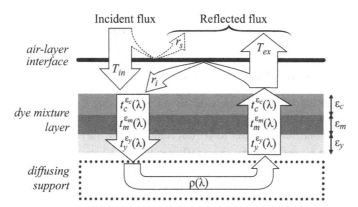

Fig. 1. Path of light in a coloring layer made of three dyes on top of a diffusing support, according to Berns' model

Finally, Berns equation is written:

$$R(\lambda) = r_s + \frac{T_{in}T_{ex}\rho(\lambda)t^2(\lambda)}{1 - r_i\rho(\lambda)t^2(\lambda)} \qquad (3)$$

When the dye layer is a mixture (or equivalently a superposition) of primary dyes, according to Beer's law (2), the internal transmittance $t(\lambda)$ is given by (2). The support's internal reflectance is deduced from the measured reflectance of the unprinted support. The internal transmittance of each primary, at unit optical thickness (maximum amount of dye), is deduced from the spectral reflectance measured on a color patch where this primary is alone.

3   Spectral Mixing Laws for Halftone Printing

Most traditional printing systems cannot transfer variable amount of ink on the support but deposit it according to a binary process. Color variations are thus produced by covering partially the surface according to a screen of patterns. this technique is called halftoning [20]. Once printed, the surface looks like a mosaic of colored areas, called *Neugebauer primaries*, resulting from the partial overlap of the primary ink patterns. For N printed inks, we have 2^N Neugebauer primaries. In classical clustered-dot or error diffusion prints, the fractional area occupied by each Neugebauer primary can be deduced from the surface coverages of the primary inks according to the Demichel equations [21], valid in all cases where the ink halftone dots are laid out independently, e.g. in stochastic screening, in error diffusion, or in mutually rotated clustered dot screens. For three primary inks with respective surface coverages c, m, and y, the surface coverages a_k of the eight primaries are respectively:

$$
\begin{aligned}
a_w &= (1-c)(1-m)(1-y) & a_{m+y} &= (1-c)my \\
a_c &= c(1-m)(1-y) & a_{c+y} &= c(1-m)y \\
a_m &= (1-c)m(1-y) & a_{c+m} &= cm(1-y) \\
a_y &= (1-c)(1-m)y & a_{c+m+y} &= cmy
\end{aligned}
\tag{4}
$$

3.1   The Yule-Nielsen Modified Spectral Neugebauer Equation

The Neugebauer equation is the only additive color mixing law applicable to printed surfaces. It relies on the simple idea that each primary k in the halftone, i.e. each area in the mosaic, contributes to the total reflectance of the surface in proportion of its surface coverage a_k, and with the same reflectance $R_k(\lambda)$ as in a large patch where it is printed alone. The spectral reflectance of a halftone print is thus written [22]

$$
R_H(\lambda) = \sum_k a_k R_k(\lambda)
\tag{5}
$$

This linear equation can be equivalently expressed in terms of tristimulus values, for example in the CIEXYZ 1931 color space:

$$
(X_H, Y_H, Z_H) = \sum_k a_k (X_k, Y_k, Z_k)
\tag{6}
$$

However, the use of the Neugebauer equation is very limited because it does not account for the possible travels of photons through different primaries, especially due to the scattering of light by the support. This phenomenon, called *optical dot gain* or *Yule-Nielsen effect* [23-24], may have considerable consequence on the spectral reflectance of the printed surface. The Neugebauer model is therefore limited to configurations without any scattering of light (e.g. transparent inks on nonscattering printed supports such as transparency films or mirrors) or where edge effects can be neglected because the primary areas are very large (very low halftone screen frequency).

In order to correct the Neugebauer model, Yule and Nielsen [23] established an empirical law that Viggiano used as a correction of the Neugebauer equation [25], yielding the Yule-Nielsen modified Spectral Neugebauer (YNSN) equation:

$$R(\lambda) = \left[\sum_k a_k R_k^{1/n}(\lambda) \right]^n \tag{7}$$

The n value is a real number, usually higher than 1, which generally increases as the printing support is more scattering or the halftone screen frequency increases [11]. However, it has been noticed that values below 1 or even negative could provide better agreement with the measurements, especially when the ink deeply penetrates the support [26-28].

The physical interpretation of the Yule-Nielsen correction has been explored along various axes, for example by modeling photon path probabilities in the different primaries [29-31]. Recently, an unsuccessful attempt to find other empirical corrections [32] suggests that this correction is the best expression of the physical reality. In most cases, its capacity to match the measured reflectance of halftones is very good, despite its disconcerting simplicity. However, the use of an exponential function in this correction is rather consistent with the physics of attenuation of light in absorbing media.

In addition to the already proposed interpretations, we add a simple one that, as far as we can see, has never been exposed. Let us first schematically consider that the reflection process of light is a succession of two events: the reflection by the support, with reflectance $\rho(\lambda)$, and the attenuation through the halftone ink layer. The reflectance of one Neugebauer primary printed alone is written

$$R_k(\lambda) = \rho(\lambda) T_k(\lambda), \tag{8}$$

where $T_k(\lambda)$ can be assimilated to an internal transmittance of the primary, and the Yule-Nielsen modified Spectral Neugebauer equation (7) is written

$$R(\lambda) = \rho(\lambda) \left[\sum_k a_k T_k^{1/n}(\lambda) \right]^n \tag{9}$$

If we subdivide the halftone layer into n identical sublayers of relative thickness $1/n$, the internal transmittance of each one, assuming that no scattering is allowed within it, is

$$\sum_k a_k T_k^{1/n}(\lambda) \tag{10}$$

where the power $1/n$ comes from the relative thickness $1/n$ of the sublayer, according to Beer's law.

The Yule-Nielsen equation (9) means that the light, while crossing the n sublayers, mixes completely between each sublayer as represented in Fig. 2 for $n = 2$: the primaries met by photons through the different sublayers are not correlated. Therefore, the Yule-Nielsen correction actually models the optical dot gain by an alternation of transmissions without scattering through the primaries and complete mixings of the transmitted light components. The n values determines the number of mixing events (which may be extended to real numbers) in the halftone layer, therefore the number of transitions between primaries statistically carried out by the photons. Note that even on transparency films where scattering is very low, the optimal n value is not 1 but rather around 2 [4].

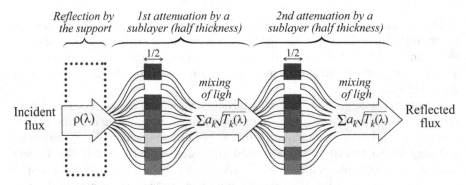

Fig. 2. Physical interpretation of the Yule-Nielsen model for $n = 2$

3.2   Multiplicative Equation for Halftone Colors

It is interesting to analyze the limit of the Yule-Nielsen modified Spectral Neugebauer model as n tends to infinity [26-28]. Let us write equation (7) as follows

$$R(\lambda) = \exp\left[n\log\left(\sum_k a_k R_k^{1/n}(\lambda)\right)\right] \qquad (11)$$

As n tends to infinity, $1/n$ tends to 0 and the terms $R_k^{1/n}(\lambda)$ tend to 1. Since the sum of the surface coverages a_k is 1, the term in the log function tends to 1, and the log function tends to its first order Taylor expansion:

$$\lim_{n\to\infty} \log\left(\sum_k a_k R_k^{1/n}(\lambda)\right) = \lim_{n\to\infty} \left(\sum_k a_k R_k^{1/n}(\lambda)\right) - 1 \qquad (12)$$

Using the first order Taylor expansion of the exponential function, we also have

$$\lim_{n\to\infty} R_k^{1/n}(\lambda) = \lim_{n\to\infty} \exp\left(\frac{1}{n}\log R_k(\lambda)\right) = \lim_{n\to\infty}\left[1 + \frac{1}{n}\log R_k(\lambda)\right] \qquad (13)$$

Finally, we can easily show from (12) and (13) that (11) tends to

$$R_{n \to \infty}(\lambda) = \lim_{n \to \infty} \exp\left[n \sum_k a_k \left(\frac{1}{n} \log R_k(\lambda)\right)\right] = \exp\left[\sum_k a_k \log R_k(\lambda)\right]$$
$$= \prod_k R_k^{a_k}(\lambda) \tag{14}$$

or, according to the notation introduced in (8), to

$$R_{n \to \infty}(\lambda) = \rho(\lambda) \prod_k T_k^{a_k}(\lambda) \tag{15}$$

This surprising result means that the Yule-Nielsen correction with infinite n transforms the additive Neugebauer equation into a multiplicative one, and the surface coverages into optical thickness as in (2). Pursuing our physical interpretation of the correction, infinite n means infinity of infinitesimal sublayers, which is comparable to a homogenous mixture of the inks for which the Beer-Lambert-Bouguer law applies. This model is particularly suitable to halftones printed on very porous supports such as cotton fabrics, in which the inks deeply penetrate and strongly spread so that the halftone patterns almost completely disappear.

3.3 The Clapper-Yule Equation

The model introduced in 1953 by Clapper and Yule [33] for the spectral reflectance of single-ink halftone prints follows the same approach as Berns' model for contones with a halftone ink layer in place of the dye mixture layer. The Clapper-Yule equation extended to multi-ink halftones is

$$R(\lambda) = r_s + \frac{T_{in} T_{ex} \rho(\lambda) \left[\sum a_k t_k(\lambda)\right]^2}{1 - \rho(\lambda) r_i \left[\sum a_k t_k^2(\lambda)\right]} \tag{16}$$

where r_s, T_{in}, T_{out}, r_i and $\rho(\lambda)$ have same meaning as in Berns' equation (3).

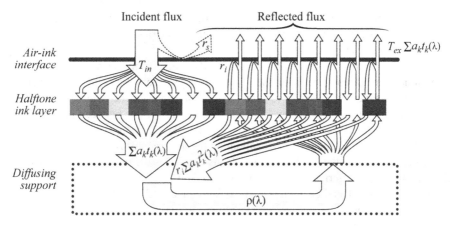

Fig. 3. Path of light in a halftone ink layer on top of a diffusing background, according to the Clapper-Yule model

The squared sum in the numerator of (16) denotes the transmissions of the incident light and the exiting light through the halftone ink layer. The sum in the denominator denotes the double attenuation of light issued from the diffusing support that is internally reflected by the interface through each primary, as represented in Fig. 3. The corresponding reflectance is $r_i \sum a_k t_k^2$. The diffusing support collects the light components issued from the primaries and mixes them completely.

As for Berns' model, the internal reflectance of the support and the internal transmittance of primaries are deduced from the spectral reflectances measured on the unprinted support and on patches where each Neugebauer primary is printed alone.

Note that both Yule-Nielsen modified Spectral Neugebauer model and the Clapper-Yule model have been transposed to transmittance, including the possibility to address duplex prints [34-37].

4   Real and Virtual Primaries

The previously introduced spectral mixing laws are adapted to classical printing systems where the number of primaries is finite: woodcut printing, offset, inkjet, electro-photography, dye sublimation… [13]. However, they appear to be too limited for new inkless printing technologies based on laser-sensitive layers being currently developed. The concept of primary needs to be reviewed. In order to better understand the challenge of calibrating these printing processes, it is useful to recall how the classical prediction models mentioned above are calibrated.

4.1   Calibration of Models for Traditional Printing Systems

The reflectances of the primaries in the Yule-Nielsen modified Spectral Neugebauer model, or their internal transmittances in the Berns and Clapper-Yule models, are directly deduced from the measured spectral reflectances of the single-primary color printed on the support. Then, in order to predict the spectral reflectance of any printable color, there is nothing else but getting the quantities (optical thicknesses or, accordingly, surface coverages) of the different primaries that have been actually transferred on the support.

In D2T2 printing, for example, we can verify that, for any printed color, we can find values for the optical thicknesses ε_c, ε_m and ε_y of the three primaries so that the spectral reflectance predicted by (3) and the measured one correctly match. According to our experiments carried out over 54 patches, the deviations between predicted and measured spectra, assessed in terms of CIELAB 1994 ΔE, were 0.43 unit in average, and 1.3 at maximum, which enables validating the accuracy of Berns' equation.

Full calibration of the predictive models also includes the correspondence between the amounts of transferred dyes or printed inks and the CMYK color coordinates of the digital layout. Detailed methods are described in [12] for halftone printing and [17] for contone printing.

4.2   Challenges of Calibrating Inkless Printing Technologies

A new generation of inkless printing techniques is currently developed where an achromatic photosensitive layer is coated on a support, then irradiated with lasers in order to reveal the colors. A first example is the laser microinscription system on silver-containing titania films presented in [14]. Many different angle- and polarization-dependent colors may be produced by varying the laser command parameters (irradiance, wavelength, polarization, exposure…). The concept of primary would need to be extended at least to angle and polarization variations.

Another example is the color laser marking (CLM) system based on the selective bleaching of a mixture of cyan, magenta and yellow dyes under laser irradiation [15]. the bleachable dye mixture is coated on a polymer substrate then overlaid by a clear polymer sheet. The laser irradiation enables bleaching uniformly the dye mixture layer over a large area (see examples in Fig. 4). The structure of the print is comparable to the contone prints and Berns' equation (3) applies.

Fig. 4. Microscopic images of areas printed with the CLM technology by using different laser wavelengths and powers. The coloring layer is nearly continuous, no halftoning is needed.

The ideal bleaching process would transform the initial colored dyes into clear ones, but in practice, new color dyes appear due to photo- or thermo-chemical mechanisms. The consequence is that the initial mixture of the three dyes with known internal transmittances is transformed into a mixture containing more dyes with unknown internal transmittances.

We tried to reproduce the classical calibration procedure explained in Section 4.1 for the D2T2 printer, by using samples where each of the three bleachable dyes cyan, magenta and yellow are coated alone. From the spectral reflectances of these samples, we deduced their respective internal transmittances. Then, for 570 other printed patches, we searched for their respective optical thicknesses in order to have the best agreement between the spectral reflectance predicted by the Berns' equation (3) and the measured one. The average CIELAB 1994 ΔE value over these 570 patches was of 4.2 units, with a maximum of 7.1 units. This poor accuracy shows that this method fails with the CLM printing whereas is was performing for the D2T2 printing. The question is therefore how to obtain effective primaries able to reconstruct the spectral space generated by the printing process. One possible solution to get them is to use a principal component analysis (PCA) [17].

4.3   Mixing Virtual Primaries Obtained by PCA

We selected a set of 130 patches printed in CLM, measured their spectral reflectances, deduced from them the 130 spectral internal transmittances of transformed dye mixtures, and finally performed the PCA on these 130 internal transmittances. The PCA is computed by creating a rectangular matrix $\mathbf{M}$ whose rows correspond to the spectral internal transmittances, then by diagonalizing the Gramian matrix $\mathbf{M}^T\mathbf{M}$ [38-39]. Most eigenvalues of $\mathbf{M}^T\mathbf{M}$ are close to zero; the number of eigenvalues with significant value indicates the dimensionality of the spectral space [40], the significance of eigenvalues being assessed by the cumulative percentage variance defined in [38]. The corresponding eigenvectors will be used as the spectral internal transmittances of virtual primaries.

The ten highest eigenvalues obtained from 130 spectral reflectances of CLM patches are shown in Table 1. The cumulative percentage variance reaches 100% with the four highest eigenvalues: the dimensionality of the spectral space generated by the CLM is therefore 4. By using the four corresponding eigenvectors as internal spectral transmittances in equations (2) and (3), and by searching for their respective optical thicknesses yielding the best agreement between the predicted and measured spectral reflectances for each of the 570 printed patches, we obtained an average CIELAB ΔE_{94} value between predicted and measured spectra of 0.55 units (maximum of 1.88 units). With six eigenvectors instead of four, the average ΔE_{94} became 0.10 unit (maximum of 0.39 unit). This represents an appreciable gain in accuracy compared to the classical method based on 3 real primaries, and shows that the spectral mixing concept can be extended to "virtual primaries" (containing however all physical information from the measured spectra used in the learning step of the model) when the "real primaries" cannot be clearly identified.

For comparison, we also tested this method from 54 CMY patches printed in D2T2. Compared to CLM printing, similar cumulative variances are achieved with one primary less (Table 1). We can estimate that the dimensionality of the spectral space in D2T2 printing is 3, which is consistent with the fact that three dyes are transferred almost independently of each other [17].

Table 1. Ten highest eigenvalues of the Gramian matrix computed from spectral reflectances of patches printed with the CLM printing process and a D2T2 printer

CLM printing process										
Eigenvalue e_i	2401	65.6	14.5	4.0	0.37	0.30	0.03	0.02	0.01	0.005
Cumulative % variance	**96.6**	**99.2**	**99.8**	**100**	100	100	100	100	100	100
D2T2 printer										
Eigenvalue e_i	529	146.4	106.0	0.12	0.11	0.03	0.01	0.008	0.002	0.001
Cumulative % variance	**67.7**	**86.4**	**100**	100	100	100	100	100	100	100

5   Conclusions

In this work, we recalled the main predictive equations for the spectral reflectance of printed surfaces: Berns' equation, applicable to contone prints, and the Yule-Nielsen modified Spectral Neugebauer and the Clapper-Yule model applicable to halftone prints, by showing explicitly how they model the spectral attenuations of fluxes in the colored primaries. We espcially reviewed the physical interpretation of the Yule-Nielsen correction for the Neugebauer equation by showing that it actually models the optical dot gain as an alternation of transmissions of light through the primaries (pure absorption without scattering and transition to other primaries), and complete mixings of the transmitted light components. We also highlighted the two limits of this model according to the value of its tunable parameter n: one limit is the additive Neubaeur equation (only case of additive color mixing applicable to printed surfaces), and the opposite limit is the multiplicative equation where the halftone ink layer tends to become a continuous ink layer. These equations can be considered as spectral mixing laws giving a more physical meaning to the usual concept of subtractive color mixing.

For the new inkless printing technologies based on laser irradiation, these classical models must be extended in order to cope with angle- and polarization dependent colors or to cope with the apparition of unknown primaries without simple correlation with the input parameters of the printing system. However, using a principal component analysis on a large set of printed samples, we can obtain the spectral parameters of a finite number of "virtual primaries" and use them in the classical mixing laws, while keeping satisfying agreement between the predicted and measured spectral reflectances of the printed samples.

Acknowledgement. This work was supported by the French National Research Agency (ANR) within the program "Investissements d'Avenir" (ANR-11-IDEX-0007), in the framework of project PHOTOFLEX n°ANR-12-NANO-0006 and the LABEX MANUTECH-SISE (ANR-10-LABX-0075) of Université de Lyon.

References

1. Wyszecki, G., Stiles, W.S.: Color science: Concepts and methods, quantitative data and formulae, 2nd edn. Wiley, New York (1982)
2. Sharma, G.: Color fundamentals for digital imaging. In: Color imaging handbook. CRC Press, New-York (2003)
3. Saunderson, J.L.: Calculation of the color pigmented plastics. J. Opt. Soc. Am. A **32**, 727–736 (1942)
4. Machizaud, J., Hébert, M.: Spectral transmittance model for stacks of transparencies printed with halftone colors. In: Proc. IS&T/SPIE Electronic Imaging Symposium, SPIE Vol. **8292**, pp. 829240.1–10 (2012)
5. Simonot, L., Hébert, M., Hersch, R.D.: Extension of the Williams-Clapper model to stacked nondiffusing colored coatings with different refractive indices. J. Opt. Soc. Am. A **23**, 1432–1441 (2006)

6. Hébert, M., Hersch, R.D., Simonot, L.: Spectral prediction model for piles of nonscattering films. J. Opt. Soc. Am. A **25**, 2066–2077 (2008)

7. Hébert, M., Machizaud, M.: Spectral reflectance and transmittance of stacks of nonscattering films printed with halftone colors. J. Opt. Soc. Am. A **29**, 2498–2508 (2012)

8. Kubelka, P.: New contributions to the optics of intensely light-scattering material, part I. J. Opt. Soc. Am. A **38**, 448–457 (1948)

9. Emmel, P.: Physical models for color prediction. G, Bala, R. Digital Color Imaging Handbook. CRC Press, New York, In Sharma (2003)

10. Wyble, D.R., Berns, R.S.: A critical review of spectral models applied to binary color printing. Color Res. Appl. **25**, 4–19 (2000)

11. Hébert, M., Hersch, R.D.: Review of spectral reflectance prediction models for halftone prints: calibration, prediction and performance. Color Res. Appl. (2014). doi:10.1002/col.21907

12. Simonot, L., Hébert, M.: Between additive and subtractive color mixings: intermediate mixing models. J. Opt. Soc. Am. A **31**, 58–66 (2014)

13. Kipphan, H.: Handbook of Print Media. Springer Verlag, Berlin (2001)

14. Crespo-Monteiro, N., Destouches, N., Bois, N., Chassagneux, F., Reynaud, S., Fournel, T.: Reversible and irreversible laser microinscription on silver-Containing mesoporous titania films. Adv. Mater. **22**, 3166–3170 (2010)

15. Lutz, N., Zinner, G.: Plastic body, which is provided in the form of a film, for example, a transfer film or laminate film or which is provided with a film of this type, and method for producing color image on or in a plastic body of this type. Patent US2004043308 (2004)

16. Williams, F.C., Clapper, F.R.: Multiple Internal Reflections in Photographic Color Prints. J. Opt. Soc. Am. **43**, 595–597 (1953)

17. Berns, R.S.: Spectral modeling of a dye diffusion thermal transfer printer. J. Electron. Imaging **2**, 359–370 (1993)

18. Hébert, M., Hersch, M.: Classical Print Reflection Models: A Radiometric Approach. J. Im. Sci. Technol. **48**, 363–374 (2004)

19. Judd, D.B.: Fresnel reflection of diffusely incident light. Journal of the National Bureau of Standards **29**, 329–332 (1942)

20. Kang, H.R.: Digital color halftoning. SPIE Publications, Washington (1999)

21. Demichel, M.E.: Procédés **26**, 17–21 (1924)

22. Neugebauer, H.E.J.: Die theoretischen Grundlagen des Mehrfarbendrucks. Zeitschrift fuer wissenschaftliche Photographie 36, 36-73 (1937). Translated into English: The theoretical basis of multicolour letterpress printing. Color Res. App. 30, 322-331 (2005)

23. Yule, J.A.C., Nielsen, W.J.: The penetration of light into paper and its effect on halftone reproduction. Proc. TAGA **3**, 65–76 (1951)

24. Ruckdeschel, F.R., Hauser, O.G.: Yule-Nielsen effect in printing: a physical analysis. Appl. Opt. **17**, 3376–3383 (1951)

25. Viggiano, J.A.S.: The Color of Halftone Tints, Proc. TAGA, 647–661 (1985)

26. Lewandowski, A., Ludl, M., Byrne, G., Dorffner, G.: Applying the Yule-Nielsen equation with negative n. J. Opt. Soc. Am. A **23**, 1827–1834 (2006)

27. Viggiano, J.A.S.: Ink Penetration, Isomorphic Colorant Mixing, and Negative Values of Yule-Nielsen n. In: Proc. IS&T 18th Color and Imaging Conference (Springfield, VA), pp. 285–290 (2010)

28. Viggiano, J.A.S.: Physical Significance of Negative Yule-Nielsen n-value. In: Proc. IS&T International Congress of Imaging Sciences (Rochester, NY), pp. 607–610 (2006)

29. Arney, J.S.: A probability description of the Yule-Nielsen effect, I: Tone reproduction and image quality in the graphic arts. J. Im. Sci. Technol. **41**, 633–636 (1997)

30. Arney, J.S., Kutsube, M.: A probability description of the Yule-Nielsen effect. II : The impact of halftone geometry : Tone reproduction and image quality in the graphic arts. Recent Progress in Digital Halftoning II 41, 637–642 (1999)
31. Ruckdeschel, F.R., Hauser, O.G.: Yule-Nielsen effect in printing: a physical analysis. Appl. Opt. **17**, 3376–3383 (1997)
32. Hébert, M.: Yule-Nielsen effect in halftone prints: graphical analysis method and improvement of the Yule-Nielsen transform. In: Proc. SPIE 9015, Color Imaging XIX: Displaying, Processing, Hardcopy, and Applications, (San Francisco, CA) 90150R (2014)
33. Clapper, F.R., Yule, J.A.C.: The Effect of Multiple Internal Reflections on the Densities of Halftone Prints on Paper. J. Opt. Soc. Am. **43**, 600–603 (1953)
34. Hébert, M., Hersch, R.D.: Reflectance and transmittance model for recto-verso halftone prints. J. Opt. Soc. Am. A **23**, 2415–2432 (2006)
35. Hébert, M., Hersch, R.D.: Reflectance and transmittance model for recto-verso halftone prints: spectral predictions with multi-ink halftones. J. Opt. Soc. Am. A **26**, 356–364 (2009)
36. Mazauric, S., Hébert, M., Simonot, L., Fournel, T.: Two-flux transfer matrix model for predicting the reflectance and transmittance of duplex halftone prints. J. Opt. Soc. Am. A **31**, 2775–2788 (2014)
37. Hébert, M., Hersch, R.D.: Yule-Nielsen based recto-verso color halftone transmittance prediction model. Applied Optics **50**, 519–525 (2011)
38. Tzeng, D.Y., Berns, R.S.: A review of principal component analysis and its applications to color technology. Color Research & Application **30**, 84–98 (2005)
39. Bugnon, T.: Flexible and Robust Calibration of the Yule-Nielsen Model for CMYK Prints. PhD Dissertation, Ecole Polytechnique Fédérale de Lausanne, Switzerland (2011)
40. Hardeberg, J.Y.: On the spectral dimensionality of object colours. In: Proc. IS&T Conference on Colour in Graphics, Imaging, and Vision (CGIV2002), pp. 480–485 (2002)

An Overview of Color Name Applications in Computer Vision

Joost van de Weijer[1]([⊠]) and Fahad Shahbaz Khan[2]

[1] Computer Vision Center Barcelona, Edifici O, Campus UAB,
Bellaterra 08193, Spain
joost@cvc.uab.es
[2] Computer Vision Laboratory, Linköping University, Linköping, Sweden

Abstract. In this article we provide an overview of color name applications in computer vision. Color names are linguistic labels which humans use to communicate color. Computational color naming learns a mapping from pixels values to color names. In recent years color names have been applied to a wide variety of computer vision applications, including image classification, object recognition, texture classification, visual tracking and action recognition. Here we provide an overview of these results which show that in general color names outperform photometric invariants as a color representation.

Keywords: Color features · Color names · Object recognition

1   Introduction

Color is one of the important characteristics of materials in the world around us. As such it is one of the important features for computer vision systems in their task to understand visual data. Its description however is complicated due to many scene accidental events such as unknown illuminant, presence of shadows and specularities, unknown acquisition system and image compression. As a result many researchers ignored color and only extracted information from the luminance channel. However, it has been shown that for many applications, ranging from image retrieval and object recognition to visual tracking and texture recognition, color description is crucial for obtaining state-of-the-art results.

There exist two main methodologies to the color description problem. The first methodology is based on reflection models which describe the interaction of light, material and sensors [5,6,8]. From these reflection models photometric invariant descriptions of the material color can be derived. Given certain assumptions these descriptors can overcome the dependence of the color description on scene accidental events. Examples are color descriptions which are invariant to illuminant color, shadow-shading and specularities[4,19,22]. The main advantage of these methods is that they do not need training data and therefore do not require a laborious and costly labeling phase. The main drawback of these

A. Trémeau et al. (Eds.): CCIW 2015, LNCS 9016, pp. 16–22, 2015.
DOI: 10.1007/978-3-319-15979-9_2

Fig. 1. Example of pixelwise color name annotation. The color names are represented by their corresponding color.

methods is that the assumptions on which they are based (for example white illumination, known acquisition device, etc) limit their application. Typically they require high-quality images without compression artifacts, and are not very effective for the medium quality images which are currently used in the many large scale data sets which have been collected from the internet.

The second methodology to color description is based on color names. Color names are words that refer to a specific color and are used by humans to communicate colors. Examples of color names are 'blue', 'crimson' and 'amber'. Humans use color names routinely and seemingly without effort. They have been primarily studied in the fields of visual psychology, anthropology and linguistics [7]. Basic color terms have been studied in the influential work of Berlin and Kay [2]. They are defined as those color names in a language which are applied to diverse classes of objects, whose meaning is not subsumable under one of the other basic color terms, and which are used consistently and with consensus by most speakers of the language. Basic color names were found to be shared between languages. However the number of basic terms varies from two in some indigenous languages to twelve in for example Russian. Most computer vision works, and also this paper, consider the eleven basic color terms of the English language: black, blue, brown, grey, green, orange, pink, purple, red, white, and yellow.

Computational color naming[1,18,23] aims to learn a mapping from pixel values to color name labels (see Fig. 1). A clear example in computer vision where color names are desired is within the context of image retrieval, where a user might want to query for images with "blue sofas". The system recognizes the color name "blue", and orders the retrieved results on "sofa" based on their resemblance to the human usage of "blue'. Later research showed that color names actually also constitute an excellent color descriptor. They where found to be robust to photometric variations, while having in general higher discriminative power than the photometric invariants.

In recent years, the two approaches to color description, namely, the physics-based and the color name methods, have been compared on a wide variety of computer vision applications. Constantly, color names where found to outperform the physics-based approaches by a significant margin. Color names have been extensively tested in image classification tasks [11,13], object recogni-

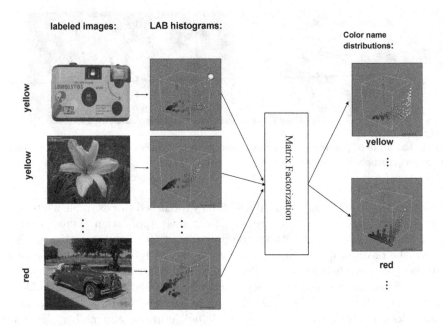

Fig. 2. Overview of approach to learn color names presented in [23]

tion [12], and action recognition [9]. Similar results where reported for texture classification[10], visual tracking [3] and person reidentification [24]. For image retrieval results for color names are reported in [16][25] and recently it was used for improved illumination estimation[20]. The main reason for this success is the high discriminative power which color names possess, while being robust to photometric variations in images.

In this paper, we first outline the different approaches which exist to computational color naming. In section 3 we present an overview of the results we obtained when comparing color names to other color representations. After which we discuss conclusion and future outlook for color name research in section 4.

2   Color Names

There are two main approaches to computational color naming, the main difference is the nature of their training data, either being calibrated or uncalibrated. In a calibrated setup, multiple subjects are asked to label hundreds of color chips within a well-defined experimental setup [15,17]. The colors are to be chosen from a preselected set of color names (predominantly the set of 11 basic color terms). Examples of color name mappings based on calibrated data are the work of Mojsilovic [18] and Benavente et al. [1]. The latter proposed a parametric method to model color names. They introduce a fuzzy model which is fitted to data obtained from psychophysical experimental data. This data is well calibrated, meaning that the color samples are presented in a controlled laboratory environment under stable viewing conditions with known illuminant. These studies are very relevant within the fields of linguistics and color science. However, for applications in computer vision which are often based on uncalibrated data, these mappings learned under perfect circumstances were often found to underperform.

In [23], we proposed a different approach to learning color name mappings, which is based on uncalibrated data obtained from 'Google image'. For this data the illuminant, acquisition system and amount of compression are unknown. An overview of this method is provided in Fig. 2. The images from 'Google images' are represented as LAB histograms after which they are joined in one large data matrix. An adapted probabilistic latent semantic analysis (PLSA) is applied to factorize the matrix into mixture coefficients and topic distributions. Here the topic distributions are the probabilities of colors to occur for a certain color name. An advantage of this method, over the calibrated mappings described above, is that it is more robust to scene accidental events, such as slight illuminant changes, shadows, image compression, etc. Therefore this approach is more popular for computer vision applications, and in the next section we provide an overview of its usage.

It is interesting to interpret color names in terms of photometric invariance theory which was developed by physics-based research to color. Color names typically are elongated along the intensity axes (or achromatic axis) of the color space, and more compact in the hue direction. As a result color names typically describe a group of colors which have similar hue but vary significantly in saturation and luminance. The hue is known to be a photometric invariant with respect to shadow, shading and specularities. Since the color names typically group colors of equal hue it can be said to be photometrically robust. Color names however significantly differ from photometric invariants along the achromatic axes. Here photometric invariance do not differ between light and dark colors and are often instable for dark and achromatic colors. On the other hand there are three color names, black, grey and white, which allow to distinguish between these sections of the color space. As a result, color names do not have the drop in discriminative power along the achromatic axis which is observed for photometric invariants [14].

3 Color Names Applications in Computer Vision

Here we provide an overview of the experiments over the last couple of years, where we have used color names and compared them to photometric invariants.

As discussed above, the main advantage of color names is that they maintain the discriminative power while possessing a certain degree of photometric robustness. In addition, they yield a very compact color representation of only eleven dimensions. This also compares favorable with respect to photometric invariants. For example the hue and opponent angle invariants of [21] are 36 dimensions. The popular color SIFTS [19] perform the SIFT operation on the

Table 1. Comparison of color-name results versus baseline (either luminance or standard RGB) and versus the best reported photometric invariant. Results are provided for several applications and different data sets. The final column indicates the performance measure which is used. The results show that color names consistently outperform the photometric invariants.

applications	data set	baseline	phot. inv.	color names	measure
image class.	flower-17 [11]	69.0	87.0	**88.0**	class. rate
	birds-200 [13]	12.9	14.0	**17.0**	class. rate
object detection	cartoons [12]	27.6	35.3	**41.7**	mAP
	pascal 2007 [12]	32.2	30.6	**34.8**	mAP
action recognition	willow[9]	66.6	67.2	**68**	mAP
	Pascal 2010 [9]	55	54.8	**56.3**	mAP
	standford-40 [9]	39	38.7	**39.8**	mAP
texture	KTH-TIPS-2a [10]	55.5	54.3	**56.8**	class. rate
	KTH-TIPS-2b [10]	42.1	**45.4**	44.2	class. rate
	FMD [10]	20.3	22.2	**25.6**	class. rate
	Texture-10 [10]	52.3	52.7	**56.0**	class. rate
visual tracking	OTB [3]	54.5	57.6	**74.0**	distance prec.

separate color channels of colorspaces. As a result the dimensionality increment is either of 128 or 256 dimensions.

When incorporating color into a computer vision application, one has to decide on the color feature to use, and on how to combine the shape and color information. Standard approaches include early and late fusion methods, but especially for image classification it was found that more complex fusion approaches can significantly improve the overall results [13] [11]. The main idea behind these more complex fusion methods is that they aim to 'bind' the color and shape information locally.

Our results of using color names for various application domains have been summarized in Table 1. The results are compared to a baseline performance, which is either the results based on luminance only or on RGB (if luminance results are not reported). In addition, the best results reported with photometric invariants for these data sets are given. One can observe that for all applications the best results are obtained with color names. It is also interesting to note that photometric invariants do not always outperform the baseline. The highest performance increases are reported for object detection and visual tracking.

Next to our efforts to evaluate color name performance several other research groups have resulted similar conclusions. A recent paper, which proposes to use 16 color names (fuchsia, blue, aqua, lime, yellow, red, purple, navy, teal, green, olive, maroon, black, gray, silver and white) for person re-identification obtains excellent results without using uncalibrated images to train. Most probably this is due to the fact that colors are grouped based on their distance to the color centers which represent these color names. As a result they do not obtain the very compact color distributions for the achromatic colors which are typical for color mapping learned from calibrated data. In addition Zheng et al. [25] report excellent image retrieval results based on color names.

4 Discussion and Future Research Directions

We have summarized recent evaluation results on color descriptors. Results on various computer vision applications, including image classification, object recognition, texture classification, visual tracking and action recognition, show that color names outperform color descriptors based on photometric invariance.

Several future research directions can be considered to further improve color representations. In a recent paper [14], we show that there is a third approach to color description. This method directly optimizes the discriminative power of the color representation given a classification problem. For the same dimensionality as the color names (11 dimensions) this method reported slightly inferior results than color names. However, for higher dimensions, this method obtained better results on various data sets. This method could be further improved by learning from larger data sets.

Also the approach of Zheng et al. [25], which extends the set of color names to 16 color names, could be further investigated. Analysis of the optimal number of color names, and the correct probabilistic representations of these overlapping color name sets should be considered. Finally, applying recent advances in convolutional neural networks (deep learning) to the problem of discriminative color representations learning is also expected to improve results.

Acknowledgments. This work is funded by the Project TIN2013-41751 of Spanish Ministry of Science and the Catalan project 2014 SGR 221.

References

1. Benavente, R., Vanrell, M., Baldrich, R.: Parametric fuzzy sets for automatic color naming. Journal of the Optical Society of America A **25**(10), 2582–2593 (2008)
2. Berlin, B., Kay, P.: Basic color terms: their universality and evolution. University of California, Berkeley (1969)
3. Danelljan, M., Shahbaz Khan, F., Felsberg, M., Van de Weijer, J.: Adaptive color attributes for real-time visual tracking. In: Proceedings of IEEE Conference on Computer Vision and Pattern Recognition (CVPR) 2014. IEEE (2014)
4. Finlayson, G.D., Schiele, B., Crowley, J.L.: Comprehensive colour image normalization. In: Burkhardt, H.-J., Neumann, B. (eds.) ECCV 1998. LNCS, vol. 1406, p. 475. Springer, Heidelberg (1998)
5. Geusebroek, J., van den Boomgaard, R., Smeulders, A., Geerts, H.: Color invariance **23**(12), 1338–1350 (2001)
6. Gevers, T., Smeulders, A.: Color based object recognition. Pattern Recognition **32**, 453–464 (1999)
7. Hardin, C., Maffi, L. (eds.): Color Categories in Thought and Language. University Press, Cambridge (1997)
8. Healey, G.: Segmenting images using normalized color. IEEE Trans. Syst., Man, Cybern. **22**, 64–73 (1992)

9. Khan, F.S., Anwer, R.M., van de Weijer, J., Bagdanov, A.D., Lopez, A.M., Felsberg, M.: Coloring action recognition in still images. International Journal of Computer Vision **105**(3), 205–221 (2013)

10. Khan, F.S., Anwer, R.M., van de Weijer, J., Felsberg, M., Laaksonen, J.: Compact color-texture description for texture classification. Pattern Recognition Letters **51**, 16–22 (2015)

11. Khan, F.S., van de Weijer, J., Vanrell, M.: Modulating shape features by color attention for object recognition. International Journal of Computer Vision (IJCV) **98**(1), 49–64 (2012). http://www.cat.uab.cat/Public/Publications/2012/SVV2012

12. Khan, F., Anwer, R., van de Weijer, J., Bagdanov, A., Vanrell, M., Lopez, A.: Color attributes for object detection. In: IEEE Conference on Computer Vision and Patter Recognition (2012)

13. Khan, F., Van de Weijer, J., Bagdanov, A., Vanrell, M.: Portmanteau vocabularies for multi-cue image representation. In: Twenty-Fifth Annual Conference on Neural Information Processing Systems (NIPS 2011) (2011)

14. Khan, R., Van de Weijer, J., Khan, F.S., Muselet, D., Ducottet, C., Barat, C.: Discriminative color descriptors. In: 2013 IEEE Conference on Computer Vision and Pattern Recognition (CVPR), pp. 2866–2873. IEEE (2013)

15. Lammens, J.: A computational model of color perception and color naming. Ph.D. thesis, Univ. of Buffalo (1994)

16. Liu, Y., Zhang, D., Lu, G., Ma, W.Y.: Region-based image retrieval with high-level semantic color names. In: Proceedings of the 11th International Multimedia Modelling Conference, MMM 2005, pp. 180–187. IEEE (2005)

17. Menegaz, G., Troter, A.L., Sequeira, J., Boi, J.M.: A discrete model for color naming. EURASIP Journal on Advances in Signal Processing 2007 (2007)

18. Mojsilovic, A.: A computational model for color naming and describing color composition of images. IEEE Transactions on Image Processing **14**(5), 690–699 (2005)

19. van de Sande, K.E.A., Gevers, T., Snoek, C.G.M.: Evaluating color descriptors for object and scene recognition. PAMI **32**(9), 1582–1596 (2010)

20. Vazquez-Corral, J., Vanrell, M., Baldrich, R., Tous, F.: Color constancy by category correlation. IEEE Transactions on Image Processing **21**(4), 1997–2007 (2012)

21. van de Weijer, J., Schmid, C.: Coloring local feature extraction. In: Proc. of the European Conference on Computer Vision **2**, pp. 334–348. Graz, Austria (2006)

22. van de Weijer, J., Schmid, C.: Applying color names to image description. In: IEEE International Conference on Image Processing (ICIP). San Antonio, USA (2007). http://www.cat.uab.cat/Public/Publications/2007/VaS2007a

23. van de Weijer, J., Schmid, C., Verbeek, J., Larlus, D.: Learning color names for real-world applications. IEEE Transactions on Image Processing **18**(7), 1512–1524 (2009). http://www.cat.uab.cat/Public/Publications/2009/VSV2009

24. Yang, Y., Yang, J., Yan, J., Liao, S., Yi, D., Li, S.Z.: Salient color names for person re-identification. In: Fleet, D., Pajdla, T., Schiele, B., Tuytelaars, T. (eds.) ECCV 2014, Part I. LNCS, vol. 8689, pp. 536–551. Springer, Heidelberg (2014)

25. Zheng, L., Wang, S., Liu, Z., Tian, Q.: Packing and padding: Coupled multi-index for accurate image retrieval. In: Proceedings of IEEE Conference on Computer Vision and Pattern Recognition (CVPR) 2014. IEEE (2014)

Optics and Computational Methods for Hybrid Resolution Spectral Imaging

Masahiro Yamaguchi[✉]

Global Scientific Information and Computing Center,
Tokyo Institute of Technology, Tokyo, Japan
yamaguchi.m.aa@m.titech.ac.jp

Abstract. The concept and computational methods for hybrid resolution spectral imaging (HRSI) are introduced. In HRSI, a high-resolution spectral image is reconstructed with combining a high-resolution RGB image and a low-resolution spectral image. An important difficulty in high-resolution spectral imaging is that the light-energy is reduced at the image sensor. Such problem can be solved by the hybrid resolution approach, since the image resolution and quality are mostly determined by the high-resolution RGB image, which can be captured by commercial high-performance cameras. Different reconstruction methods suitable for a hybrid resolution system are reviewed and the performance of those methods is discussed. The hybrid resolution spectral video system is also demonstrated.

Keywords: Spectral imaging · Multispectral imaging · Hybrid resolution · Color reproduction · Low-resolution spectral sensor · Piecewise Wiener · Regression

1   Introduction

A spectral imaging technology will be more widely adopted if high-resolution imagery can be acquired in video-rate with a compact and easy-to-handle imaging device.

Multispectral and hyperspectral imaging has been applied in remote-sensing [1], industrial inspection [2], security, biomedical imaging [3-5], digital archive of cultural heritage, and color reproduction [6-9]. Spectral video is also promising in those fields [10-12]. However, there are still some limitations in spectral video, such as the scanning time, the signal-to-noise (S/N) ratio, the less amount of light energy incident on an image sensor, and the processing of huge amount of data. There have been reported snapshot spectral camera systems recently [13-17], but it is yet difficult to capture high-resolution spectral video with a compact and handy camera system.

In the author's group, a hybrid-resolution spectral imaging (HRSI) have been developed for the solution to this problem. In HRSI, a low-spatial-resolution spectral (LR-Spec) image and a high-spatial-resolution 3-band image (HR-RGB) are captured simultaneously, and a spectral image with high-resolution in both spectral and spatial dimensions is reconstructed, as shown in fig. 1. The image reconstruction method is a key technology in HRSI, and this paper introduces some methods developed in our group, along with the optical systems for this purpose.

© Springer International Publishing Switzerland 2015
A. Trémeau et al. (Eds.): CCIW 2015, LNCS 9016, pp. 23–32, 2015.
DOI: 10.1007/978-3-319-15979-9_3

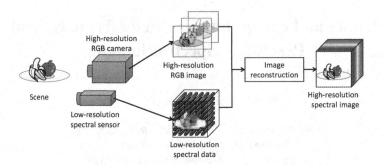

Fig. 1. The concept of hybrid resolution spectral imaging

2   Optical Systems for Spectral Imaging

Classical devices for capturing multispectral or hyperspectral images require spatial or spectral scanning, for example, filter-wheel cameras [6] and push-broom type sensors with diffraction grating [2]. Liquid crystal tunable filters [4] are also used for spectral scanning. Nevertheless, single-shot (or snapshot) imaging is expected for photographing moving objects or video imaging. Single-shot imaging is possible by using multiple sensors and dichroic-mirrors, and multiband video systems were demonstrated [11,12]. But the number of spectral channels is limited, as well as the optics design becomes difficult because the optical path becomes longer for the dichroic-mirror-based spectral imaging.

Advanced spectral imaging techniques suitable for video or single-shot imaging have been studied recently, such as Fourier Transform Imaging Spectrometer (FTIS) [13], Computed Tomography Imaging Spectrometer (CTIS) [14,15], Coded Aperture Snapshot Spectral Imaging (CASSI) [16], and Image Mapping Spectrometer (IMS) [17]. They enable the single-shot capture, but the spatial resolution is reduced.

For the application of spectral imaging to color reproduction, the display of realistic image is important, and high-resolution spectral imaging is crucial. One of the difficulties in high-resolution spectral imaging is the reduced light energy on the image sensor. It is known that the signal-to-noise (S/N) ratio is highest in the dichroic-mirror-based optical system, but the narrower the spectral bandwidth is, the less light intensity can be detected. In our previous 6-band high-definition video experiment [6, 11], the lens aperture was set larger so that enough light energy could be exposed to all the six image sensors. Then the depth of field became shallow, and the captured images were sensed as rather blurred. Moreover, the light intensity was sometimes not satisfactory yielding poor S/N ratio. Therefore, a method to breakthrough the trade-off between the spatial resolution and the image quality is needed for high-resolution spectral imaging.

3   Hybrid-Resolution Spectral Imaging System

The concept of HRSI is shown in fig. 1. It consists of two input devices; one with high-spatial-resolution but small number of spectral channels, and another one with high-spectral-resolution but low-spatial-resolution. Then the image data captured by those two devices are fused to derive an image with high spatial and spectral resolution. In the case of aiming at spectrum-based color reproduction, the former device with high-spatial-resolution can be a conventional RGB (Red, Green, Blue) camera.

The image quality including S/N ratio and sharpness is mainly depends on the former imaging device, i.e., a high-resolution RGB camera. It is possible to employ wide variety of high-performance digital cameras for both still and video imaging. The LR-Spec imaging device is used for improving the spectral and color fidelity, and thus this is a practical way to obtain high-resolution high-quality spectral images. Obviously there is a limitation if the target object is very small and has unique spectral characteristics, but in the application to color reproduction, the color difference in a small object is hardly noticed by human vision. Hence the hybrid-resolution approach is especially suitable for spectrum-based color imaging applications.

The idea of HRSI was originally introduced in remote sensing applications [18,19]. High-resolution spectral images are obtained by an image fusion of a low-resolution multispectral image and a panchromatic high-resolution image, or a low-resolution hyperspectral image and a high-resolution image with small number of bands.

We proposed the application of this concept to spectral color imaging [20-25]. In the earlier papers, the LR-Spec image was captured by scanning the fiber-based spectrometer. In [24, 25], we reported the hyperspectral video imaging with quasi-real-time spectrum-based color reproduction, using a low-resolution spectral sensor (LRSS) as described in chapter 5. Cao, Ma et. al., also reported spectral video system based on the similar approach [26, 27].

There are two ways for capturing HR-RGB and LR-Spec images, one is to use different cameras (a) and another way is to combine two systems using a beam splitter (b). In satellite or airborne imaging, (a) is suitable because the object is located very far from the two cameras, and the disparity can be ignored. If the objects are three-dimensional and located near the camera, the disparity between the two cameras should be taken into account. In such case, (b) seems to be better because the pixel-wise registration is possible. But the optical system becomes complicated, the amount of light energy is reduced by the beam splitter, and the handiness and the image quality are lost. If the method for reconstructing a spectral image is robust to the image registration error, the optical system (a) is preferable.

4   Reconstruction Methods for HRSI

The optical system as shown in fig.1 enables the simultaneous acquisition of an HR-RGB image and an LR-Spec image. Then, how can we reconstruct a spectral image with both spatially and spectrally high-resolution? In this subsection, let us firstly discuss the spectral estimation from the RGB data with the assistance of the spectral dataset obtained from the LR-Spec image.

Spectral Estimation with the Aid of Spectral Measurements
When the number of channels is not satisfactory high in a spectral imaging device, the spectral reconstruction is needed at each pixel of a spectral image. In color reproduction applications, it was reported that the surface spectra can be represented

by small number of parameters by a linear model [28]. Then it is possible to reconstruct continuous spectrum from the measurement data of small number of spectral channels, e.g., RGB 3-channels. Various reconstruction techniques have been presented until now, including linear and nonlinear methods.

If we consider that continuous spectral data are sampled in N-wavelengths, then the spectral data can be represented as a vector in an N-dimensional space. In the linear model, the reconstructed spectra are located within the 3-dimensional (3D) subspace as shown in fig.2 (a). For example, in Wiener estimation method, which is one of commonly used technique, the 3D subspace for reflectance estimation is determined by the spectral sensitivity of the input device, the illuminant spectrum, and the covariance matrix of the object spectra. As it is not always possible to obtain the covariance matrix for specific objects to be imaged, a mathematical model is sometimes employed, e.g., the covariance matrix is derived based on Markov model [29]. In this case, the signals of closer wavelengths are considered to be more correlated, and the spectral distribution is assumed to be smooth. Although it is mostly true for various cases, it is more preferable employ the covariance matrix generated from the target object itself.

Thus, the LR-Spec data can be utilized to produce the covariance matrix of spectral characteristics of the target object, i.e., Wiener estimation [fig. 2 (b)]. It is also possible to derive the basis functions from the LR-Spec data by principal component analysis (PCA). The basis functions becomes adaptive to the target object as they are obtained from the measurement data. However, since only one set of three basis functions is used in the entire image, the accuracy of reconstructed spectra is limited especially when there are various objects that have different spectral characteristics in a scene.

Spatio-Spectral MAP Estimation

In fact, the LR-Spec image holds the information outside the subspace spanned by the three basis functions derived by the PCA of the covariance matrix. In order to make use of the information that lies outside the subspace, a method based on maximum a posteriori probability (MAP) was proposed [20]. This method is called spatio-spectral MAP (ss-MAP) estimation hereafter. The estimated spectral image $\hat{\mathbf{f}}$ is given by

$$\hat{\mathbf{f}} = \operatorname{argmax}_{\mathbf{f}} \; P(\mathbf{f}|\mathbf{g}, \mathbf{r}) \tag{1}$$

where $\mathbf{f}$, $\mathbf{g}$, and $\mathbf{r}$ represent the original spectral distribution of the target object, the HR-RGB image, and the LR-Spec image, respectively. Under the assumption that the spatial and spectral correlation is separable, the solution of eq.(1) becomes the form:

$$\hat{\mathbf{f}} = \mathbf{M_s}\,\mathbf{g} + \mathbf{M_r}\,\mathbf{r} \tag{2}$$

where $\mathbf{M_s}$ and $\mathbf{M_r}$ express the estimation operators based on spectral and spatial correlation, respectively. The first term is the same as the method described in the previous paragraph, shown in fig. 2 (b). The second term is the estimation in the $(N-3)$ dimensional subspace that is orthogonal to the three basis functions, derived from the spatial correlation of the HR-RGB image [Fig. 3 (a)]. Therefore, the location information of the LR-Spec image is exploited, and the component that is orthogonal to the 3D subspace spanned by the basis functions can be determined by this method. A problem in this method is the calculation cost.

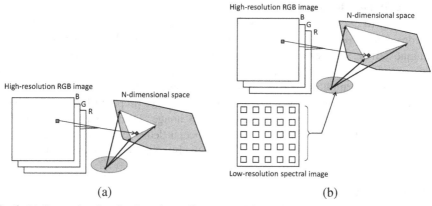

Fig. 2. (a) Spectral estimation based on a linear model from an RGB image. (b) LR-Spec image is used to derive the optimal basis functions.

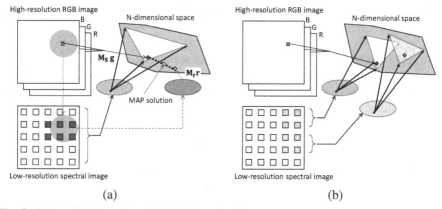

Fig. 3. Schematic illustration of (a) MAP estimation and (b) piecewise Wiener estimation in hybrid resolution spectral imaging

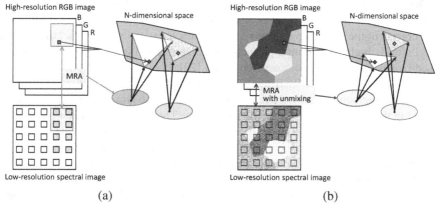

Fig. 4. Schematic illustration of modified MRA-based spectral estimation methods. (a) Locally weighted regression (LW-MRA), and (b) class-based regression with spectral unmixing.

Piecewise Wiener Estimation

Another way to overcome the limit of the 3D subspace is to use different sets of basis functions depending on the location in the image. Piecewise Wiener (PW) estimation technique utilize different estimation matrices derived from the spectral measurements near the target pixel, as shown in fig. 3 (b) [21]. Then the estimation accuracy is improved when multiple classes of objects are present in the image. The computational cost is not very high, where multiple matrices are prepared from the LR-Spec image and applied to each pixel of the HR-RGB image. Then it is possible to implement the method in real-time without using special dedicated hardware. In practice, adjacent blocks should be overlapped to avoid the block artifact at the boundary.

Regression-Based Reconstruction Methods

Multiple regression analysis (MRA) has also been applied to the spectral estimation from multiband or RGB data, and can be applied to HRSI. In contrast to the above methods like ss-MAP and PW estimation that employ the spectral sensitivity of the input device to derive estimation matrices, it is not needed in regression-based methods. It is beneficial as the accurate spectral sensitivity measurement is not an easy task.

To apply MRA to HRSI, the pixel correspondence is required. Since the pixel aperture of LRSS is often larger than the RGB imager, a virtual low-resolution RGB image is generated from its high-resolution version, to attain the correspondence in the low-resolution pixels. Then MRA is applied to derive a matrix for spectral estimation, and the matrix is applied to each pixel of the RGB image to generate a high-resolution spectral image. In principle, the performance is equivalent to the Wiener estimation of fig. 2 (b), except that the spectral sensitivity is not explicitly needed in MRA process.

It is also possible to apply the concept similar to the PW technique in MRA, which was reported in [25]. As shown in fig. 4 (a), the image is divided into multiple blocks, and the regression coefficient matrix is derived for each block. The spectral data from LRSS are weighted depending on the distance from the center of each block. Then different matrices are applied to every location in the image.

The method of fig. 4 (a) is based on the idea that the correlation of spectral characteristics is higher if two pixels are closer. However, there are often cases where multiple objects in the scene have same spectral characteristics. In such case, the spectral correlation is high even if multiple objects are apart from each other. Then a class-based reconstruction technique was proposed [22]. Fig. 4 (b) shows the overview of the method. Firstly an HR-RGB image is segmented based on the color information, where each segment is not necessarily aggregated in the image; multiple separated objects in the image can belong to the same class. Then the class of each pixel in the LR-Spec image is determined from the corresponding region in the image, and MRA is applied to each class. But there is a question: how do we handle the case when the pixel in the LR-Spec image is larger and corresponds to the pixels of multiple classes in HR-RGB image? In the method presented in [22], the spectral unmixing is applied to a pixel that belongs to multiple classes and MRA is adopted to the unmixed classes.

Bilateral and Trilateral Interpolation

Moreover, there have been reported hybrid systems for spectral video using bilateral and trilateral interpolation [26, 27]. The spectrum of a pixel in high-resolution spectral image is interpolated from neighboring pixels of LR-Spec data, with weighting based on the Euclidian distances in both the spatial domain and the RGB color space. In the video application, the interpolation was done in temporal direction as well after an optical flow is adopted. The interpolation technique is designed for the system in which the image set consists of RGB pixels with the spectral measurements and RGB pixels that do not have correspondence to the spectral data. It is expected to extend the interpolation method in future to the case when the pixel aperture sizes are different in RGB and spectral images, like the instances shown in figs. 2-4.

5   Experiments

Performance of Different Reconstruction Methods

In [21], the performance of the PW and ss-MAP estimation was compared and it was shown that the estimation accuracy was almost equivalent, while the computational cost in ss-MAP estimation was much higher. The accuracy of PW estimation was shown to be significantly higher than 3-band cameras without low-resolution spectral measurement, and Wiener estimation using the low-resolution spectral data. Although the accuracy depends on the image content, PW technique gives better results especially in the images that hold multiple objects of various colors. The results of the class-based regression method with spectral unmixing were reported in [22], where the performance is similar to PW, but sometimes better accuracy is achieved depending on the constituents in the image.

The accuracy of the image registration between HR-RGB and LR-Spec images is not serious in Wiener and PW techniques, where pixel-wise registration is needed in MRA or LW-MRA. Bilateral and trilateral interpolation technique also requires high-accuracy registration. In practice, a reconstruction method that is robust to the image registration error is expected.

Experiments Using a Hybrid Resolution Spectral Video System

We have demonstrated a hybrid resolution spectral video system [24] that employs a LRSS system [3], shown in fig. 5. It should be noted that the pixel size in the LRSS is considerably large, where the 2D fiber array corresponds a set of pixels. It is an important issue for achieving higher sensitivity in the LRSS. In the video system, the reproduction of a color or gray-scale image is not difficult even though spectral processing, because the spectral processing is linear and only 3×3 or 1×3 matrix multiplications are required for image reproduction. It is possible to reproduce an image with spectrum-based color reproduction and single wavelength image in almost real-time, and if a certain point on the image is clicked by a mouse, the spectral distribution at the pixel is exhibited in another window.

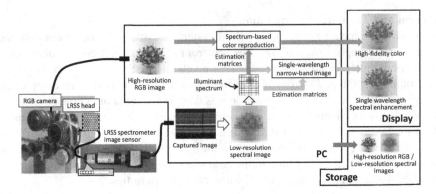

Fig. 5. The spectral data from 68 fibers are captured by an LRSS, and after the calibration and the rearrangement, a LR-Spec image is produced. In PW estimation or LW-MRA technique, 3×3 or 1×3 matrices are applied to the HR-RGB image as they are basically linear processing, thus the computational cost is not so high and real-time reproduction is possible.

Table 1 shows the results on the evaluation of color reproduction accuracy. The error was slightly large in PW estimation using LRSS data. We consider this unexpected larger error is caused by the error in the spectral sensitivity of the RGB camera. In MRA and LW-MRA, the spectral sensitivity data is not used in the estimation process, and the error became smaller. Additionally, the color differences are larger because the difference was calculated from objects that have color variation measured by a spectroradiometer and the HRSI system. Despite of those issues in the experiment, it can be confirmed that the LW-MRA gives the best performance among the tested methods. The image quality was basically determined by the HR-RGB camera, and good-quality results were obtained.

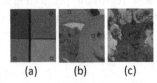

(a)   (b)   (c)

Fig. 6. (a)-(c) Three images used in the experiment. The small squares in the images indicate the regions used in the color difference calculations.

Table 1. Color estimation error (average CIELAB ΔE) in the estimated colors under D50 from the spectral images captured under artificial sunlight (Seric Solax XC-100AF). (a)-(c) indicate the images shown in figs. 6 (a)-(c).

Image	Wiener (Markov)	Wiener (LRSS)	PW (LRSS)	MRA	LW-MRA
(a)	13.1	13.0	9.6	7.5	3.4
(b)	12.5	9.1	8.1	5.5	5.2
(c)	12.4	7.9	5.6	8.8	5.5

6   Conclusion

This paper introduces the concept of HRSI and the algorithms for reconstructing a spectral image. The HRSI enables to reconstruct a high-resolution spectral image from LR-Spec and HR-RGB images. As the image quality mainly depends on the HR-RGB image in HRSI, it becomes possible to obtain high-resolution and high-quality spectral images by a single-shot. It should be mentioned that the hybrid resolution approach is not suitable for the application that requires to detect small regions with abnormal spectral characteristics that cannot be distinguished by the HR-RGB image.

From the review of different reconstruction methods and the experimental comparison presented in this paper, it is needed to undertake more comparative evaluations to explore a practical reconstructing method for HRSI. Then it is also expected to explore the applications of the hybrid-resolution systems that enables to capture high-resolution and high-quality spectral images.

Acknowledgement. The author expresses deep acknowledgement to Yuri Murakami, D. Eng, who has been conducting the research introduced in this paper. Also the author wish to acknowledge Keiichiro Nakazaki, Asami Tanji, and Kunihiko Ietomi for their great contribution to the experimental implementation. This research is partly supported by National Institute of information and Communications Technology (NICT) and Japan Society for the Promotion of Science KAKENHI (23135509, 25135712).

References

1. Anuta, P.E., MacDonald, R.B.: Crop surveys from multiband satellite photography using digital techniques. Remote Sensing of Environment **2**, 53–67 (1971)
2. Hyvarinen, T., Herrala, E., Dall Ava, A.: Direct sight imaging spectrograph: A unique add-on component brings spectral imaging to industrial applications. Proc. SPIE **3302**, 165–175 (1998)
3. Matsuoka, H., Kosai, Y., Saito, M., Takeyama, N., Suto, H.: Single-cell viability assessment with a novel spectro-imaging system. J. Biotechnol. **94**, 299–308 (2002)
4. Levenson, R., Cronin, P.J., Pankratov, K.K.: Spectral imaging for brightfield microscopy. Proc. SPIE **4959**, 27–33 (2003)
5. Yamaguchi, M., Murakami, Y., Hashizume, H., Haneishi, H., Kanno, Y., Komiya, Y.: High-fidelity color video reproduction of open surgery by six-band camera. Proc. SPIE **7627**, 762707 (2010)
6. Hill, B., Vorhagen, F.W.: Multispectral image pick-up system. US Patent 5, 319, 472 (1994)
7. Burns, P.D., Berns, R.S.: Analysis of multispectral image capture. In: Proc. IS&T/SID 4th Color Imaging Conference, pp. 19–22 (1996)
8. Tominaga, S.: Multichannel vision system for estimating surface and illumination functions. J. Opt. Soc. Am. A **13**, 2163–2173 (1996)
9. Yamaguchi, M., Haneishi, H., Ohyama, N.: Beyond red-green-blue (RGB): spectrum-based color imaging technology. J. Imaging Sci. Technol. **52**, 010201 (2008)
10. Everitt, J.H., Escobar, D.E., Cavazos, I., Noriega, J.R., Davis, M.R.: A three-camera multispectral digital video imaging system. Remote Sensing of Environment **54**(3), 333–337 (1995)
11. Ohsawa, K., Ajito, T., Fukuda, H., Komiya, Y., Haneishi, H., Yamaguchi, M., Ohyama, N.: Six-band HDTV camera system for spectrum-based color reproduction. J. Imaging Sci. Technol. **48**, 85–92 (2004)
12. Leitner, R., De Biasio, M., Arnold, T., Dinh, C.V., Loog, M., Duin, R.P.W.: Multi-spectral video endoscopy system for the detection of cancerous tissue. Pattern Recognition Letters **34**(1), 85–93 (2013)

13. Hirai, A., Inoue, T., Itoh, K., Ichioka, Y.: Application of multiple-image Fourier transform spectral imaging to measurement of fast phenomena. Opt. Rev. **1**, 205–207 (1994)
14. Okamoto, T., Yamaguchi, I.: Simultaneous acquisition of spectral image information. Opt. Lett. **16**, 1277–1279 (1991)
15. Descour, M.R., Volin, C.E., Dereniak, E.L., Thome, K.J., Schumacher, A.B., Wilson, D.W., Maker, P.D.: Demonstration of a high-speed nonscanning imaging spectrometer. Opt. Lett. **22**, 1271–1273 (1997)
16. Wagadarikar, A.A., Pitsianis, N.P., Sun, X., Brady, D.J.: Video rate spectral imaging using a coded aperture snapshot spectral imager. Optics Express **17**(8), 6368–6388 (2009)
17. Gao, L., Kester, R.T., Nagen, N., Tkaczyk, T.S.: Snapshot image mapping spectrometer (IMS) with high sampling density for hyperspectral microscopy. Opt. Express **18**, 14330–14344 (2010)
18. Price, J.C.: Combining panchromatic and multispectral imagery from dual resolution satellite instruments. Remote Sens. Environ. **21**, 119–128 (1987)
19. Eismann, M.T., Hardie, R.C.: Application of the stochastic mixing model to hyperspectral resolution enhancement. IEEE Trans. Image Process. **42**, 1924–1933 (2004)
20. Murakami, Y., Ietomi, K., Yamaguchi, M., Ohyama, N.: Maximum a posteriori estimation of spectral reflectance from color image and multipoint spectral measurements. Appl. Opt. **46**(28), 7068–7082 (2007)
21. Murakami, Y., Yamaguchi, M., Ohyama, N.: Piecewise Wiener estimation for reconstruction of spectral reflectance image by multipoint spectral measurements. Appl. Opt. **48**(11), 2188–2202 (2009)
22. Murakami, Y., Yamaguchi, M., Ohyama, N.: Class-based spectral reconstruction based on unmixing of low-resolution spectral information. JOSA A **28**(7), 1470–1481 (2011)
23. Murakami, Y., Yamaguchi, M., Ohyama, N.: Hybrid-resolution multispectral imaging using color filter array. Opt. Express **20**(7), 7173–7183 (2012)
24. Murakami, Y., Nakazaki, K., Yamaguchi, M.: Hybrid-resolution spectral video system using low-resolution spectral sensor. Opt. Express **22**(17), 20311–20325 (2014)
25. Nakazaki, K., Murakami, Y., Yamaguchi, M.: Hybrid-Resolution spectral imaging system using adaptive regression-based reconstruction. In: Elmoataz, A., Lezoray, O., Nouboud, F., Mammass, D. (eds.) ICISP 2014. LNCS, vol. 8509, pp. 142–150. Springer, Heidelberg (2014)
26. Cao, X., Tong, X., Dai, Q., Lin, S.: High resolution multispectral video capture with a hybrid camera system. In: Proc. IEEE Conf. on Computer Vision and Pattern Recognition, CVPR, pp. 297–304 (2011)
27. Ma, C., Cao, X., Wu, R., Dai, Q.: Content-adaptive high-resolution hyperspectral video acquisition with a hybrid camera system. Opt. Lett. **39**, 937–940 (2014)
28. Maloney, L.T.: Evaluation of linear models of surface spectral reflectance with small numbers of parameters. J. Opt. Soc. Am. A **3**(10), 1673–1683 (1986)
29. Pratt, W.K., Mancill, C.E.: Spectral estimation techniques for the spectral calibration of a color image scanner. Appl. Opt. **15**, 73–75 (1976)

Relative Pose Estimation and Fusion of 2D Spectral and 3D Lidar Images

Zoltan Kato[1]($\boxtimes$) and Levente Tamas[2]

[1] Institute of Informatics,
University of Szeged, P.O. Box 652, H-6701 Szeged, Hungary
kato@inf.u-szeged.hu
[2] Robotics Research Group, Technical University of Cluj-Napoca,
Dorobantilor street 73, 400609 Cluj-Napoca, Romania
levente.tamas@aut.utcluj.ro

Abstract. This paper presents a unified approach for the relative pose estimation of a spectral camera - 3D Lidar pair without the use of any special calibration pattern or explicit point correspondence. The method works without specific setup and calibration targets, using only a pair of 2D-3D data. Pose estimation is formulated as a 2D-3D nonlinear shape registration task which is solved without point correspondences or complex similarity metrics. The registration is then traced back to the solution of a non-linear system of equations which directly provides the calibration parameters between the bases of the two sensors. The method has been extended both for perspective and omnidirectional central cameras and was tested on a large set of synthetic lidar-camera image pairs as well as on real data acquired in outdoor environment.

1 Introduction

In the past years there was a considerable research effort invested in the fusion of heterogeneous image data acquired from 2D and 3D sensors [24]. The need for fusing such sensory data is common to various research fields including remote sensing [17], medical image processing [3,12,20], mobile robotic applications [6], urban autonomous driving [5], geodesic information fusion [27], cultural heritage documentation [1], or entertainment related commercial depth cameras[2]. One of the most challenging issues is the fusion of 2D RGB imagery with other

This research was partially supported by the European Union and the State of Hungary, co-financed by the European Social Fund through project TAMOP-4.2.2.A-11/1/KONV-2012-0073 (*Telemedicine-focused research activities in the fields of Mathematics, Informatics and Medical sciences*); as well as by Domus MTA Hungary. The laser data of the *Bremen Cog* was provided by Amandine Colson from the German Maritime Museum, Bremerhaven, Germany. The authors gratefully acknowledge the help of Csaba Benedek from DEVA Lab., SZTAKI in providing us with preprocessed Velodyne Lidar scans. The catadioptric camera was provided by the Multimedia Technologies and Telecommunications Research Center of UTCN with the help of Camelia Florea.

A. Trémeau et al. (Eds.): CCIW 2015, LNCS 9016, pp. 33–42, 2015.
DOI: 10.1007/978-3-319-15979-9_4

3D range sensing modalities (*e.g.* Lidar) which can be formulated as a camera calibration task. Internal calibration refers to the self parameters of the camera, while external parameters describe the *pose* of the camera with respect to a world coordinate frame. The problem becomes more difficult, when the RGB image is recorded with a non-conventional camera, such as central catadioptric or dioptric (*e.g.* fish-eye) panoramic cameras. This paper focuses on the extrinsic parameter estimation for a range-camera sensor pair, where the 3D rigid motion between the two camera coordinate systems is determined. Due to the different functionality of the ranger (*e.g.* lidar) and central camera, the calibration is often performed manually, or by considering special assumptions like artificial markers on images, or establishing point matches. These procedures tend to be laborious and time consuming, especially when calibration has to be done more than once during data acquisition. In real life applications, however, it is often desirable to have a flexible one step calibration without such prerequisites.

Based on our earlier works [25, 26], this paper presents a region based calibration framework for spectral 2D central cameras and 3D lidar. Instead of establishing point matches or relying on artificial markers or recorded intensity values, we propose a relative pose estimation algorithm which works with segmented planar patches. Since segmentation is required anyway in many real-life image analysis tasks, such regions may be available or straightforward to detect. The main advantage of the proposed method is the use of regions instead of point correspondence and a generic problem formulation which allows to treat several types of cameras in the same framework. Basically, we reformulate pose estimation as a shape alignment problem, which is accomplished by solving a system of nonlinear equations. The method has been quantitatively evaluated on a large synthetic dataset both for perspective [26] and omnidirectional [25] cameras, and it proved to be robust and efficient in real-life situations.

1.1   Related Work

There are various techniques applied for camera calibration, *e.g.* point or line correspondence finding [13], intensity image based correlation [19], use of specific artificial land-marks [8] or mutual information extraction and parameter optimization[11]. The extrinsic calibration of 3D lidar and low resolution color camera was first addressed in [28] which generalized the algorithm proposed in [29]. This method is based on manual point feature selection from both sensory data and it assumes a valid camera intrinsic model for calibration. A similar manual point feature correspondence based approach is proposed in [21]. There are also extensions to the simultaneous intrinsic-extrinsic calibration presented in the work [16] which used the intensity information from lidar to find correspondences between the 2D-3D domains. Other works are based on the fusion of IMU or GPS information in the process of 2D-3D calibration [18], mainly in the initialization phase of the calibration [27]. Recently there has been an increasing interest in various calibration problem setups ranging from high-resolution spatial data registration [13] to low-resolution, high frame rate depth commercial cameras such as Kinect [9], or in the online calibration during different measurements in time such as in case of a traveling mobile robot [19].

The most commonly used non-perspective central camera systems, especially for robotics and autonomous driving, are using omnidirectional (or panoramic) lenses. The geometric formulation of such systems were extensively studied [15,22,23]. The internal calibration of such cameras depends on these geometric models. Although different calibration methods and toolboxes exist [10,14,22] this problem is by far not trivial and is still in focus [23]. While internal calibration can be solved in a controlled environment, using special calibration patterns, pose estimation must rely on the actual images taken in a real environment. There are popular methods dealing with point correspondence estimation such as [22] or other fiducial marker images suggested in [10], which may be cumbersome to use in real life situations. This is especially true in a multimodal setting, when omnidirectional images need to be combined with other non-conventional sensors like lidar scans providing only range data. The Lidar-omnidirectional camera calibration problem was analyzed from different perspectives: in [21], the calibration is performed in natural scenes, however the point correspondences between the 2D-3D images are selected in a semi-supervised manner. The method in [16] tackles calibration as an observability problem using a (planar) fiducial marker as calibration pattern. In [19], a fully automatic method is proposed based on mutual information (MI) between the intensity information from the depth sensor and the omnidirectional camera. Also based on MI, [27] performs the calibration using particle filtering. However, these methods require a range data with recorded intensity values, which is not always possible and often challenged by real-life lighting conditions.

2   Region-Based Calibration Framework

Consider a lidar camera with a 3D coordinate system having its origin $\mathbf{O}$ in the rotation center of the laser sensor, x and y axes pointing to the right and down, respectively, while z is pointing away from the sensor. Setting the world coordinate system to the lidar's coordinate frame, we can always express a 3D lidar point $\mathbf{X}$ with its homogeneous world coordinates $\mathbf{X} = (X_1, X_2, X_3, 1)^T$.

A classical perspective camera sees the same world point $\mathbf{X}$ as a homogeneous point $\mathbf{x} = (x_1, x_2, 1)^T$ in the image plain obtained by a perspective projection $\mathbf{P}$:

$$\mathbf{x} = \mathbf{PX} = \mathbf{KR}[\mathbf{I}|\mathbf{t}]\mathbf{X}, \tag{1}$$

where $\mathbf{P}$ is the 3×4 camera matrix, which can be factored into the well known $\mathbf{P} = \mathbf{KR}[\mathbf{I}|\mathbf{t}]$ form, where $\mathbf{I}$ is the identity matrix, $\mathbf{K}$ is the 3×3 upper triangular *calibration* matrix containing the camera intrinsic parameters, while $\mathbf{R}$ and $\mathbf{t}$ are the rotation and translation, respectively, aligning the camera frame with the world coordinate frame. A classical solution of the calibration problem is to establish a set of 2D-3D point matches using a special calibration target [9,16], and then solve for $\mathbf{P}$ via a system of equation based on (1) or the minimization of some error function. When a calibration target is not available, then solutions typically assume that the lidar points contain also the laser reflectivity value (interpreted as a gray-value), which can be used for intensity-based matching or registration [13,21].

However, in many practical applications (*e.g.* infield mobile robot), it is not possible to use a calibration target and most lidar sensors will only record depth information. Furthermore, lidar and camera images might be taken at different times and they need to be fused later based solely on the image content. Therefore the question naturally arises: what can be done when neither a special target nor point correspondences are available? Herein, we present a solution for such challenging situations. In particular, we will show that by identifying a single planar region both in the lidar and camera image, the extrinsic calibration can be solved. When two such non-coplanar regions are available then the full calibration can be solved. Of course, these are just the necessary minimal configurations. The more such regions are available, a more stable calibration is obtained.

Hereafter, we will focus only on the relative pose $(\mathbf{R}, \mathbf{t})$ estimation, hence we assume that for perspective cameras $\mathbf{K}$ is known. As for omnidirectional cameras, the intrinsic parameters and relative pose is discussed below.

2.1 Omnidirectional Camera Model

A unified model for central omnidirectional cameras was proposed by Geyer and Daniilidis [7], which represents central panoramic cameras as a projection onto the surface of a unit sphere. This formalism has been adopted and models for the internal projection function have been proposed by Micusik [15] and subsequently by Scaramuzza [22] who derived a general polynomial form of the internal projection valid for any type of omnidirectional camera. In this work, we will use the latter representation.

Let us first see the relationship between a point $\mathbf{x}$ in the omnidirectional image $\mathcal{I}$ and its representation on the unit sphere $\mathcal{S}$ (see Fig. 1). Note that only the half sphere on the image plane side is actually used, as the other half is not visible from image points. Following [22], we assume that the camera

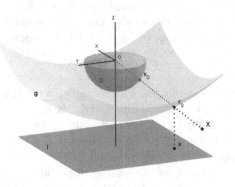

Fig. 1. Omnidirectional camera model

coordinate system is in $\mathcal{S}$, the origin (which is also the center of the sphere) is the projection center of the camera and the z axis is the optical axis of the camera which intersects the image plane in the *principal point*. To represent the nonlinear (but symmetric) distortion of central omnidirectional optics, [22] places a surface g between the image plane and the unit sphere $\mathcal{S}$, which is rotationally symmetric around z. Herein, as suggested by [22], we will use a fourth order polynomial $g(\|\mathbf{x}\|) = a_0 + a_2\|\mathbf{x}\|^2 + a_3\|\mathbf{x}\|^3 + a_4\|\mathbf{x}\|^4$ which has 4 parameters representing the internal parameters (a_0, a_2, a_3, a_4) of the camera. The bijective mapping $\Phi : \mathcal{I} \rightarrow \mathcal{S}$ is composed of 1) lifting the image point $\mathbf{x} \in \mathcal{I}$ onto the g surface by an orthographic projection

$$\mathbf{x}_g = \begin{bmatrix} \mathbf{x} \\ a_0 + a_2\|\mathbf{x}\|^2 + a_3\|\mathbf{x}\|^3 + a_4\|\mathbf{x}\|^4 \end{bmatrix} \tag{2}$$

and then 2) centrally projecting the lifted point $\mathbf{x}_g$ onto the surface of the unit sphere $\mathcal{S}$:

$$\mathbf{x}_{\mathcal{S}} = \Phi(\mathbf{x}) = \frac{\mathbf{x}_g}{\|\mathbf{x}_g\|} \tag{3}$$

Thus the omnidirectional camera projection is fully described by means of unit vectors $\mathbf{x}_{\mathcal{S}}$ in the half space of $\mathbb{R}^3$.

The projection of a 3D world point $\mathbf{X} \in \mathbb{R}^3$ onto $\mathcal{S}$ is basically a traditional central projection onto $\mathcal{S}$ taking into account the extrinsic pose parameters $(\mathbf{R}, \mathbf{t})$ acting between the camera (represented by $\mathcal{S}$) and the world coordinate frame. Thus for a world point $\mathbf{X}$ and its image $\mathbf{x}$ in the omnidirectional camera, the following holds on the surface of $\mathcal{S}$:

$$\Phi(\mathbf{x}) = \mathbf{x}_{\mathcal{S}} = \Psi(\mathbf{X}) = \frac{\mathbf{R}\mathbf{X} + \mathbf{t}}{\|\mathbf{R}\mathbf{X} + \mathbf{t}\|} \tag{4}$$

2.2 Pose Estimation

Our solution for the relative pose is based on the 2D shape registration approach of Domokos *et al.* [4], where the alignment of non-linear shape deformations are recovered via the solution of a special system of equations. Here, however, the calibration problem yields a 2D-3D registration problem in case of a perspective camera and a restricted 3D-3D registration problem on the spherical surface for omnidirectional cameras. These cases thus require a different technique to construct the system of equations.

2.3 Relative Pose of Perspective Cameras

Since correspondences are not available, (1) cannot be used directly. However, individual point matches can be integrated out yielding the following integral equation:

$$\int_{\mathcal{D}} \mathbf{x}d\mathbf{x} = \int_{\mathcal{P}\mathcal{F}} \mathbf{z}d\mathbf{z}, \tag{5}$$

where $\mathcal{D}$ corresponds to the region visible in the *camera* image and $\mathbf{P}\mathcal{F}$ is the image of the *lidar region* projected by the camera matrix $\mathbf{P}$. The above equation corresponds to a system of 2 equations only, which is clearly not sufficient to solve for all parameters of the camera matrix $\mathbf{P}$. Therefor we adopt the general mechanism proposed in [4] to construct new equations. Indeed, (1) remains valid when a function $\omega : \mathbb{R}^2 \rightarrow \mathbb{R}$ is acting on both sides of the equation

$$\omega(\mathbf{x}) = \omega(\mathbf{PX}), \tag{6}$$

and the integral equation of (5) becomes [26]

$$\int_{\mathcal{D}} \omega(\mathbf{x}) d\mathbf{x} = \int_{\mathbf{P}\mathcal{F}} \omega(\mathbf{z}) d\mathbf{z}. \tag{7}$$

Adopting a set of nonlinear functions $\{\omega_i\}_{i=1}^{\ell}$, each ω_i generates a new equation yielding a system of ℓ independent equations. Hence we are able to generate sufficiently many equations. The parameters of the camera matrix $\mathbf{P}$ are then simply obtained as the solution of the nonlinear system of equations (7). In practice, an overdetermined system is constructed, which is then solved by minimizing the algebraic error in the *least squares sense* via a standard *Levenberg-Marquardt* algorithm.

Note that computing the integral on the right hand side of (7) involves the actual execution of the camera projection $\mathbf{P}$ on $\mathcal{F}$, which might be computationally unfavorable. However, choosing power functions for ω_i [26]:

$$\omega_i(\mathbf{x}) = x_1^{n_i} x_2^{m_i}, \quad n_i \leq 3 \text{ and } m_i \leq 3 \tag{8}$$

and using a triangular mesh representation $\mathcal{F}^{\triangle}$ of the lidar region $\mathcal{F}$, we can adopt an efficient computational scheme. First, let us note that this particular choice of ω_i yields the 2D geometric moments of the projected lidar region $\mathbf{P}\mathcal{F}$. Furthermore, due to the triangular mesh representation of $\mathcal{F}$, we can rewrite the integral adopting ω_i from (8) as [26]

$$\int_{\mathcal{D}} x_1^{n_i} x_2^{m_i} d\mathbf{x} \quad = \quad \int_{\mathbf{P}\mathcal{F}} z_1^{n_i} z_2^{m_i} d\mathbf{z} \quad \approx \quad \sum_{\forall \triangle \in \mathcal{F}^{\triangle}} \int_{\triangle} z_1^{n_i} z_2^{m_i} d\mathbf{z}. \tag{9}$$

The latter approximation is due to the approximation of $\mathcal{F}$ by the discrete mesh $\mathcal{F}^{\triangle}$. The integrals over the triangles are various geometric moments which can be computed using efficient recursive formulas [26].

2.4   Relative Pose of Spherical Cameras

For omnidirectional cameras, we have to work on the surface of the unit sphere as it provides a representation independent of the camera internal parameters. Therefore the system of equation has the following form [25]:

$$\iint_{\mathcal{D}_S} \omega(\mathbf{x}_S) \, d\mathcal{D}_S = \iint_{\mathcal{F}_S} \omega(\mathbf{z}_S) \, d\mathcal{F}_S \tag{10}$$

$\mathcal{D}_S$ and $\mathcal{F}_S$ denote the surface patches on $\mathcal{S}$ corresponding to the omni and lidar planar regions $\mathcal{D}$ and $\mathcal{F}$, respectively. To get an explicit formula for the above integrals, the surface patches $\mathcal{D}_S$ and $\mathcal{F}_S$ can be naturally parameterized via Φ and Ψ over the planar regions $\mathcal{D}$ and $\mathcal{F}$. Without loss of generality, we can assume that the third coordinate of $\mathbf{X} \in \mathcal{F}$ is 0, hence $\mathcal{D} \subset \mathbb{R}^2$, $\mathcal{F} \subset \mathbb{R}^2$; and $\forall \mathbf{x}_S \in \mathcal{D}_S : \mathbf{x}_S = \Phi(\mathbf{x}), \mathbf{x} \in \mathcal{D}$ as well as $\forall \mathbf{z}_S \in \mathcal{F}_S : \mathbf{z}_S = \Psi(\mathbf{X}), \mathbf{X} \in \mathcal{F}$ yielding the following form of (10) [25]:

$$\iint_{\mathcal{D}} \omega(\Phi(\mathbf{x})) \left\| \frac{\partial \Phi}{\partial x_1} \times \frac{\partial \Phi}{\partial x_2} \right\| dx_1 \, dx_2 = \iint_{\mathcal{F}} \omega(\Psi(\mathbf{X})) \left\| \frac{\partial \Psi}{\partial X_1} \times \frac{\partial \Psi}{\partial X_2} \right\| dX_1 \, dX_2 \quad (11)$$

where the magnitude of the cross product of the partial derivatives is known as the surface element. Adopting a set of nonlinear functions $\{\omega_i\}_{i=1}^{\ell}$, each ω_i generates a new equation yielding a system of ℓ independent equations. Although arbitrary ω_i functions could be used, power functions are computationally favorable [4, 26] as these can be computed in a recursive manner:

$$\omega_i(\mathbf{x}_S) = x_1^{l_i} x_2^{m_i} x_3^{n_i}, \text{ with } 0 \le l_i, m_i, n_i \le 2 \text{ and } l_i + m_i + n_i \le 3 \quad (12)$$

2.5 Algorithm Summary

The summary of the numerical implementation of the proposed method is presented in Algorithm 1. Note that normalization is critical in the perspective case to ensure a numerically stable solution (see [4, 26] for details). In the omnidirectional case, we use the coordinates on the spherical surface which are already normalized as $\mathcal{S}$ is a unit sphere.

Algorithm 1. The proposed calibration algorithm

Input: 3D point cloud and 2D binary image representing the same region, and the internal camera parameters (either $\mathbf{K}$ or (a_0, a_2, a_3, a_4)).
Output: Relative pose $(\mathbf{R}, \mathbf{t})$.
1: For perspective cameras, normalize 3D points into the unit cube and the 2D points into the unit square centered in the origin. For omnidirectional cameras, project 3D points and 2D image pixels onto the surface of $\mathcal{S}$ using (3) and (4).
2: Triangulate the region represented by the 3D point cloud.
3: Construct the system of equations. For perspective cameras, use (9) with the polynomial ω_i functions of (8), whereas for omnidirectional cameras, use (11).
4: Initialize the relative pose $(\mathbf{I}, \mathbf{0})$ for perspective cameras and follow the initialization procedure from [25] for omnidirectional cameras.
5: Solve the nonlinear system of equations using the Levenberg-Marquardt algorithm

6: Unnormalize the solution.

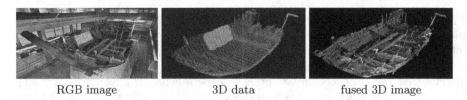

RGB image   3D data   fused 3D image

Fig. 2. Cultural heritage use case example with the *Bremen Cog*. Segmented planar regions are shown in yellow (best viewed in color).

Fig. 3. Dioptric (fish eye) and lidar images with segmented area marked in yellow, and the fused images after pose estimation (best viewed in color)

3   Discussion

In this paper a method for relative pose estimation of central cameras has been presented. The method is based on a point correspondence-less registration technique, which allows reliable estimation of extrinsic camera parameters. The presented algorithms have been applied to various datasets. Three representative examples are shown in Fig. 2, Fig. 4, and Fig. 3. The perspective images in Fig. 2 and Fig. 4 were obtained with a commercial camera while the omnidirectional images were captured with a catadioptric lens in Fig. 4 and a fish-eye in Fig. 3, respectively. After the raw data acquisition, the segmentation was performed in both domains. Finally, the estimated transformation was used to fuse the depth

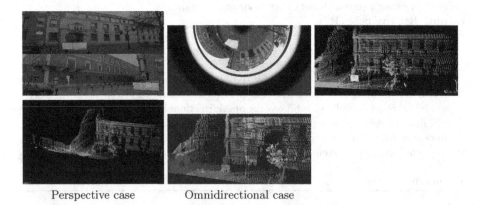

Perspective case   Omnidirectional case

Fig. 4. Perspective, catadioptric and lidar images with segmented area marked in yellow, and the fused images after pose estimation (best viewed in color)

and RGB data by reprojecting the point cloud on the image plane using the internal and external camera parameters, and thus obtaining the color for each point of the 3D point cloud. The method proved to be robust against segmentation errors, but a sufficiently large overlap between the regions is required for better results.

References

1. Boochs, F., Bentkowska-Kafel, A., Degrigny, C., Karaszewski, M., Karmacharya, A., Kato, Z., Picollo, M., Sitnik, R., Trémeau, A., Tsiafaki, D., Tamas, L.: Colour and space in cultural heritage: Key questions in 3D optical documentation of material culture for conservation, study and preservation. In: Ioannides, M., Magnenat-Thalmann, N., Fink, E., Žarnić, R., Yen, A.-Y., Quak, E. (eds.) EuroMed 2014. LNCS, vol. 8740, pp. 11–24. Springer, Heidelberg (2014)
2. Bouaziz, S., Pauly, M.: Dynamic 2D/3D registration for the kinect. In: ACM SIGGRAPH 2013 Courses, SIGGRAPH 2013, pp. 21:1–21:14. ACM, New York (2013)
3. Cao, T., Zach, C., Modla, S., Czymmek, D.P.K., Niethammer, M.: Multi-modal registration for correlative microscopy using image analogies. Medical Image Analysis **18**(6), 914–926 (2014)
4. Domokos, C., Nemeth, J., Kato, Z.: Nonlinear Shape Registration without Correspondences. IEEE Transactions on Pattern Analysis and Machine Intelligence **34**(5), 943–958 (2012)
5. Geiger, A., Lauer, M., Wojek, C., Stiller, C., Urtasun, R.: 3D Traffic Scene Understanding From Movable Platforms. IEEE Transactions on Pattern Analysis and Machine Intelligence **36**(5), 1012–1025 (2014)
6. Geiger, A., Moosmann, F., Car, O., Schuster, B.: Automatic camera and range sensor calibration using a single shot. In: International Conference on Robotics and Automation, pp. 3936–3943. IEEE (2012)
7. Geyer, C., Daniilidis, K.: A unifying theory for central panoramic systems and practical implications. In: Vernon, D. (ed.) ECCV 2000. LNCS, vol. 1843, pp. 445–461. Springer, Heidelberg (2000)
8. Gong, X., Lin, Y., Liu, J.: Extrinsic calibration of a 3D lidar and a camera using a trihedron. Optics and Lasers in Engineering **51**(4), 394–401 (2013)
9. Herrera, C.D., Kannala, J., Heikkila, J.: Joint depth and color camera calibration with distortion correction. IEEE Transactions on Pattern Analysis and Machine Intelligence **34**(10), 1–8 (2012)
10. Kannala, J., Brandt, S.S.: A Generic Camera Model and Calibration Method for Conventional, Wide-Angle, and Fish-Eye Lenses. IEEE Transactions on Pattern Analysis and Machine Intelligence **28**(8), 1335–1340 (2006)
11. Li, Y., Ruichek, Y., Cappelle, C.: Optimal extrinsic calibration between a stereoscopic system and a lidar. IEEE Transactions on Instrumentation and Measurement **62**(8), 2258–2269 (2013)
12. Markelj, P., Tomaževič D., Likar, B., Pernuš, F.: A review of 3D/2D registration methods for image-guided interventions. Medical Image Analysis 16(3), 642–661 (2012). Computer Assisted Interventions
13. Mastin, A., Kepner, J., Fisher III, J.: Automatic registration of lidar and optical images of urban scenes. In: IEEE Computer Society Conference on Computer Vision and Pattern Recognition, pp. 2639–2646. IEEE, Miami (June 2009)

14. Mei, C., Rives, P.: Single view point omnidirectional camera calibration from planar grids. In: International Conference on Robotics and Automation, pp. 3945–3950. Roma, Italy (April 2007)
15. Mičušík, B., Pajdla, T.: Para-catadioptric camera auto-calibration from epipolar geometry. In: Asian Conference on Computer Vision, Seoul, Korea South, vol. 2, pp. 748–753 (January 2004)
16. Mirzaei, F.M., Kottas, D.G., Roumeliotis, S.I.: 3D LIDAR-camera intrinsic and extrinsic calibration: Identifiability and analytical least-squares-based initialization. International Journal of Robotics Research **31**(4), 452–467 (2012)
17. Mishra, R., Zhang, Y.: A review of optical imagery and airborne lidar data registration methods. The Open Remote Sensing Journal **5**, 54–63 (2012)
18. Nunez, P., Drews, P., Rocha, R., Dias, J.: Data fusion calibration for a 3D laser range finder and a camera using inertial data. In: European Conference on Mobile Robots, Dubrovnik, Croatia, pp. 31–36 (September 2009)
19. Pandey, G., McBride, J.R., Savarese, S., Eustice, R.M.: Automatic targetless extrinsic calibration of a 3D lidar and camera by maximizing mutual information. In: AAAI National Conference on Artificial Intelligence, pp. 2053–2059. Toronto, Canada (July 2012)
20. Pluim, J., Maintz, J., Viergever, M.: Mutual-information-based registration of medical images: a survey. IEEE Transactions on Medical Imaging **22**(8), 986–1004 (2003)
21. Scaramuzza, D., Harati, A., Siegwart, R.: Extrinsic self calibration of a camera and a 3D laser range finder from natural scenes. In: International Conference on Intelligent Robots and Systems, pp. 4164–4169. San Diego, USA (October 2007)
22. Scaramuzza, D., Martinelli, A., Siegwart, R.: A flexible technique for accurate omnidirectional camera calibration and structure from motion. In: International Conference on Computer Vision Systems, Washington, USA, pp. 45–51 (January 2006)
23. Schoenbein, M., Strauss, T., Geiger, A.: Calibrating and centering quasi-central catadioptric cameras. In: International Conference on Robotics and Automation, Hong-Kong, China, pp. 1253–1256 (June 2014)
24. Stamos, I.: Automated registration of 3D-range with 2D-color images: an overview. In: 2010 44th Annual Conference on Information Sciences and Systems (CISS), pp. 1–6 (March 2010)
25. Tamas, L., Frohlich, R., Kato, Z.: Relative pose estimation and fusion of omnidirectional and lidar cameras. In: ECCV Workshop on Computer Vision for Road Scene Understanding and Autonomous Driving (ECCV-CVRSUAD). Lecture Notes in Computer Science, pp. 1–12, Zurich, Switzerland (September 2014)
26. Tamas, L., Kato, Z.: Targetless calibration of a lidar - perspective camera pair. In: International Conference on Computer Vision, Bigdata3dcv Workshops, Sydney, Australia, pp. 668–675 (December 2013)
27. Taylor, Z., Nieto, J.: A mutual information approach to automatic calibration of camera and lidar in natural environments. In: Australian Conference on Robotics and Automation, Wellington, Australia, pp. 3–8 (December 2012)
28. Unnikrishnan, R., Hebert, M.: Fast extrinsic calibration of a laser rangefinder to a camera. Tech. rep. Carnegie Mellon University (2005)
29. Zhang, Q.: Extrinsic calibration of a camera and laser range finder. In: International Conference on Intelligent Robots and Systems, pp. 2301–2306. IEEE, Sendai (September 2004)

Representation of Cultural Objects by Image Sets with Directional Illumination

Lindsay W. MacDonald[(✉)]

3D Impact Research Group, Faculty of Engineering, University College London,
London, England
lindsay.macdonald@ucl.ac.uk

Abstract. In a dome illumination system, many different images can be captured in pixel register from the same viewpoint, each illuminated from a different direction. This is a much richer representation than a single image, and has many applications in cultural heritage for the digitising and display of objects that are flattish with surface relief, such as coins, medals, fossils, rock art, incised tablets, bas reliefs, engravings, canvas paintings, etc. The image sets can be used in three ways: (1) visualisation by interactive movement of a virtual light source over the enclosing hemisphere; (2) 3D reconstruction of the object surface; (3) modelling of the specular highlights from the surface and hence realistic rendering.

Keywords: Illumination · Surface normals · 3D reconstruction · Specular model

1 Dome Photography

It has long been recognised that illumination incident at low angles can help to visualise the relief on surfaces. In the study of canvas paintings it has been used for examining the artist's technique [1], identification of retouching [2] and detection of forgery [3]. In astronomy the oblique direction of the sun's rays has shown the structure of craters on the moon [4]. In archaeology raking light has been used to reveal inscriptions on marble and stone that were otherwise invisible [5]. In palaeographic studies of incised wooden and lead curse tablets from the Roman empire, directional illumination has been used to enhance the marks left by the stilus [6]. Generally it has been employed in an empirical way, with the observer or photographer moving the object relative to the light source (or vice versa) until the desired effect was achieved.

Directional lighting has also been key to the measurement of angular reflectance distributions from the surfaces of materials. In a gonioreflectometer, by moving the source of illumination relative to the sample and/or detector, the bidirectional reflectance distribution function (BRDF) can be obtained. Ward developed an automated system for BRDF measurement with a movable light source and rotating sample, under a hemispherical mirror [7]. Malzbender showed how directional illumination could be used in a systematic way for digital photography [8]. He built an illumination dome at HP Labs from an acrylic hemisphere of diameter 18 inches (45 cm) with 24 fixed flash lights. The camera was mounted at the 'north pole' and the object placed on a horizontal surface beneath. This enabled sets of 24 images to be taken in pixel register.

© Springer International Publishing Switzerland 2015
A. Trémeau et al. (Eds.): CCIW 2015, LNCS 9016, pp. 43–56, 2015.
DOI: 10.1007/978-3-319-15979-9_5

The UCL Dome is an acrylic hemisphere of nominal diameter 1030 mm, fitted with 64 flash lamps, each mounted on a separate circuit board (Fig. 1). The lamps are distributed around the hemisphere, arranged in three tiers of 16, one tier of 12, and one tier of 4 lights at approximately equal intervals. The lowest tier produces raking light across the equatorial plane (<10°), whereas the highest tier is nearly polar (>80°). The Nikon D200 digital camera is mounted on a rigid steel frame above the dome.

Fig. 1. (left) Hemispherical dome with the camera mounted above the north pole, with 64 flash lights on circuit boards, connected by 'daisy chain' ribbon cables; (right) flash lamp firing

Because both the camera mounting point and the lamp positions are fixed, the dome geometry can be characterised precisely. Although the original concept design called for the flash lights to be placed at regular intervals over the surface of the hemisphere, the positions of the lamps in the actual dome, as constructed, differ from the ideal. Three techniques were employed for the geometric calibration of flash light positions in the dome: (1) the shadow cast

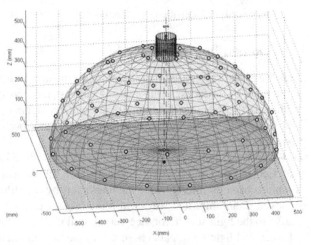

Fig. 2. Coordinates of 64 flash lamp centroids plotted on hemispherical dome, with representation of lens and sensor (top)

by a vertical pin onto graph paper; (2) multi-image photogrammetry with retro- reflective targets; and (3) multi-image photogrammetry using the flash lights themselves as targets. It was found that although photogrammetric methods could locate individual target coordinates to an accuracy of 20 microns, the uncertainty of locating the centroids of the flash lights was approximately 1.5 mm [9]. This result is considered satisfactory for photometric imaging purposes.

2   Visualisation of Surfaces

The set of images from the dome can be used to visualize the effect of moving a virtual light source over the object, illuminating its surface from any angle in the hemisphere. The question is how to interpolate the 64 angles of the lights in the dome to achieve a continuous movement? One approach would be to make an azimuthal equidistant projection of the lamp coordinates onto the equatorial plane and then to triangulate the network (Fig. 3). The image intensity could then be estimated as a weighted linear combination of the three nearest neighbours of the projected virtual light source. Better results could be obtained by fitting surface patches to the intensity distribution.

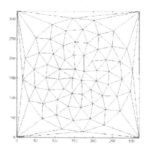

Fig. 3. Delaunay triangulation of X,Y coordinates of azimuthal equidistant projection of dome lamps

An alternative approach is to fit a continuous function to all intensity values over the hemisphere. Malzbender showed that the intensity distribution over all angles of the hemisphere could be approximated by a biquadratic function with six parameters, in a method he called polynomial texture mapping (PTM). Singular value decomposition (SVD) is applied to determine the projection of each of the lamp vectors onto the biquadratic components, and then regression with least-squares minimisation to obtain the six coefficients for each pixel [9]. PTM assumes separability of the reconstruction function, with a constant 'base colour' per pixel modulated by an angle-dependent luminance factor:

$$I = L(\Theta_i, \Phi_i, u, v)R(u, v) \tag{1}$$

for $R(u,v)$ and similarly for $G(u,v)$ and $B(u,v)$. The dependence of the luminance on light direction is modelled by the biquadratic function:

$$L(u, v; l_u, l_v) = a_0 l_u^2 + a_1 l_v^2 + a_2 l_u l_v + a_3 l_u + a_4 l_v + a_5 \tag{2}$$

where (l_u, l_v) are projections of the normalised light vector into the local texture coordinate system (u, v) and L is the resultant luminance. A separate set of six coefficients $(a_0\text{-}a_5)$ is fitted to the image data for each pixel and stored in the PTM file at the same spatial resolution as each of the original images. For reconstruction in the viewer software, the position of the virtual light source is expressed in coordinates (u, v) and the intensity of every pixel calculated by Eq. (2). The PTM has the same spatial resolution as each of the original images, but has a low resolution in the angular space of incident illumination, because the n directions of the image set are approximated by only 6 coefficients at each pixel.

PTM has found favour with the museum and cultural heritage community because it provides a convenient and attractive way to visualise objects in collections. The interactive control of lighting direction in the viewer software facilitates perception of the surface structure compared to static photographs, thereby enhancing the legibility of surface relief and inscriptions [10]. The illusion of a 3D surface lit by a movable light source is compelling, even though there is no underlying 3D representation.

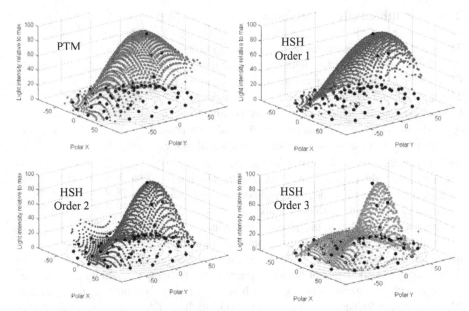

Fig. 4. Angular distributions of intensity, plotted in the azimuthal equidistant projection, for four approximations to the measured intensity distribution. The black dots represent actual reflected intensity of the 64 lamps. All intensities are normalised to a maximum of 100.

An improved method of fitting the directional distributions was introduced by Gautron *et al* [11] by limiting the domain of the orthogonal basis functions of spherical harmonics to a hemisphere instead of the full sphere. These hemispherical harmonic (HSH) functions provide a more compact and accurate way of representing hemispherical distributions than the biquadratic function used in PTM. They have since been widely adopted for a variety of computer graphic applications where only half of the spherical distribution needs to modelled, such as the representation of BRDFs, environment map rendering of non-diffuse surfaces and global-illumination computation.

HSH components are expressed as functions of angles for azimuth θ and co-latitude φ over the hemisphere [12]. Good results are obtained with sixteen components, which include four first-order, five second-order and seven third-order terms. Fitting of the coefficients follows the same SVD-based procedure as for PTM, and can be applied to the image luminance (weighted sum of R,G,B channels) to provide the angular modulation at each pixel of a constant R,G,B colour value. These components can be conveniently visualised by projecting the hemisphere onto a plane through an azimuthal equidistant projection. Comparison of the HSH and PTM renderings (Fig. 4) shows that HSH (2nd-order with nine coefficients) gives a better representation of the directionality of the surface, with higher contrast for local gradients.

How many images are needed to give an accurate rendering of the angular reflectance distribution in PTM or HSH? Ideally one should capture images with illumination from all necessary angles but no more. The challenge is to reduce the number of photographic image samples that need to be acquired while preserving the power of the digital model to represent the object realistically. A full BRDF analysis requires a systematic sampling of a four-dimensional space, with both illumination and view angles able to range over the full hemisphere. In the PTM and RTI scenarios, the view direction is always fixed (usually at the zenith, perpendicular to the centre of the object surface) and only the illumination direction is variable.

Gunawardane *et al* analysed the sampling of both view and lighting directions and whether methods for interpolation could be improved if both view and lighting information were available [13]. They conducted a data-driven study in which a test object was illuminated by a hemispherical dome with 64 tungsten lights. The object sat on a turntable and a full set of 64 images was captured for 360 rotational angles of the object, at 1° intervals for a total of 23,040 images. The complete image set was then sub-sampled for intervals of

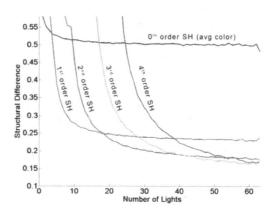

Fig. 5. Error vs number of lights for four orders of hemispherical harmonics (Gunawardane, 2009)

both lighting and view angles and the errors calculated between HSH fittings of both the full and subsampled image sets. The results (Fig. 5) indicated that the minimum number of lamps is approximately 10, 20, 36 and 56 for the 1st to 4th harmonic orders respectively. The pitfall in interpolation of images from different lighting directions was found to be that errors in flow vectors caused pixels to move to incorrect positions, producing visible tearing artifacts and structural discontinuities.

Drew *et al* observed that for non-Lambertian phenomena matrix factorisation methods can produce inaccurate surface normals and lighting directions [14]. Because the basic PTM method relies on a matte surface and linear regression, it fails to model phenomena such as inter-reflections, specularities and shadows. Increasing the degree of the PTM polynomial model, for example by the use of HSH basis functions, may help to model these effects but at the expense of degrading the interpolated results at non-sampled light directions due to over-fitting. For finding the matte part of the photometric model, they used the Least Median of Squares (LMS) method, which provides automatic identification of outliers, both specular highlights and shadows. Knowledge of the inlier pixel values means that the recovered surface albedo, chromaticity and surface normals are robust, in the sense of ignoring outlier contributions and thus more accurately mapping surface reflectance, colour and shape. They also altered the polynomial used in PTM so as to generate a subset of three regression coefficients that is exactly correct in the case when the inliers are Lambertian.

Brady *et al* developed an alternative method of visualizing the relief of incised tablets, called shadow stereo, after observing how a professional palaeographer examined a stilus tablet, holding it horizontally on his upturned palm to be illuminated at a grazing angle, and slowly rotating it to change the angle of elevation [15].

3   3D Reconstruction

The image sets captured in the dome contain information about the geometry of the object surface. The photometric stereo technique enables the normal at each point to be determined for a single viewpoint, using the principle that the intensity of reflected light depends on the angle of incidence of the light onto the surface and the reflectance factor. With a perfectly Lambertian surface and in the absence of noise, only three intensity values $[I_1, I_2, I_3]$ from non-coplanar light sources with unit direction vectors $[\mathbf{L}_1, \mathbf{L}_2, \mathbf{L}_3]$ would be sufficient to solve for both the normal direction $\mathbf{N}$ and the surface albedo ρ:

$$I_i = \rho \mathbf{L}_i \cdot \mathbf{N} = \rho \, |L_i| \cos \alpha_i \tag{3}$$

where α_i is the angle between the normal and lamp vector i. In practice, normals calculated in this way from three light directions exhibit an unacceptable level of noise and vary widely according to the particular combination of lamps selected. Better results can be obtained for noisy image data by calculating normals for many triplets of light sources. By selecting suitable combinations of three lamps, candidates for the normal can be calculated for every pixel. For a non-Lambertian surface, however, the above method gives incorrect results, because the effect of surface gloss is to exaggerate the apparent gradient of the surface.

A new method for estimating normals has been developed, which is robust and adapts to the presence of both shadows and surface gloss [12]. First all of the intensity values at a pixel are extracted from the image set and treated as a vector. The intensity values are then sorted into ascending order and the cumulative sum calculated. The subset of lamps is selected for which the normalised cumulative values lie between two thresholds, nominally 0.10 and 0.25. These thresholds are chosen to select a region of the sorted distribution that follows the slope of the cumulative sorted cosine, i.e. related to the diffuse component of the reflection. Fig. 6 shows the results of applying the technique to a 19th-century terracotta roundel of Chopin, and the derived gradients $P = (\partial I / \partial x)$ and $Q = (\partial I / \partial y)$, encoded in false colour.

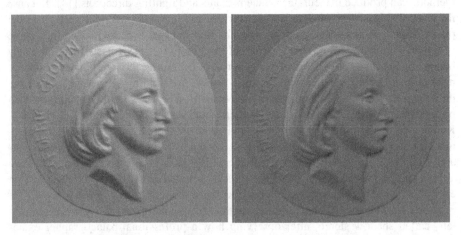

Fig. 6. (left) Photometric normal vectors in false colour (Nx red, Ny green, Nz blue); (right) False colour composite of gradients (P red, Q green)

A novel method for integrating the gradients to reconstruct height was introduced by Frankot & Chellappa [16], using the Fourier transform to regularise (i.e. to enforce integrability of) the gradients in the frequency domain. This is neatly implemented in Matlab by a few lines of code, taken from the library developed by Kovesi [17].

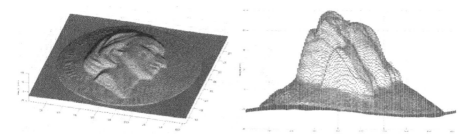

Fig. 7. (left) Oblique view and (right) elevation of Chopin surface reconstructed by the basic Frankot & Chellappa integration of gradients in the frequency domain

Applying this technique to the Chopin gradients (Fig. 6 right) yields a 3D surface that is continuous and is recognisably Chopin, but is distorted over the whole area with the height greatly amplified. Fig. 7 (left) shows an oblique view, which looks very plausible, but when the same structure is viewed in elevation (Fig. 7 right) it is seen that the height range is from -27.6 to +79.9, an overall maximum height of 107.5 mm, compared with the true maximum height above the baseplane of 22.5 mm. Also there is a false undulation of the base with a period of approximately one cycle over the whole width. The problem is that although the photometric gradients give a good representation of the spatial frequencies in the surface, right up to the Nyquist frequency, they are not accurate for very low frequencies of a few cycles over the full object diameter. Such frequencies are represented in the Fourier plane by only a few sample points close to the (shifted) origin. Errors in these frequencies can result in 'curl' or 'heave' in the baseplane, even though the superimposed higher spatial frequencies may be accurate.

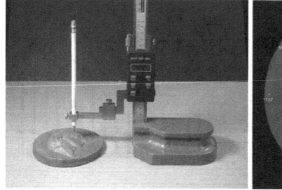
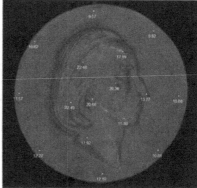

Fig. 8. (left) Using a height measuring gauge; (right) Heights of selected points in mm, superimposed on an image of the Chopin terracotta taken under all lights in Tier 3

The solution is to replace the inaccurate low frequencies of the photometric normals by the more accurate low frequencies of a surface constructed from a few known heights [18]. This can be conveniently achieved from the values measured by a digital height gauge (Fig. 8) by first interpolating them to produce a smooth 'hump' and then transforming into the frequency domain by an FFT (Fig. 9).

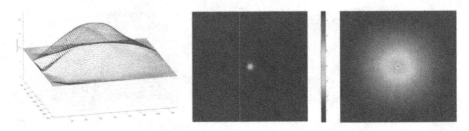

Fig. 9. (left) Smooth surface of hump produced by interpolation of measured points; (centre and right) Log(power) distribution of spatial frequencies of hump and photometric gradients

The low spatial frequencies of the gradients from the Frankot-Chellappa integration are replaced by the corresponding frequencies from the hump. Rather than an abrupt change at a given threshold frequency, they are blended over a radial distance in the range 1.5 to 4.0 pixels by a linear interpolation function (Fig. 10 left). The power of the high frequencies from the gradients is scaled by the ratio of the low/high power in the region affected, in order to maintain the correct overall power distribution.

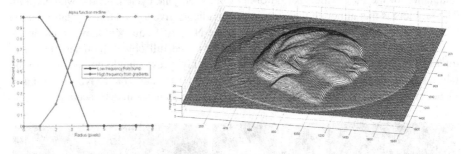

Fig. 10. (left) Cross-over of low and high frequency components; (right) Reconstructed surface

Differences between the 16 values measured by the height gauge and the reconstructed values at the same positions are well distributed (Fig. 11), ranging from -1.31 to +1.92 mm with mean zero, mean-of-absolutes 0.61 and stdev 0.83. Even better results can be obtained by using the point cloud from a 3D scanner to provide the geometric basis of the low frequency components in the reconstruction.

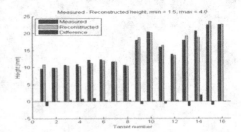

Fig. 11. Measured and reconstructed heights and their differences (mm)

4   Specular Modelling

The image sets captured in the dome, illuminated from 64 known directions over the hemisphere, contain information about the directionality of reflection from an object surface. The aim is to model the luminance variation at each point on the object surface as a function of the angle of illumination, in such a way that the reconstructed images are indistinguishable from the original photographs. This would also enable views of the object to be 'relit' for a continuous range of illumination angles in between those of the fixed lamps in the dome.

The decorative test object used in this study was a polished brass dish, 125 mm in diameter, embellished in the Damascene fashion with inlaid copper and silver arabesques (Fig. 12 left). There is a significant trade-off in choosing the exposure setting when photographing the object in the dome: if too low then most of the non-specular pixels are of very low intensity (as in this case) and hence greatly affected by sensor noise; if too high then most of the specular pixels are over-exposed, producing the maximum output value and causing blooming in neighbouring pixels by spill-over of photoelectrons in the sensor.

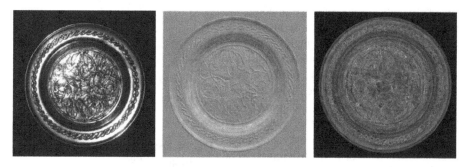

Fig. 12. Damascene dish: (left) image illuminated by four lamps in tier 5 of dome; (centre) normal vectors in false colour; (right) albedo

The normal vector and albedo were computed for every pixel (Fig. 12 centre and right). The normals are quite subtle because most of the surface is horizontal and the relief of the decoration is shallow. The albedo is surprisingly dark and chromatic, representing the diffuse 'base colour' of the metal without any specular component.

The 'specular quotient' is calculated as the ratio between the actual intensity for each lamp direction and the intensity that would be produced by a perfect diffuser in the same direction. The more shiny the surface, the greater the quotient value (Fig. 13 left). The specular direction vector is calculated as a weighted sum of the lamp vectors exceeding a threshold, multiplied by the corresponding specular quotient values. The same weighted sum gives the colour of the specular reflection (Fig. 13 right). For most materials this would be the same colour as the illumination, i.e. white, but for metals the specular component carries the colour of the metal. Here for the Damascene dish the colours of the brass, copper and silver are clearly defined.

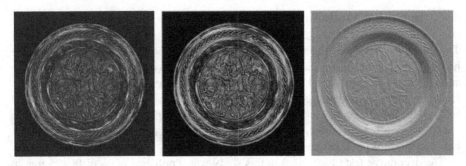

Fig. 13. (left) Specular quotient = ratio of specular/diffuse intensities; (centre) specular colour; (right) Specular direction vectors in false colour

The resulting specular direction vectors (Fig. 13 right) have the same general appearance as the normals (Fig. 12 centre) but are more chromatic because the specular gradients are greater with respect to the view vector. In conventional practice in computational photography it is almost universally assumed that the specular angle should be exactly double that of the normal, and for a perfect mirror this would of course be true. But the surfaces of real objects have a meso-structure with fine texture and granularity. One pixel as sampled by the camera may span a number of micro-facets at different angles, which reflect light differently from the incident illumination.

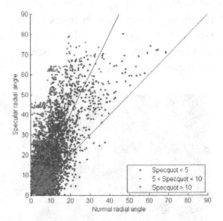

Fig. 14. Specular vs normal angles, classified by quotient value

The approach taken here is to use the ideal specular (at double the angle of the normal) as a guide to where the specular angle should be. A weighted sum is taken of all lamp vectors within a cone of 45° around this direction, weighted by their quotient values. It is clear from scatter-plotting the specular vs normal angles for a random selection of 10,000 pixels (Fig. 14) that there is a considerable amount of variation around the line of slope 2 (i.e. specular angle = 2x normal angle), which is a genuine indication of the roughness of the surface. Pixels with low values of specular quotient (blue in the figure) generally have a greater scatter. Some clustering onto the five tier angles of the dome is evident in the pixels of high quotient values (red in the figure). The figure suggests that the maximum normal angle that can be quantified by the photometric stereo technique is c.35°, with corresponding maximum specular angle of c.70°.

In the general case the bidirectional reflectance distribution function (BRDF) has four degrees of freedom, giving the reflectance of the surface at any viewpoint when illuminated from any direction. In the case of dome imaging, however, the viewpoint is fixed with the camera always at the 'north pole' of the hemisphere and the object lying in the equatorial plane. So the problem is simplified to finding a two-dimensional function of the reflectance factor toward the camera, given the normal and lamp vectors. A further simplification is to assume that the function of reflectance is isotropic and therefore rotationally symmetric, i.e. dependent only on the radial angle ω from the peak but not on the phase angle around the peak. The required function needs to be positive, continuous and monotonic, with a peak at $\omega = 0$ and asymptotic to zero as $\omega \to 90°$ (excluding the Fresnel component at grazing angles).

The model adopted to fit the specular peak is based on the Lorentzian function, because it naturally conforms to the observed shape and is mathematically convenient [12]. In particular the broad flanks enable the scattered light at perispecular angles to be modelled more effectively than the Gaussian function, which falls too quickly to zero. The comparison can be seen by fitting both functions empirically to the distribution (Fig. 15). An offset in the X axis has been made to accommodate the horizontal scatter, and the scale factors (divisors of X value) are different. But it is clear that the Gaussian approaches zero too rapidly and therefore underestimates the reflected intensity in the

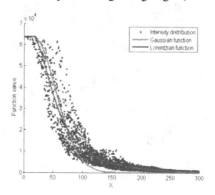

Fig. 15. Comparison of Gaussian and Lorentzian functions against a real distribution of reflected intensities

critical intermediate angles between peak and flank. The Lorentzian can be written as a function of three variables:

$$f(x) = \frac{a}{1+\left(\frac{x}{s}\right)^2} + c \tag{4}$$

where a is the amplitude of the peak, s is the scale factor (horizontal spread), and c is a constant (uplift).

5   Specular Classification

A detail of the specular colour image of the Damascene dish shows clearly that the specular highlights of the three metallic components carry the colour of the metal (Fig. 16 left). Scatter-plotting 10,000 points chosen at random by their colours and locations in RGB space shows (Fig. 16 right) that they lie in an oblate region around the long diagonal of the colour cube, i.e. the neutral axis. There is a surprising amount of colour variation for what appears to be a surface composed of only three materials, and the tonal variation is continuous from black to the lightest points at about 0.7 of full range.

The pixel colours are converted from RGB via XYZ to CIELAB, assuming the sRGB colour space and the CIE standard 2° observer with D65 white point. Plotting the same points on the a^*–b^* chromatic plane shows that the colours of the three metals, brass, copper and silver, have distinctly different hue angles (Fig. 17). This provides the opportunity to segment the image pixels into four categories, corresponding to the three metals plus black.

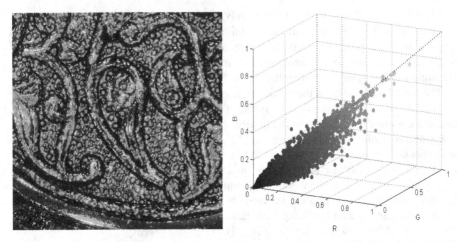

Fig. 16. (left) Detail of specular colour image of Damascene dish, size 500x500 pixels; (right) scatter plot of 10,000 pixels in R,G,B colour space

The simple way to classify is by hue angle around the centroid of the three category centres, where reddish colours in the range [-45°, +70°] correspond to copper; the yellow-greenish colours in [70°, 180°] to brass; and the slightly bluish colours in [180°, -45°] to silver. A more effective method is to categorise each pixel by its nearest distance to one of the focal colours for the three metals. The resulting 'posterised' image is equivalent to a K-means classification with four cluster centres (including black).

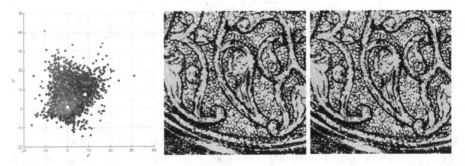

Fig. 17. (left) 10,000 pixels plotted on the CIELAB a*–b* chromatic plane, with centroids for the three metals; (centre) classification by hue angle; (right) classification by nearest colour

The ability to classify different regions of a heterogeneous surface according to their gloss enables each region to be modelled and rendered in a different way. This is an important capability for objects that are made of multiple materials, such as inlays, and also for objects that were once homogeneous but have weathered variably across the surface. It is interesting to consider whether metals could be classified in the same way.

In an attempt to differentiate the specular curves of the three metals in the Damascene dish, the map generated by image classification (Fig. 17 right) was used to select 500 random samples of each of the three metals. Curves were fitted by the Lorentzian model and plotted in superimposition (Fig. 18 left). All three sets of curves show a

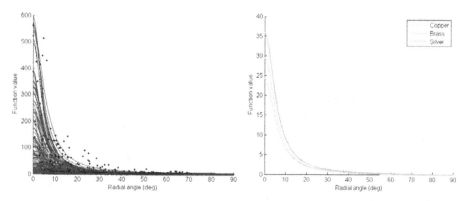

Fig. 18. (left) Specular curves fitted by the Lorentzian model to 500 pixels of silver on the Damascene dish; (right) Characteristic curves for the three metals for peak amplitudes >15

similar behaviour, with a few cases having peak values of very high amplitude, in excess of 500, but the majority much lower.

Taking the median of each parameter in the sets for each metal for those cases where the amplitude exceeds 15, and using the median parameter values in the Lorentzian model gives the indicative curves of Fig. 18 right. The ordering of amplitude is: silver highest, copper second and brass lowest, but the relative differences are small and the variance of the curves for individual pixels is so great that these curves could not be used as a reliable diagnostic to determine the type of metal. The colour in the albedo and specular highlights is a much more reliable guide. All that one can say in this case is that the freshly polished silver is likely to be slightly brighter in the specular highlights than the other two metals.

6   Conclusion

A set of images in pixel register under controlled directional lighting provides a much richer representation of an object than a single image, because it contains information about both the topography and specularity of the surface. With appropriate metadata, including the directions of the incident light sources, camera position and lens distortion, such a dataset can be considered as a valid archival representation of the object, with many applications for education, conservation and interpretation.

Through an interactive visualisation technique, such as PTM, the sense of materiality of the object can be conveyed much more strongly than through a static image display. This is an example of how, as Witcomb says, "multimedia installations in museums can enhance ... the 'affective' possibilities of objects" [19]. They can "act as releasers of memory in much the same way as objects can make unconscious memories conscious. This they achieve through their power to affect us by 'touching' us or 'moving' us."

Acknowledgements. Thanks to colleagues in the 3DImpact Research Group, especially Stuart Robson, Mona Hess and Ali Ahmadabadian, for assistance and encouragement in this research.

References

1. Rosen, D., Marceau, H.: A Study in the Use of Photographs in the Identification of Paintings. Technical Studies in the Field of the Fine Arts **6**(2), 75–105 (1937)
2. Ruhemann, H.: Criteria for distinguishing additions from original paint. Studies in Conservation **3**(4), 145–161 (1958)
3. Stolow, N.: The Canadian art fraud case. Canadian art 94 (1964)
4. Phillips, J.: Notices of Some Parts of the Surface of the Moon. Phil. Trans. Royal Society of London **158**, 333–345 (1868)
5. Engelbach, R.: A foundation scene of the second dynasty. The Journal of Egyptian Archaeology, 183–184 (1934)
6. Bowman, A.K., Brady, J.M., Tomlin, R.S.O.: Imaging incised documents. Literary and Linguistic Computing **12**(3), 169–176 (1997)
7. Ward, G.J.: Measuring and modeling anisotropic reflection. In: Proc. 19th Conf. on Computer Graphics (Siggraph), pp. 265–272. ACM (1992)
8. Malzbender, T., Gelb, D., Wolters, H.: Polynomial texture maps. In: Proc. 28th Conf. on Computer Graphics (Siggraph), pp. 519–528. ACM (2001)
9. MacDonald, L.W., Ahmadabadian, A.H., Robson, S.: Determining the coordinates of lamps in an illumination dome. In: Proc. SPIE Conf. on Videometrics, Munich (2015)
10. Earl, G., Martinez, K., Malzbender, T.: Archaeological applications of polynomial texture mapping: analysis, conservation and representation. J. Archaeological Science **37**(8), 2040–2050 (2010)
11. Gautron, P., Krivanek, J., Pattanaik, S., Bouatouch, K.: A novel hemispherical basis for accurate and efficient rendering. In: Eurographics Symposium on Rendering Techniques, pp. 321–330 (2004)
12. MacDonald, L.W.: Colour and directionality in surface reflectance. In: Proc. Conf. on Artificial Intelligence and Simulation of Behaviour (AISB). Goldsmiths College (April 2014)
13. Gunawardane, P., Wang, O., Scher, S., Rickards, I., Davis, J., Malzbender, T.: Optimized image sampling for view and light interpolation. In: Proc. 10th Intl. Conf. on Virtual Reality, Archaeology and Cultural Heritage (VAST), Eurographics, vol. 10, pp. 93–100 (2009)
14. Drew, M., Hel-Or, Y., Malzbender, T., Hajari, N.: Robust estimation of surface properties and interpolation of shadow/specularity components. Image and Vision Computing **30**(4), 317–331 (2012)
15. Brady, M., et al.: Shadow stereo, image filtering and constraint propagation. In: Bowman, A.K., Brady, M. (eds) Images and Artefacts of the Ancient World, pp. 15–30 (2005)
16. Frankot, R.T., Chellappa, R.: A method for enforcing integrability in shape from shading algorithms. IEEE Trans. on Pattern Analysis & Machine Intell. 10(4), 439–451 (1988)
17. Kovesi, P.: Shapelets correlated with surface normals produce surfaces. In: Proc. Tenth IEEE Intl. Conf. on Computer Vision, vol. 2, pp. 994–1001 (2005)
18. Tominaga, R., Ujike, H., Horiuchi, T., Surface reconstruction of oil paintings for digital archiving. In: Proc. IEEE Southwest Symp. on Image Analysis and Interpretn., pp. 173–176 (2010)
19. Witcomb, A.: The materiality of virtual technologies: A new approach to thinking about the impact of multimedia in museums. In: Cameron, F., Kenderine, S. (eds) Theorizing Digital Cultural Heritage: A Critical Discourse, pp. 35–48. The MIT Press (2007)

Color Reproduction

Descriptor-Based Image Colorization and Regularization

Dmitry Kuzovkin[1,2], Christel Chamaret[1], and Tania Pouli[1(✉)]

[1] Technicolor Research and Innovation, Rennes, France
{christel.chamaret,tania.pouli}@technicolor.com
[2] Jean Monnet University, Saint-Étienne, France
kuzovkin.dmitry@gmail.com

Abstract. We propose a new, fully automatic method for example-based image colorization and a robust color artifact regularization solution. To determine correspondences between the two images, we supplement the PatchMatch algorithm with rich statistical image descriptors. Based on detected matches, our method transfers colors from the reference to the target grayscale image. In addition, we propose a general regularization scheme that can smooth artifacts typical to color manipulation algorithms. Our regularization approach propagates the major colors in image regions, as determined through superpixel-based segmentation of the original image. We evaluate the effectiveness of our colorization for a varied set of images and demonstrate our regularization scheme for both colorization and color transfer applications.

Keywords: Colorization · Regularization · Color transfer

1 Introduction

Colorization — the process of adding color to grayscale content — is crucial for giving a new lease of life to legacy movies or photographs. Historically, colorization has been a time-consuming, manual task, however in recent years, automated solutions have emerged for colorizing content. Existing automatic colorization solutions rely on a user-provided reference image [16], a palette specifying the colors the image should obtain [11] or set of strokes [10] drawn directly on the image to define colors.

Our work falls within the first category, known as *example-based colorization*, and relies on a reference color image with semantically similar content to the target grayscale image. To transfer color information from the reference to the target, our method finds correspondences using a modified version of the PatchMatch algorithm [2]. Although typically this algorithm considers only color information in the image, this often does not provide enough distinguishing information when the two images are not depicting the same scene. To that end, we supplement PatchMatch with a series of statistical descriptors that provide a rich representation of the structure in the two images.

© Springer International Publishing Switzerland 2015
A. Trémeau et al. (Eds.): CCIW 2015, LNCS 9016, pp. 59–68, 2015.
DOI: 10.1007/978-3-319-15979-9_6

In addition to our colorization method, we propose a novel regularization scheme to remove artifacts typical to such color manipulations. In processes such as colorization or color transfer, small discontinuities in the luminance (e.g. due to compression artifacts) may lead to corresponding anomalies in chromaticities. To remove such artifacts, regularization methods aim to smoothly propagate colors within coherent regions. Our solution relies on superpixel segmentation and subsequent merging to robustly divide the image into coherent areas. A stroke is automatically created for each region and propagated depending on adjacent luminance information [10].

Experiments conducted on various types of images demonstrate that our method can provide visually appealing colorization results in different scenarios, competitive with the state of the art, at a lower computational cost. Additionally, we demonstrate the usefulness of our regularization approach in the context of color modification methods. Our work offers the following contributions:

- A novel, fully automatic colorization approach
- A combination of image descriptors that allows using a wider set of images as references in colorization
- A regularization scheme for correcting artifacts typically seen after color processing such as colorization or color transfer

2 Related Work

Given a reference color image, example-based methods aim to find correspondences with the grayscale target in order to define how colors should be distributed. Earlier methods rely only on luminance information to determine correspondences [16], which can often fail when corresponding areas (e.g. sky) do not have corresponding luminance. Additionally, small irregularities in the luminance can lead to spatial consistency issues.

To address some of these limitations, the higher-level context of each pixel needs to be considered. Irony *et al.* [8] use a supervised classification scheme based on image features and can provide plausible colorization results, however it requires manual segmentation into corresponding regions, making it ill-suited for automatic colorization. To obtain better correspondences, Charpiat *et al.* [4] further exploit the idea of feature descriptors by using SURF descriptors incorporated into a probability estimation model. Probabilistic information is also used by Bugeau *et al.* [3], where a variational energy minimization framework is employed to simultaneously find candidate colors and regularize results.

The closest to our approach is the work of Gupta *et al.* [7], which relies on a cascade feature matching scheme to find correspondences between reference and target images. The spatial consistency of matching is improved by a voting step, which is based on mean-shift segmentation together with k-means clustering. Each segment is assigned with a color, and obtained colors are used to produce micro-scribbles in the center of each segment. These are propagated across the entire image using the algorithm by Levin et al. [10]. In contrast to their approach, we use a smaller and more general set of descriptors, allowing us to colorize using a less restrictive selection of reference images. At the same time, we take advantage of the robustness of the PatchMatch algorithm to obtain correspondences, which leads to more accurate assignment of colors as will be shown in Section 5. Finally, we ensure a better propagation of colors in our regularization scheme by creating large skeleton-based strokes that span coherent areas in the image. The following sections will describe our colorization solution and regularization scheme in detail.

3 Colorization

The general scheme of the proposed method is shown in Figure 1. The input is represented by two images: a target grayscale image I_t to be colorized, and a reference color image I_r. The images are smoothed using a Gaussian filter before analysis to remove small artifacts, such as noise or painterly texture, that might influence the matching step (w = 5x5, $\sigma = 1.0$). Then, our method finds correspondences between the intensity channels of the two images (Y_t and Y_r respectively), using their descriptor representations. The obtained correspondences are used to map chroma information from the reference to the target image, producing an initial colorization result. Finally, a regularization step (Section 4) is applied to suppress color artifacts that might be present in the initial result.

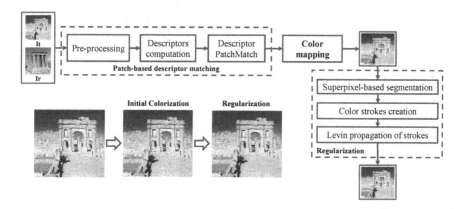

Fig. 1. Overview of the proposed colorization framework

3.1 Descriptor Computation

Intensity information by itself is not sufficient to provide reliable matches between similar but not identical objects in images, as it has been demonstrated since the pioneer work by Welsh *et al.* [16]. Even for identical objects, illumination changes or other factors might significantly affect their appearance. Image descriptors can enrich the available intensity information and represent object structures and textures in a more robust way. Thus, the influence of changes in object appearance is reduced, and more accurate matching can be achieved.

Our approach computes 38-dimensional descriptors D_t and D_r for the target and reference images respectively by concatenating grayscale intensity, texture gradients and histogram of oriented gradients descriptors. The descriptor vector for a pixel p is given by:

$$D(p) = D_{HoG}(p) \cup D_{tg}(p) \cup Y(p), \tag{1}$$

where $D_{HoG}(p)$ is the 31-D histogram of oriented gradients descriptor, $D_{tg}(p)$ is 6-D texture gradients descriptor and $Y(p)$ is the intensity for that pixel.

Grayscale Intensity. Although intensity information is not invariant to global changes in illumination between the two images, it can still provide useful information to guide matching. Therefore, in our algorithm the intensity $Y(p)$ of each pixel is used as an auxiliary descriptor.

Texture Gradients. Texture information around each pixel can help describe the local structure in the scene. To make use of such information we include texture gradients in our descriptor, relying on the approach of Martin *et al.* [13]. To compute this descriptor, responses for several filters are first collected for each pixel and categorized according to a set of representative precomputed responses known as textons [12]. Textons identify the presence of image structures, such as bars, corners or various levels of contrast. Once textons are computed, a disc is considered around each pixel and for each half of the disc, a texton histogram is computed. The distance between the histograms of each half, computed for 6 different orientations, forms the 6-D vector $D_{tg}(p)$.

Histogram of Oriented Gradients. The final descriptor used in our method is the histogram of oriented gradients (HoG), denoted by D_{HoG}, which is aimed at representing local object appearance and shape by the distribution of intensity gradients and edge directions [5][1]. To compute the HoG for a given pixel p, first, horizontal and vertical gradients are computed at that location. To compute the histogram for each pixel, a cell (4x4 pixels in our case) is considered around it, and the gradient of each pixel within the cell is allocated to one of 9 orientation bins. These responses are then locally normalized and processed into contrast-sensitive, contrast-insensitive and texture features, which are combined into a 31-dimensional HoG descriptor.

3.2 Descriptor PatchMatch

Once the descriptors D_r and D_t are computed for the reference and target images, correspondences can be determined between them. We rely on the Patch-Match algorithm [2] for this task but apply it on the 38-D space spanned by our descriptor. PatchMatch computes an approximate nearest neighbor field (NNF),

---

[1] We use the implementation from Yamaguchi: http://www3.cs.stonybrook.edu/~kyamagu/software/misc/dense_hog.m.

which provides dense, global correspondences between image patches. The Patch-Match algorithm works over image patches, but the final correspondence field is created at the pixel level. Given a pixel p_t in the target image, NNF provides us the matching pixel p_r in the reference image:

$$NNF(D_t \longleftrightarrow D_r) : p_t \to p_r \tag{2}$$

Descriptor-based matching is able to provide matches not only between same objects, but also between generally similar objects. In our approach, Patch-Match is used with a patch size of 9x9 pixels and 5 iterations, following the recommendations in [2], as after 4-5 iterations the NNF typically converges.

3.3   Color Mapping

Using the correspondences determined through PatchMatch, colors can be mapped from the reference to the target image. This is performed in the $YCbCr$ space and information from the Cb and Cr channels of the reference I_r are used to populate the corresponding channels of the target I_t, while intensity information in I_t is left unchanged. Given the correspondences defined by Eq. (2), chromatic information for a pixel p_t is given by:

$$C\{b|r\}_t(p_t) = C\{b|r\}_r(p_r) \tag{3}$$

After reconstructing the Cb and Cr channels of I_t, the image is converted back to RGB, producing an initial colorization result I_c. Although the global assignment of colors in I_c is correct in most cases at this stage of our algorithm, small local artifacts can appear, due to inaccurate correspondences. To correct such artifacts, a regularization step takes place, described in the next section.

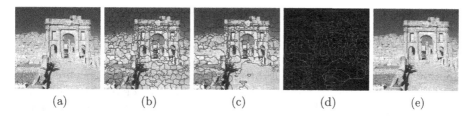

(a)   (b)   (c)   (d)   (e)

Fig. 2. Regularization of the colorization result. (a) Initial colorization without regularization. (b) SLIC superpixels. (c) Superpixel-based segmentation. (d) Resulting color strokes. (e) Final regularized colorization after stroke propagation.

4   Regularization of Color Artifacts

To regularize color artifacts, first, the target image I_t is segmented using a superpixel-based approach. Then, strokes that span each segment are created and assigned with colors representing the color distribution of the corresponding segments from the initial colorization result I_c. The color strokes are marked on the I_t and propagated to the rest of the pixels using Levin's approach [10]. The results of main regularization steps are shown in Figure 2.

4.1   Superpixel-Based Segmentation

The first step of our regularization scheme segments I_c into coherent areas based on intensity information. Using the SLIC method [1], the segmentation starts from the computation of a set of n superpixels $S = [s_1, ..., s_n]$ which span the image, where adjacent similar pixels form coherent superpixel units.

To avoid oversegmentation of large homogeneous regions, the obtained superpixels are further processed, producing a coarser set of segments S_{seg}. To compute each segment $s_{seg,i}$, adjacent superpixels with similar statistics are merged together, forming larger segments. Merging is based on the DBSCAN clustering algorithm [6], where for each superpixel s_i a set of adjacent superpixels N_i is considered. If a distance ϵ between s_i and an adjacent superpixel s_j does not exceed threshold T, s_j is taken as a new point of a cluster. Any other superpixel reachable from s_j is taken as part of the cluster as well. For grayscale images, ϵ is a distance based on simple statistics expressed by the mean and variance of the intensity within considered superpixels.

$$s_{seg,i} = s_i \bigcup_{j \in N_i} s_j \mid \epsilon < T, \quad \text{where} \quad \epsilon = \sqrt{(\mu_{s_j} - \mu_{s_i})^2 + (\sigma_{s_j} - \sigma_{s_i})^2}, \quad (4)$$

For the choice of parameters in this step, we use the values that provide a reasonable trade-off between over- and undersegmentation, given the lack of color information. The initial set of superpixels is computed using $n = 250$, and the threshold T in the clustering step is set to 2.75. Higher value of n would provide more detailed segmentation causing preservation of undesirable artifacts, whereas higher value of T might lead to excessive merging and diffusion of colors.

4.2   Color Stroke Creation and Propagation

Each segment obtained from the previous step is used to create a continuous stroke, which spans that segment and contains the dominant color of that area. The created strokes serve as input to the stroke-based colorization approach of Levin *et al.* [10], where colors of strokes placed on the grayscale image are smoothly propagated to the rest of the image. Since the stroke colors are taken from our initial colorization result I_c, this process smooths colors within coherent areas, removing wrong local assignments that might have created artifacts before.

The color propagation method of Levin *et al.* [10] relies on the premise that nearby pixels with similar intensities are likely to have the same color. Previous approaches that automatically create strokes for this process opt for microstrokes placed in the center of each area [7]. In practice, we have found that larger strokes that span the area to be colorized can lead to better coverage once propagated. Based on that, to create strokes we compute the binary skeleton of each segment using the thinning morphological operation [9].

To determine the color of a stroke, the Cb and Cr values of each pixel within a segment are quantized into 48 clusters using k-means clustering, and the major chromatic component of a segment is assigned to the stroke. This clustering step is necessary to determine a single representative color for each region. Figure 2(d) shows the color strokes for an image as colorized skeleton shapes.

5   Colorization Evaluation

We compare results obtained from our method with the results of previous
example-based colorization methods. Figure 3 depicts the final results of our
combined colorization and regularization approach as well as results from the
methods of Gupta *et al.* [7], Charpiat *et al.* [4] and Welsh *et al.* [16]. Input
images are taken from [7] and represent typical scenes with semantically similar content, but demonstrating different characteristics of intensity, textures and
overall appearance.

Fig. 3. Comparison with existing example-based colorization methods. Represented
methods: Gupta *et al.* [7], Charpiat *et al.* [4], Welsh *et al.* [16].

Due to complex image content, the method by Welsh *et al.* [16] fails in almost
all cases since it is based only on direct intensity matching. Charpiat's method
[4], which is based on SURF descriptors and multimodal probability distribution
estimation, is more robust to differences in intensity. It can produce successful
matches between identical or very similar objects in input images, as it can be
seen on landscape images in rows (b) and (d). However, this method can fail
when changes of visual features are more significant, as shown in examples (a)
and (c). In contrast to the previously discussed methods, our approach and the
approach by Gupta *et al.* [7] lead to comparable results with fewer artifacts and
a more satisfactory colorization.

Additional comparisons with Gupta *et al.* [7] are shown in Figure 4 to assess
the effectiveness of our descriptors. Despite the similarities in the input images,
the descriptors used in [7] cannot accurately determine correspondences for
ambiguous areas, such as the clouds seen in row (a), where our method preserves the white of the clouds. Similarly, our method is robust to global changes
as shown in row (b). In this case the input images vary significantly in global

luminance and contrast, even though they depict the same structures. Our texture and gradient based descriptors successfully determine correspondences in this case. Similar observations can be made about the last example (c), where the same objects are depicted but with changes in pose.

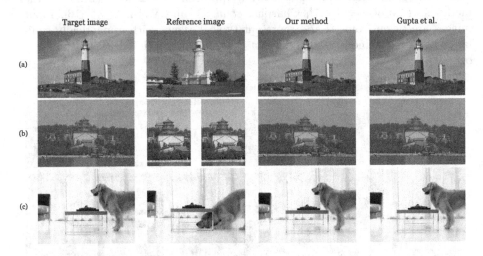

Fig. 4. Additional comparisons with method by Gupta *et al.* [7]. The intensity of the reference image is also shown in example (b). Our method preserves the white of the clouds (a) and can successfully colorize images despite global luminance and contrast changes (b) or changes in pose (c).

Our method achieves qualitative improvements and more robust performance over the state of the art for a large selection of images, while offering a 2 to 4-fold computational improvement against the method by Gupta et al. [7].

6   Color Artifact Removal by Regularization

Application of the proposed regularization method is not limited to colorization. Our method can also be applied for artifact suppression in a more general scenario of color manipulations, e.g. color transfer. In Figure 5, an image (a) is recolored according to the reference image (b), using the color transfer method by Pitié *et al.* [14]. In this case, the result (c) shows distinctive color artifacts, which can be regularized with our approach requiring only minimal adjustments. To regularize artifacts in this case, the original color image is considered for the superpixel segmentation process, while the recolored result serves as input for the computation of strokes. As the original image here contains color information, all three channels are used for the superpixel segmentation and clustering, leading to more accurate results. Given the additional color information, we found that a larger number of superpixels could be used in this case: we set $n = 750$, allowing the segmentation to follow image edges more closely. At the same time, a higher threshold was used for DBSCAN ($T = 5$ in this case), allowing for smaller clusters to form, therefore better respecting image detail.

After the segmentation, color strokes are automatically created and propagated as described in Section 4. Note that the colors of strokes are extracted from the result of color transfer, but the strokes are marked onto the luminance channel of the original artifact-free image, to allow for smoother propagation. Figure 5 shows a comparison of our regularized result as well as those of competing methods [14,15]. In contrast to other solutions, we only regularize in the chromatic domain, leaving luminance information unchanged.

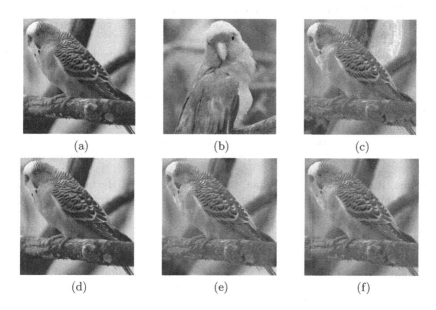

(a)   (b)   (c)

(d)   (e)   (f)

Fig. 5. Regularization of color transfer artifacts. (a) Original image. (b) Reference image. (c) Color transfer by Pitié *et al.* [14]. Regularization using (d) our method, (e) regraining method [14] and (f) TMR filter [15].

7   Conclusions

We presented a new, automatic method for colorizing grayscale images. Our method combines advantages of example-based and stroke-based techniques, requiring minimal levels of user interaction. Using descriptor representations of the input images, the matching step can provide meaningful correspondences between images, even under global contrast and illumination changes or differences in scene structure. In addition, we proposed a robust regularization scheme for reducing artifacts due to color manipulations, which we demonstrated in the context of colorization and color transfer. We applied our technique to several image pairs with varied content and compared our results to the state of the art, showing that the proposed colorization method is competitive with recent methods, providing robust colorization at a lower computational time.

References

1. Achanta, R., Shaji, A., Smith, K., Lucchi, A., Fua, P., Susstrunk, S.: Slic superpixels compared to state-of-the-art superpixel methods. IEEE Transactions on Pattern Analysis and Machine Intelligence **34**(11), 2274–2282 (2012)
2. Barnes, C., Shechtman, E., Goldman, D.B., Finkelstein, A.: The generalized patchmatch correspondence algorithm. In: Daniilidis, K., Maragos, P., Paragios, N. (eds.) ECCV 2010, Part III. LNCS, vol. 6313, pp. 29–43. Springer, Heidelberg (2010)
3. Bugeau, A., Ta, V.T., Papadakis, N.: Variational exemplar-based image colorization. IEEE Transactions on Image Processing **33**, 1–9 (2013)
4. Charpiat, G., Hofmann, M., Schölkopf, B.: Automatic image colorization via multimodal predictions. In: Forsyth, D., Torr, P., Zisserman, A. (eds.) ECCV 2008, Part III. LNCS, vol. 5304, pp. 126–139. Springer, Heidelberg (2008)
5. Dalal, N., Triggs, B.: Histograms of oriented gradients for human detection. In: IEEE Computer Society Conference on Computer Vision and Pattern Recognition, CVPR 2005, vol. 1, pp. 886–893. IEEE (2005)
6. Ester, M., Kriegel, H.P., Sander, J., Xu, X.: A density-based algorithm for discovering clusters in large spatial databases with noise. In: Kdd, vol. 96, pp. 226–231 (1996)
7. Gupta, R.K., Chia, A.Y.S., Rajan, D., Ng, E.S., Zhiyong, H.: Image colorization using similar images. In: Proceedings of the 20th ACM International Conference on Multimedia, pp. 369–378. ACM (2012)
8. Irony, R., Cohen-Or, D., Lischinski, D.: Colorization by example. In: Proceedings of the Sixteenth Eurographics conference on Rendering Techniques, pp. 201–210. Eurographics Association (2005)
9. Kong, T., Rosenfeld, A.: Topological Algorithms for Digital Image Processing. Machine Intelligence and Pattern Recognition, Elsevier Science (1996)
10. Levin, A., Lischinski, D., Weiss, Y.: Colorization using optimization. In: SIGGRAPH 2004, pp. 689–694. ACM, New York (2004)
11. Lin, S., Ritchie, D., Fisher, M., Hanrahan, P.: Probabilistic color-by-numbers: suggesting pattern colorizations using factor graphs. ACM Trans. Graph. **32**(4), 37 (2013)
12. Malik, J., Belongie, S., Leung, T., Shi, J.: Contour and texture analysis for image segmentation. International Journal of Computer Vision **43**(1), 7–27 (2001)
13. Martin, D.R., Fowlkes, C.C., Malik, J.: Learning to detect natural image boundaries using local brightness, color, and texture cues. IEEE Transactions on Pattern Analysis and Machine Intelligence **26**(5), 530–549 (2004)
14. Pitié, F., Kokaram, A.C., Dahyot, R.: Automated colour grading using colour distribution transfer. Computer Vision and Image Understanding **107**(1), 123–137 (2007)
15. Rabin, J., Delon, J., Gousseau, Y.: Removing artefacts from color and contrast modifications. IEEE Transactions on Image Processing **20**(11), 3073–3085 (2011)
16. Welsh, T., Ashikhmin, M., Mueller, K.: Transferring color to greyscale images. In: ACM Transactions on Graphics (TOG), vol. 21, pp. 277–280. ACM (2002)

Experimental Analysis for Modeling Color
of Halftone Images

G.M. Atiqur Rahaman[1(✉)], Ole Norberg[2], and Per Edström[1]

[1] Department of Natural Sciences, Mid Sweden University, Örnsköldsvik, Sweden
gmatiqur@gmail.com, per.edstrom@miun.se
[2] Department of Applied Physics and Electronics, Umeå University, Umeå, Sweden
ole.norberg@umu.se

Abstract. Reflectance models such as the monochrome Murray–Davies (MD) and the Neugebauer color equations make inaccurate predictions owing to changes in reflectance or tristimulus values (TSVs) of halftone dots and the paper between the dots. In this paper, we characterize the change of micro-TSVs as a function of printed area in spectral halftone image by a power function and compare its prediction efficiency using theoretically and experimentally measured limiting TSVs assuming dots of uniform thickness. We found that experimentally accounting for dot thickness variations as solid and mixed areas more precisely explained the single-model parameter that captured the observed lateral light scattering effect. The results showed that incorporating empirically modeled TSVs of the dots and the paper between dots, as well as introducing a new term addressing mixed area in the MD equation, produced CIE ΔE_{ab}^* in the range 1.22–1.76, and the overall gain was more than 1 ΔE_{ab}^*.

Keywords: Spectral image · Halftone · Color · Light scattering · Murray-Davies

1   Introduction

In printing, the surface coverage of ink is varied to reproduce different tones or lightness levels in a halftone image. A halftone reflection prediction model establishes the correct relation between the reflectance of printed surfaces and the amount of printed ink to render the reproduction system reliable [1]. The prediction is mainly made by using the measured average reflectance of a set of halftone patches. Successful models account for the observed effect because of lateral light scattering within the substrate as a function of printed dot coverage. Furthermore, accounting for the ink-spreading effect generates more accurate results. However, currently available empirical models find the connection to the classical Murray–Davies (MD) model for monochrome [2] because the MD model is theoretically successful in establishing a linear relation between the fractional coverage of fulltone ink (a) and the average reflectance of the halftone image by assuming uniform thickness and constant reflectance of the ink and the paper, as follows:

$$R_{halftone} = a\,R_{ink} + (1 - a)\,R_{paper} \tag{1}$$

© Springer International Publishing Switzerland 2015
A. Trémeau et al. (Eds.): CCIW 2015, LNCS 9016, pp. 69–80, 2015.
DOI: 10.1007/978-3-319-15979-9_7

In principle, the formula represents the conservation of energy by summing up all light reflected off the components. In practice, this equation predicts values different from the actual values because of mechanical and optical dot gains. The following correction was subsequently made to the equation by adding an empirical factor, known as the Yule–Nielsen *n-value,* to account for the optical dot gain [2]:

$$R_{halftone}^{1/n} = a\,R_{ink}^{1/n} + (1 - a)\,R_{paper}^{1/n} \tag{2}$$

The *n-value* improves prediction accuracy but explains light interactions for only a limited class of cases [3]. Furthermore, the linearity of the MD model is lost. This can be traced to the false assumption of the constant reflectance of the ink and the paper over the entire surface. Internal changes in reflectance values were subsequently characterized mathematically by an additional parameter to account for the effect of variations in colorimetric values surrounding the dot boundary [4]. Modification was made to Eq. 1 by retaining its original form but accommodating variable reflectances [4].

P.G. Engeldrum empirically studied changes in the reflectance of dots and the paper between dots in halftone prints, and reported results in terms of the International Commission on Illumination's (CIE) tristimulus values (TSVs) [5]. He showed that paper TSVs are linear mixtures of plain paper and a limiting TSV, whereas dot TSVs are linear mixtures of fulltone ink and the same limiting TSV. The limiting TSV refers to the TSVs of the paper when the dot coverage approaches 1.0 or the TSVs of the dots when the coverage approaches zero. The limiting value was theoretically calculated as identical to the product of the reflectance of the paper and the spectral transmittance of the ink [4, 5]. If T represents the TSV (X, Y, or Z), T_{limit} the limiting TSV, and p represents the exponent, the equations proposed by Engeldrum to characterize the changes of the TSVs of the paper and the dots, respectively, are as follows:

$$T_{pap}(a) = (T_{paper} - T_{limit})\,(1 - a)^p + T_{limit} \tag{3}$$

$$T_{dot}(a) = T_{limit} - (T_{limit} - T_{ink})\,a^p \tag{4}$$

Eq. 1 was modified to incorporate these changes as a function of fractional coverage to calculate the average tint of the halftone image as formulated in Eq. 5:

$$T_{halftone}(a) = a\,T_{dot}(a) + (1 - a)\,T_{pap}(a) \tag{5}$$

The accuracy of Eqs. 3-4 is determined by the accuracy of fitting the exponent p to the measured data. The parameter p is described in order to capture the light scattering effect as a function of paper light spread function, dot geometry, and screen frequency. However, P.G. Engeldrum assumed ink dots of uniform thickness, and the results were based on halftone prints of low screen frequency [5]. However, we show in the current study that a numerically calculated T_{limit} does not optimally fit the data for medium or high screen frequency.

In a previous study [6], we reported using experimental image analysis that effective dot area in a single-ink halftone image consists of a solid ink area and a mixed area. Solid ink refers to the dot part close to fulltone density, and mixed area refers to the periphery or edge of the dot, where ink thickness varies and light diffusion adds blurriness. Due to variation in reflectance values in these two parts, we proposed in [6] an extension of Eq. 1 (formulated in Eq. 6 in TSV) to adjust the amount of lights, primarily assuming constant reflectance of fulltone ink and paper:

$$T_{halftone} = a_{paper}\, T_{paper} + a_{solid}\, T_{solid} + a_{mix}\, T_{mix} \tag{6}$$

The contribution of the current study is twofold. First, to the best of the author's knowledge, this study is the first to characterize changes of color in the mixed area, in addition to those in the paper and the solid ink, by analyzing single-colorant halftone microscale spectral images. Second, the accuracy of the extended MD halftone model is studied by incorporating variable colorimetry and preserving the law of conservation of energy that is suitable for explaining the physics behind the formula. Cyan, magenta, and yellow inks on two types of paper with different screen frequencies for the same printing technology are analyzed. The limiting case is measured separately for paper and dots, and the effects of solid ink as well as the mixed area are analyzed using Eqs. 3-6. The crucial parameter, i.e., the model exponent, and the relevant accuracies of the modified MD model are reported in terms of CIE ΔE_{ab}^*.

The research here is motivated to gain greater insight into the interactions between halftone ink, paper, and light, and a linear model is chosen for this background study in support with the principle of conservation of energy. A microscopic analysis should allow us to systematically discover the relevant parameters, properly relate them, and to formulate the ultimate predictions with more subtle explanations of the non-linearity. This advanced understanding can help to improve state-of-the-art spectral printing systems incorporating the variations of the colorimetry of the paper and the ink in existing models that characterize multichannel printers.

2   Materials and Methods

2.1   Samples

A sequence of halftone patches of cyan, magenta, and yellow ink was printed on coated and uncoated papers of different optical and surface properties. The range of ink surface coverage was 0%, 3%, 10%, 20%, ..., 90%, 95%, and 100%. The halftone screen frequency was 175 *lpi* for coated paper and 144 *lpi* for uncoated paper, as is suitable for optimized print and color quality. Rotated screen amplitude modulated (AM) halftone cell produced ink dots to form the image structure on the paper.

The thickness and grammage values of the coated and uncoated paper were 0.12 mm and 150 gsm, and 0.22 mm and 200 gsm, respectively. The samples were printed using a commercial prepress printer (*HP indigo 5000*) that used liquid electro-photographic ink to produce images with sharp edges, uniform gloss, and thin layers.

2.2   Measurements

A microscopic spectral camera system was used to capture the images of halftone dot patterns and to perform measurements at the pixel level. The measurements required in this study for each colorant were: (1) the microspectral reflectance of the solid ink, the mixed area, and the paper between the dots, (2) the corresponding fractional ink coverages, (3) the overall reflectance of halftone tints, and (4) the transmittance of the dots. The imaging setup consisted of a microscope (*Nikon Eclipse MA200*) with a CRi Nuance spectral camera attached to it. The ring-shaped illumination from the halogen lamps approximately made an 8^0 angle, whereas the detection angle was 0^0. The spatial resolution given the chosen objective was approximately 1 µm and the captured area was approximately 1 mm × 1.3 mm. The spectral resolution of the camera varied from 420 nm to 700 nm in increments of 10 nm, its bit depth was 12, and all images were directly stored as radiance images.

The spectral reflectance of each pixel was obtained by dividing the spectral radiance image by the spectral radiance image of a reference white (Spectralon Standard), and the values were multiplied by the known reflectance factors of the reference. The square root of the measured reflectance value of the fulltone image divided by the reflectance of the bare paper gave the transmittance value of the ink. Pixel reflectance was classified into that of the paper, the mixed area, and the solid ink based on the segmentation of the corresponding RGB image. The RGB image was captured at the same time and under the same conditions as the spectral radiance images. The segmentation results were also used to calculate respective fractional coverage as the ratio of the corresponding number of pixels to the total number of pixels in the image.

For segmentation, the RGB image was first converted to CMY(K) space because cyan, magenta, and yellow ink in the corresponding space provide the best contrast with the paper. The segmentation technique was based on hierarchical cluster analysis [7], which calculated two optimal threshold values to segment the gray-level image into three regions. The dynamic threshold selection technique began with the assumption that each nonempty gray level of an image histogram was a cluster. Following this, clusters closest to one another were merged together in the next level; this continued up to three levels. The mean and variance values of existing clusters and clusters formed after the possible merging operation were used to measure the distance of cluster center. The highest gray-level values in the three remaining clusters at the end of the iterative merging process were chosen as the optimal threshold values. The details of the mathematical formulation and the calculation are provided in [8, 9].

3   Results

The segmented images were used as masks to collect reflectance spectra from the corresponding spectral image. The mean spectrum of each class defined the characteristic spectral reflectance of the relevant area type. The reflectance spectra were converted to TSVs for D50 illumination and 1931 standard observers. The measured micro-TSVs of the dots and the paper between the dots as a function of printed coverage for the coated paper are shown in the xy-chromaticity diagram in Fig. 1. The coordinates of the theoretical limit represent TSVs of the paper when the fractional area approaches 1.0 or those of the dots when the fractional area approaches zero [5]. The chromaticity values of the paper between the dots are close to those of the bare paper, which is represented by the central convergent point that connects the limit through a straight line. The chromaticity values of the dots are at the other end of the graph. According to [5], all dot chromaticity values should lie between the limit and the fulltone, but the chosen set of samples did not exhibit this behavior because the limiting case crossed a few dot coverages. Nevertheless, the results of the linear mixtures of TSVs [5] for both the paper and the dots are still valid because their chromaticity values fall on a line connecting the bare paper or fulltone ink to the limit.

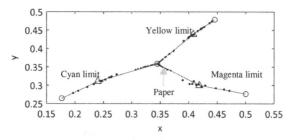

Fig. 1. CIE *xy*-chromaticity coordinates of white paper and fulltone ink (circles), paper between ink dots and fractional inks (dots), and the theoretical limits (triangles)

3.1   Full Dots and the Theoretical Limit

A nonlinear least-squares optimization technique was applied in order to fit Eqs. 3-4 to the measured data shown in Fig. 1. The performance of the characterization technique to predict TSVs as a function of fractional coverage is shown for the paper between the dots as well as for the dots in Figs. 2 and 3, respectively. The data points represent the measured CIE X, Y, and Z micro-TSVs and the lines through the points represent the predicted values. The TSVs of the paper between the dots at coverage 1.0 are the limiting values shown in the plots. Because of high color variation in the paper between the cyan and magenta dots, the predictions were not as good as for the yellow dots. Note the impact on prediction performance of a distracted data point for the cyan ink in Fig. 3.

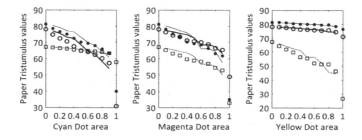

Fig. 2. The CIE X (circles), Y (dots), and Z (squares) TSVs of coated paper between the dots as a function of dot area. The lines represent the predicted values.

Table 1 lists all parameters fitted to the data for coated paper. The paper exponent was correlated with the light spread function of the paper. The exponent *p* to account for light scattering varied between 0.172 and 0.262, with an average value of 0.216

(root mean square (*rms*) error 1.65). For uncoated paper, the value of p ranged from 0.660 to 1.20, with an average value of 0.590 (*rms* error 2.88). However, the dot exponent p recorded notably higher values such that the average value of p was 10.5 (*rms* error 2.76) for the coated paper and 7.17 (*rms* error 2.54) for the uncoated paper.

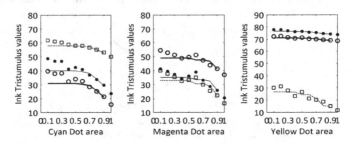

Fig. 3. The CIE X (circles), Y (solid dots), and Z (squares) TSVs of ink dots on coated paper as a function of fractional coverage. The lines represent the predicted values.

The average dot exponent p was consistently largest for cyan dots and lowest for yellow dots depending on the magnitude and uniformity of TSV changes as a function of printed area (Fig. 3). Although p was described in [5] as the parameter to capture the complex interaction of light as a function of paper spread function and halftone cell frequency, the large dot exponent value in this study indicates that it may also reveal spatial variations in reflectance around the dot edge as an effect of ink spread, absorption, and light diffusion.

Table 1. Parameters of power function fittings to the data (coated paper)

		Paper between dots					Dots			
		$T_{pap}-T_{limit}$	T_{limit}	p	*rms* error		$T_{limit}-T_{dot}$	T_{limit}	p	*rms* error
Cyan	X	47.21	30.96	0.202	2.82		15.14	30.95	15.06	4.66
	Y	41.19	40.08	0.193	2.29		16.45	40.07	14.18	4.42
	Z	9.44	57.90	0.172	0.44		7.85	57.89	14.63	1.87
Magenta	X	29.11	49.05	0.217	2.01		12.04	49.05	11.85	2.79
	Y	46.15	35.12	0.215	3.35		14.68	35.12	12.58	3.46
	Z	34.38	32.96	0.205	2.28		16.39	32.96	10.72	3.55
Yellow	X	6.98	71.19	0.238	0.56		2.58	71.18	5.21	0.66
	Y	4.70	76.56	0.242	0.36		2.89	76.56	5.01	0.68
	Z	40.59	26.75	0.262	3.27		15.06	26.75	5.27	2.81

Table 2 lists the prediction accuracy of average halftone tints in terms of CIE ΔE^*_{ab} calculated by the modified MD equation (Eq. 5) proposed in Ref. [5]. This data also serves as a metric of goodness for the fitting procedure. However, the average prediction error was lowest for cyan ink even though the data-fitting error for it was the largest. Therefore, Eq. 5 should be corrected for better explanation, and prediction accuracy of overall halftone tints.

Table 2. Prediction performance of the halftone model (Eq. 5) in terms of average CIE ΔE^*_{ab}

	Uncoated Paper		Coated Paper	
	Average	Maximum	Average	Maximum
Cyan	1.94	2.91	1.32	2.33
Magenta	3.86	7.89	2.95	7.15
Yellow	2.49	4.68	2.83	7.09

3.2 Full Dots and Measured Individual Limits

The TSVs of the paper between the dots given 99% coverage (reference 95%) and of the dots given 2.4% coverage (reference 3%) were measured and considered as limiting cases for the paper and the dot (Fig. 4). For comparison, the theoretical limit was also calculated numerically. Fig. 4 shows that the measured limits were close to one another, but at a notable distance from the theoretical value.

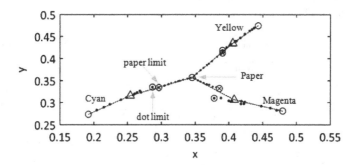

Fig. 4. CIE *xy*-chromaticity coordinates of measured paper limit (circled crosses), the dot limit (circled dots), and the theoretical limit (triangles)

The same optimization procedure was applied to fit the same set of measured data but with distinct measured limits. Table 3 lists the parameters fitted to the measured data. The use of measured limits improved the prediction accuracy of both the dot and the paper TSVs in comparison with the theoretical limit in terms of *rms* difference. Fig. 5 compares the difference in the characterization performances as a function of the limits.

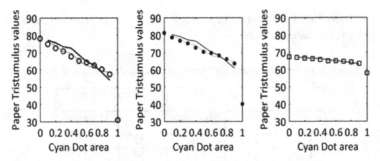

Fig. 5. Measured and predicted CIE X (circles), Y (dots), and Z (squares) TSVs of paper between the ink dots. The lines represent the predicted values (gray line: measured limit).

The exponent increased for the paper and significantly decreased in value for the dots, suggesting a dependency of the exponent on the limiting value. Note the drastic changes, especially in the value of the dot exponent p. Its value for coated paper ranged from 2.01 to 4.97, with an average of 4.08 (rms error 2.33), and that for uncoated paper ranged from 1.13 to 4.75, with an average of 2.37 (rms error 1.86). The value of p for the paper varied between 0.58 and 1.05, with an average of 0.83 (rms error 1.01) for the coated paper, and between 0.76 and 2.14, with an average of 1.25 (rms error 1.47), for uncoated paper.

Table 3. Parameters of power function fittings to the data (coated paper) with measured limits

		Paper between dots				Dots			
		T_{pap}-T_{limit}	T_{limit}	p	rms error	T_{limit}-T_{dot}	T_{limit}	p	rms error
Cyan	X	20.82	57.34	0.84	1.22	23.90	39.71	4.94	2.77
	Y	17.70	63.56	0.81	0.99	25.04	48.67	4.91	2.89
	Z	3.90	63.43	0.71	0.22	11.76	61.80	4.63	1.48
Magenta	X	12.58	65.58	0.97	1.16	17.50	54.51	4.97	2.86
	Y	19.41	61.85	1.05	1.81	20.82	41.27	5.60	3.62
	Z	14.39	52.94	0.94	1.33	23.47	40.04	4.58	3.85
Yellow	X	3.67	74.49	0.73	0.37	3.67	72.28	2.19	0.45
	Y	2.72	78.54	0.58	0.30	4.20	77.88	2.01	0.43
	Z	21.16	46.17	0.87	1.72	18.3	30.07	2.95	2.64

Table 4 reports improvements over the results listed in Table 2 for evaluating the modified MD equation (Eq. 5). Although the measured limits improved the characterization of internal changes of micro-TSVs, note that prediction of average TSVs of the halftone patch was not remarkably different (Table 4). Even overall prediction accuracy decreased for cyan and magenta colorants for the coated paper. This result also indicates that the modified MD equation (Eq. 5) needs to be corrected to improve average tint predictions.

Table 4. Prediction accuracy of the halftone model (Eq. 5) in CIE ΔE_{ab}^{*} with measured limits

	Uncoated Paper			Coated Paper		
	Average	Maximum	**Improvements**	Average	Maximum	**Improvements**
Cyan	1.90	3.78	0.04	1.72	3.48	-0.40
Magenta	3.25	9.65	0.61	3.25	6.46	-0.30
Yellow	2.46	5.14	0.03	2.78	8.9	0.05

3.3   Dot Segmentation into Solid ink and Mixed Area

The full dot was separated as solid dot and mixed area for an advanced analysis of color change within the ink region. The limiting TSVs for the paper (called limit-1) were the same as before, measured using 95% reference coverage, and the TSVs of the solid area comprising 3% reference ink were taken as the limit of the solid dots (called limit-2). Since the xy-coordinates of the mixed area frequently occupied the space between limit-1 and limit-2, these two limits were used to characterize the change of TSVs of the mixed area. This change is prominent for the magenta and yellow colorants in Fig. 6, which also shows that changes in the coordinates of solid inks were smaller, less scattered, and oriented more straightly than the full dots, as shown in Fig. 1. This means that the mixed area significantly affects the change of colorimetric values of a halftone image.

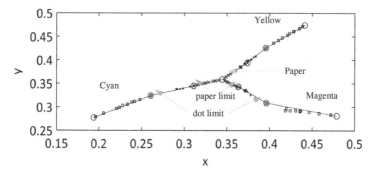

Fig. 6. CIE xy-chromaticity coordinates of solid ink (squares), mixed area (dots), the measured solid ink limit (circled square) and paper limit (circled cross)

In Eq. 3, T_{paper} was replaced by T_{limit1}, and T_{limit} by T_{limit2} to predict the changes of the mixed TSVs by fitting p to the measured data, as listed in Table 5 and illustrated in Fig. 7. For both coated and uncoated paper, the Y TSV in case of yellow colorants produced an unrepresentative value of p to reduce the number of ignorable rms errors. Therefore, in order to avoid misleading values, this particular p was replaced by the average p of X and Z TSVs. However, the average of X, Y, and Z exponents required to characterize the changes in the mixed area on coated paper ranged from 0.046 to 0.186 with an overall average of 0.106, and on uncoated paper from 0.069 to 0.334 with an average of 0.175. The low exponent value indicated small changes of color in the mixed area. The coated paper had smaller color variations in the mixed area because the ink spread and absorption was less than on uncoated paper. Therefore, the exponent manifested the effect of ink spread and penetration properties of the halftone imaging system. Fig. 7 shows small changes of TSVs in mixed area and random variations in X for cyan or Y for magenta due to possible noise or measurement errors.

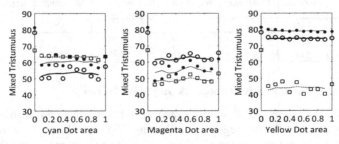

Fig. 7. Measured and predicted CIE TSVs X (circles), Y(dots), and Z (squares) of the mixed area as a function of printed area in coated paper. The lines represent the predicted values.

Table 5. Parameters of power function fittings for the dot and mixed TSVs (coated paper)

		Mixed area				Solid dots			
		$T_{limit1}-T_{limit2}$	T_{limit1}	p	rms error	$T_{limit2}-T_{solid}$	T_{limit2}	p	rms error
Cyan	X	18.51	57.34	0.110	2.95	19.94	38.83	0.792	1.91
	Y	15.33	63.56	0.105	2.48	21.22	48.22	0.838	1.97
	Z	1.61	63.43	0.043	0.87	10.24	61.82	1.13	0.84
Magenta	X	9.30	65.58	0.186	1.62	16.85	56.28	0.612	1.76
	Y	18.06	61.85	0.195	3.20	20.64	43.78	0.519	2.32
	Z	11.00	52.94	0.178	1.71	22.17	41.93	0.650	2.17
Yellow	X	1.96	74.49	0.024	0.58	3.70	72.53	0.696	0.23
	Y	0.45	78.54	0.046	0.54	4.11	78.08	0.776	0.24
	Z	13.41	46.17	0.068	2.85	19.56	32.75	0.636	1.06

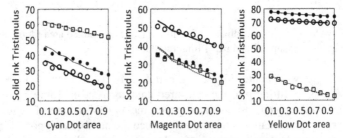

Fig. 8. Measured and predicted CIE X (circles), Y(dots), and Z (squares) TSVs of solid ink on coated paper. The lines represent the predicted values.

The average solid dot exponents required to account for light scattering on coated paper were ranged from 0.593 to 0.920 with an overall average of 0.738, and on uncoated paper ranged from 0.622 to 0.700 with an average of 0.655. Thus, the recorded values were comparable to the values of exponents of the paper between the dots in order to correlate the effect of the light spread function and the halftone cell frequency. For example, a higher dot exponent for coated paper was because of the higher screen frequency of 175 *lpi*. Fig. 8 shows that the characterization performance of solid ink TSVs change was also convincing.

The halftone tint prediction accuracy, evaluated by Eq. 6, which also includes the effect due to the mixed area [6], is shown in Fig. 9 and listed in Table 6. The average accuracy for both coated and uncoated papers was identical at 1.53 ΔE_{ab}^*. Except for cyan on coated paper, all other ink-paper combinations recorded better prediction accuracies than the values in Table 2. The highest improvement was 2.64 ΔE_{ab}^* and the global improvement was slightly higher than $1\Delta E_{ab}^*$.

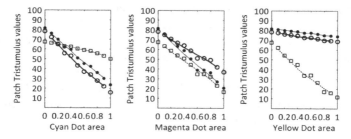

Fig. 9. Measured and predicted CIE TSVs X (circles), Y(dots), and Z (squares) of halftone patches in coated paper. The lines represent the predicted values.

Table 6. CIE ΔE_{ab}^* of the extended MD model (Eq. 6) that includes the effect of mixed area

	Uncoated Paper			Coated Paper		
	Average	Maximum	**Improvements**	Average	Maximum	**Improvements**
Cyan	1.76	2.96	0.18	1.56	3.08	-0.24
Magenta	1.22	3.29	2.64	1.75	4.71	1.20
Yellow	1.62	2.92	0.87	1.29	2.94	1.54

4   Conclusions

The change of colorimetric values of the halftone dots was larger than the paper between the dots for the electroink printing technology. The color of the dots or the paper between the dots was a mixture of colorimetric values of fulltone ink or base paper, respectively, and a limiting value. The simulated common limit used for characterizing the changes did not match with the measured limit. The measured distinct limits for the paper and the dots produced better characterization accuracy than a numerically calculated limit. However, the only empirical parameter – the model exponent – captured light scatter in the paper between the dots, but high values for the dots were not appropriate to explain the cause and effect. Nevertheless, the characterization of the dot area segmented into solid and mixed areas produced exponents comparable to the paper exponents. Notably, the low exponent value indicated small changes of color in the mixed area as a function of printed coverage. Thus, the corresponding exponent manifested variation in ink thickness due to ink spreading and penetration of the halftone imaging system. In general, the empirical model parameter was a function of paper properties, inks, and halftone screen frequency.

A modified MD halftone equation to incorporate the variable colorimetry of the dots and the paper produced overall tint prediction accuracy ranging from 1.32 to 3.86 with an average of 2.56 CIE ΔE_{ab}^* using a theoretical limit. Although the use of measured limits improved characterizations of paper or the dot TSVs, the overall tint prediction accuracy was not significant. However, linearly adding the effect due to the mixed area in an expanded MD model yielded accuracy values ranging from 1.22 to 1.76 with an average of 1.53 ΔE_{ab}^*. The overall gain was more than 1 ΔE_{ab}^*. Therefore, segmenting the inked area into solid ink and mixed area generates more accurate predictions and better explanations of observed color changes.

This study showed that an expanded MD equation that follows the law of conservation of energy can predict halftone tints with satisfactory accuracy. Therefore, incorporating the concepts of dot area fragmentation, the change of paper and dot reflectance variations in the Neugebauer equations, for instance, should yield better prediction accuracy for color halftone prints. Testing these concepts for multicolor halftone images and rendering them practically useful require a simple method based on traditionally measured reflectance values.

Acknowledgements. EU Marie Curie Initial Training Networks (ITN) N-290154 (CP7.0) supported this research. We would like to thank Prof. Markku H. Kasari of University of Eastern Finland for providing advanced color measurement devices for this study.

References

1. Hébert, M., Hersch, R.D.: Review of spectral reflectance models for halftone prints: Principles, Calibration, and Prediction accuracy. COLOR Research and Application (2014), doi: 10.1002/col.21907
2. Wyble, D.R., Berns, R.S.: A Critical Review of Spectral Models Applied to Binary Color Printing. COLOR Research and Application 25(1), 4–19 (2000)
3. Lewandowski, A., Ludl, M., Byrne, G., Dor, G.: Applying the Yule-Nielsen equation with negative n. J. Opt. Soc. Am. 23, 1827–1834 (2006)
4. Arney, J.S., Engeldrum, P.G., Zeng, H.: An expanded Murray-Davies model of tone reproduction in halftone imaging. J. of Imaging Sci. Technol. 39(6), 502–508 (1995)
5. Engeldrum, P.G.: The Color between the Dots. J. of Imaging Sci. Technol. 38(6), 545 (1994)
6. Rahaman, G.M.A., Norberg, O., Edström, P.: Extension of Murray-Davies tone reproduction model by adding edge effect of halftone dots. In: Proc. SPIE 9018: 90180F (2014)
7. Arifin, A.Z., Asano, A.: Image segmentation by histogram thresholding using hierarchical cluster analysis. Elsevier Pattern Recognition Letter 27(13), 1515 (2006)
8. Demirkaya, O., Asyali, M.H.: Determination of image bimodality thresholds for different intensity distributions. Elsevier Signal Processing: Image Communication 19(6), 507 (2004)
9. Otsu, N.: A threshold selection method from gray-level histograms. IEEE Trans. Systems, Man and Cybernetics 9, 62 (1979)

Development of a Dynamic Relighting System for Moving Planar Objects with Unknown Reflectance

Ryosuke Nakahata, Keta Hirai, Takahiko Horiuchi, and Shoji Tominaga[✉]

Graduate School of Advanced Integration Science, Chiba University, Chiba, Japan
horiuchi@faculty.chiba-u.jp

Abstract. Relighting is a technique to modify an image to account for alternate illumination conditions. Conventionally, the reflectance characteristics of an object are provided, and a relighted image is calculated using input light source information. In this paper, we propose a dynamic relighting system for moving planar objects with unknown reflectance. By acquiring the surface spectral reflectance of moving objects, our system is able to reproduce accurate colors on a display device. In the reflectance acquisition, we use a programmable light source that can produce any spectral curve. The surface spectral reflectance of an object in a darkroom is obtained based on the lighting technique with five spectral basis functions that are generated by the programmable light source. The acquired reflectance and user-input illumination information are used to calculate accurate CIEXYZ values of the relighted image. Finally, CIEXYZ values are accurately transformed to RGB values. In the experiment, illuminant A and D65 are used as the illuminants for relighting. As a result, by comparing a computer simulation with actual experiments with real objects, we observe an average color difference ΔE^*_{ab} of approximately 7. This system operates at a rate of 1 frame per second. In addition, in this study, we have implemented another relighting system for objects under an environmental lighting condition by determining the spectral power distribution of the illumination source.

Keywords: Relighting · Spectral reflectance estimation · Color reproduction · Dynamic system · Illuminant estimation

1 Introduction

In general, when looking at an object, brightness and color in human perception depend on the type of the light source. Relighting is a technique to change the illumination environment within an image. Relighting is used in industrial product design to simulate the appearance of objects under a variety of light sources.

In previous studies, relighting has been implemented by various approaches. Zhen et al. [1] proposed a relighting method for human faces by changing the coefficients of the spherical harmonic function of the radiance environment map. This approach is based on the acquisition of three-dimensional model of a human face using a morphing model. Then the human face was relighted using this three-dimensional shape. The light source environments were approximated by a spherical harmonic function as a basis function. They performed this process in real time by only estimating the

© Springer International Publishing Switzerland 2015
A. Trémeau et al. (Eds.): CCIW 2015, LNCS 9016, pp. 81–90, 2015.
DOI: 10.1007/978-3-319-15979-9_8

diffuse reflection. Debevec et al. [2] acquired a large number of shading images by using a lighting device called Light Stage. They were able to realize relighting under any illumination condition. However, these conventional methods perform poorly with RGB signals, as there is a limitation in the color reproduction accuracy. Accurate color reproduction is extremely important in relighting technology. In this regard, spectral imaging may perform better. Manakov et al. [3] have proposed a relighting technique that uses a multiband camera for obtaining spectral information. Park et al. [4] proposed a relighting technique by obtaining surface spectral reflectance of target objects from multispectral illumination with various types of LEDs. However, these relighting techniques using spectral information require a significant amount of time to acquire spectral reflectance of object surfaces. Then, the relighted objects are processed offline. Real-time relighting based on spectral information has not yet been established.

In this study, a dynamic relighting system is proposed for moving planar objects with unknown reflectance. We develop a high-speed spectral reflectance acquisition technique based on spectral basis lighting. In the proposed system, we assume that the target object is flat, and that the input illumination for relighting is a collimated light source. Under these conditions, our system can dynamically relight objects. In order to display an accurate color image, the tristimulus CIEXYZ values are calculated using the acquired surface spectral reflectance and the input illuminant spectrum. Finally, we display an RGB image sequence that has been properly transformed from the CIEXYZ values.

2   Proposed System

2.1   System Configuration and Processing Flowchart

In this study, we use a high-speed spectroscopic imaging system [5]. Figure 1 shows the configuration of the proposed system. The system is configured with a programmable light source device (Optronic Laboratories OL490), high-speed CMOS monochrome camera (EPIX SV642M), and a control computer. The advantage of this programmable light source is the ability to acquire a spectral image in real time by synchronizing with the frame rate of the camera. This source can be switched faster than the LCD-based light source. We also use a high-speed monochrome CMOS camera SV643M (resolution: 640 × 476 pixel, quantization bits: 10bit, frame rate: 200fps). The display used in the present study is EIZO ColorEdge (CG 221). The color gamut of the display is Adobe RGB. The CPU has an Intel Core i5-3470 3.2GHz and 3.48GB of RAM.

Figure 2 shows our processing flowchart. The sequence is:

1: Irradiate the object with the spectral basis illumination to acquire the corresponding pixel values of the target objects.
2: Calculate the spectral reflectance from the pixel values (See details in Section 2.2). In order to reduce the calculation time, we calculate the reflectance in 31-dimensional wavelengths in 10 nm intervals over the visible wavelength range from 400 nm to 700 nm.

3: Load the light source information. The light source for relighting is determined by the user in advance.

4: Calculate the tristimulus values (CIE XYZ) using the loaded light source information, the recovered spectral reflectance of objects, and the color matching functions. In our dynamic process, we can change the relighting conditions by reloading a variety of light sources. (See Section 2.3)

5: Convert CIE XYZ to RGB values. We properly reproduce a relighted RGB image on the display. (See also Section 2.3)

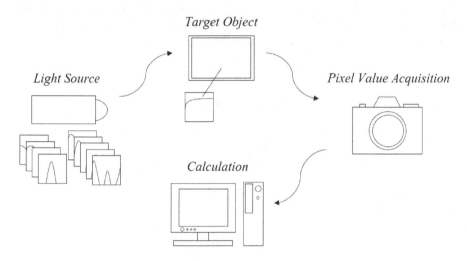

Fig. 1. Configuration of the proposed system

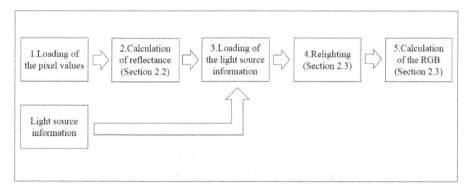

Fig. 2. Algorithm of the proposed system

2.2   Reflectance Estimation Method

The reflectance estimation used in this study is described in [6]. We use an orthogonal basis $\psi_m(\lambda)$ to represent the surface spectral reflectance. The surface spectral reflectance $S(\lambda)$ can be expressed as

$$S(\lambda)=\sum_{m=1}^{M} w_m \psi_m(\lambda) \quad (m = 1,2,...,M) \tag{1}$$

where M is the number of principal components of the orthogonal basis, w_m are the weights of the basis and λ indicates the wavelength. In this study, we selected five spectral basis functions, i.e., $M = 5$. The basis functions were computed from a spectral reflectance database with 507 samples. Figure 3 shows the five orthogonal basis functions. We were unable to irradiate with the light source that is calculated from Eq. (1), because the orthogonal basis can include negative values. In this study, we irradiated with an orthogonal basis light source divided into positive and negative functions. We estimate the spectral reflectance using acquired values:

$$\psi_m(\lambda)=\psi_m^{+}(\lambda)-\psi_m^{-}(\lambda), \tag{2}$$

$$w_m = O^{+}(t_m)-O^{-}(t_m) \tag{3}$$

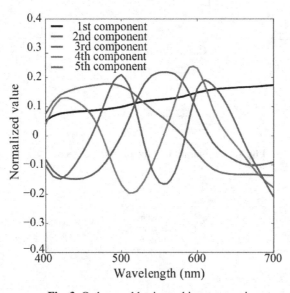

Fig. 3. Orthogonal basis used in our experiment

We divided the orthogonal basis into positive and negative elements from Eq. (2). We determined the camera output $O^{+}(t_m), O^{-}(t_m)$ by irradiating with an illumination light source calculated from Eq. (1). We estimated the surface spectral reflectance by substituting Eq. (3) into Eq. (1). Using this method, the dynamic range of the base is retained, without the need to generate a flat offset value. Figure 4 shows the illumination designed in this study. The figure shows the waveforms of nine orthogonal bases with the negative values inverted and which are divided by the spectral sensitivity of the camera $R(\lambda)$. The solid lines are the waveforms that are divided by the spectral sensitivity $R(\lambda)$ of the camera in the positive original orthogonal basis; a dashed lines are the waveforms that are divided by spectral sensitivity $R(\lambda)$ of the camera to reverse the negative component. The second to fifth main components require illumination of two sources each, in order to design the illumination light source from a total of nine waveforms.

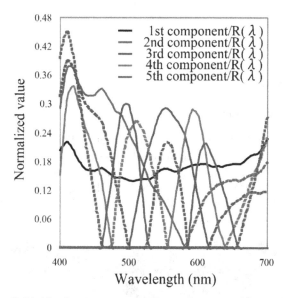

Fig. 4. Waveforms divided by the camera sensitivity are decomposed into positive and negative orthogonal basis (Solid line: Waveforms obtained by dividing the camera sensitivity are the positive values of the principal component. Dashed line: Waveforms divided by the camera sensitivity are the inverted negative values of the main component.)

2.3   Principle of Relighting

In general, the tristimulus values (CIE XYZ) at a certain point on the object surface are obtained by Eq. (4).

$$\begin{bmatrix} X \\ Y \\ Z \end{bmatrix} = \int S(\lambda)E_T(\lambda)\begin{bmatrix} \bar{x}(\lambda) \\ \bar{y}(\lambda) \\ \bar{z}(\lambda) \end{bmatrix}d\lambda \qquad (4)$$

Where $S(\lambda)$ is the acquired surface spectral reflectance of the object described in the previous section, $E_T(\lambda)$ is the spectral power distribution of the light source for relighting as input by the user, and $(\bar{x}(\lambda), \bar{y}(\lambda), \bar{z}(\lambda))$ is the color-matching function. We calculate CIE XYZ from Eq. (1) and the estimated reflectance. We then converted to RGB from the CIE XYZ values. After that, we displayed the image on the monitor. By setting the light source information $E_T(\lambda)$ appropriately in Eq. (1), the image is relighted. The relighting is performed assuming the two-dimensional, light source used is collimated.

We compute the monitor RGB by substituting CIE XYZ into Eq. (5). $\mathbf{M}_{3\times3}$ is the matrix used to convert RGB from CIE XYZ in this display. We also used a correcting LUP (Look Up Table) for the RGB values.

$$\begin{bmatrix} R \\ G \\ B \end{bmatrix} = \mathbf{M}_{3\times3} \begin{bmatrix} X \\ Y \\ Z \end{bmatrix} \tag{5}$$

3   Experiments

3.1   Experimental Setup

To verify the accuracy of the proposed system, an X-Rite Mini ColorChecker was used as a target object for relighting under the illuminant D65 and illuminant A. The object was moved to the left and right at a constant speed of 20 mm/sec by a stepping motor (Sigma Koki TSDM60-20). Figure 5 shows the experimental setup. The system is configured with a programmable light source, a high-speed CMOS monochrome camera, and a calibrated monitor.

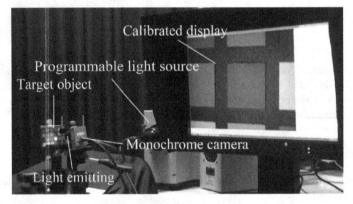

Fig. 5. Relighting system

3.2   Relighting Accuracy

In order to verify the accuracy of the relighting system, an X-Rite Mini ColorChecker was compared by setting the illuminant D65 illuminant A and re-lighting. We show the results in Fig.6. The system can process the data dynamically, and display a moving object with relighting on the calibrated monitor. Figure 7 shows the results for a moving object.

The results of the measurement are summarized in Table 1 showing CIE 1976 ΔE^*_{ab} color differences with respect to the 24 colors of the ColorChecker. The average color difference is 7.17 for illuminant A and 6.55 for illuminant D65, respectively. Table 2 shows CIE 1976 ΔE^*_{ab} color difference of spectral reflectance estimation with respect to the 24 colors of the ColorChecker and color reproduction error of the display. The accuracy of this study is due to the errors on reflectance estimation (Section 2.2) and color reproduction of the display (Section 2.3). In this study, the spectral reflectance with respect to moving object is estimated with an average color difference of about 5.36. In Ref. [6], the spectral reflectance with respect to a stationary object is estimated with an average color difference of about 2.5. The accuracy of our experiment is lower than Ref. [6], probably due to noise and variations in the lighting. The color reproduction error of the display is a 2.1. Total speed of the proposed system was 1 fps (frame per second).

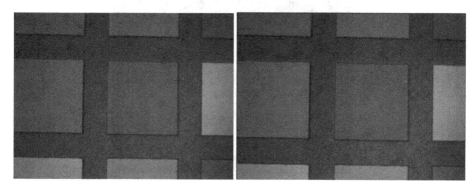

Fig. 6. Relighting result (Left: Illuminant A, Right: Illuminant D65)

Fig. 7. Relighting result for moving object (ColorChecker is moving from right to left.)

Table 1. Color reproduction error in this system

	Illuminant A	Illuminant D65
Average color difference ΔE^*ab	7.17	6.55
Maximum color difference ΔE^*ab	14.1	15.5
Minimum color difference ΔE^*ab	3.11	1.93

Table 2. Color differences of spectral reflectance estimation and color reproduction of the display

	Reflectance estimation	Color reproduction of display
Average color difference ΔE^*ab	5.36	2.1

3.3 Relighting of Commonly used Objects

We tested our relighting system using a real-world object. The target light sources were illuminant A and illuminant D65. Figure 8 shows a real sample object of a piece of cloth. Figure 9 shows the relighting result. The system is able to reproduce the appearance under a different light source illumination on the monitor. This demonstrates that our system is capable of relighting commonly used objects.

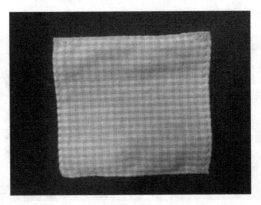

Fig. 8. Target object

Fig. 9. Relighting results for a plaid cloth (Left: A light source, Right: D65 light source)

3.4 Relighting Under Environment Lighting Condition

The spectral power distribution by illuminating with a different light source is given by the product of the spectral distribution of the light source and the surface spectral reflectance of the object. Therefore, the surface spectral reflectance of the object can be estimated by detecting the spectral distribution of the light source. By using a reference object in the image with known surface spectral reflectance, the spectral distribution of the light source can be detected.

In this study, we conducted an experiment using artificial sunlight as the environmental light source. Figure 10 shows the setup of the experiment. We used X-Rite Mini ColorChecker as the moving object and a white patch was used as the reference for detecting the spectral distribution of the light source. Figure 11 shows one experimental result. The left figure shows an input image taken under artificial sunlight, and the right figure shows a relighting result under the illuminant D65.

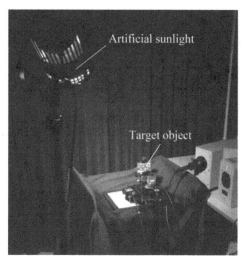

Fig. 10. Experimental setup under environment lighting condition

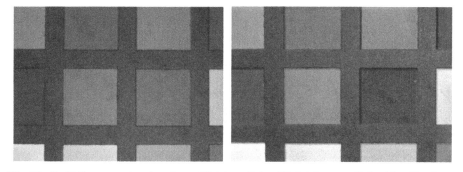

Fig. 11. (Left) Image captured under artificial sunlight. (Right) Image relighted by illuminant D65.

4   Conclusion

In this study, we have constructed a dynamic relighting system for moving planar objects with unknown reflectance. The averaged color difference ΔE^{*}_{ab} between the measured value and the true colors of X-Rite Mini ColorChecker was 7.17 for the illuminant A, and 6.55 for the illuminant D65. We demonstrated the capability of our system by relighting to a real object, in this case a piece of cloth.

One problem with the proposed system is the low processing speed of 1 fps. This could be improved in the future by using a GPU and multi-core CPU system. Since the application to glossy objects is very difficult, we will address to glossy object in the future. By using an RGB-D camera, a relighting system for an object with a complicated shape could be tackled as a future problem.

References

1. Wen, Z., Liu, Z., Huang, T.S.: Face relighting with radiance environment maps. In: Proc. CVPR, pp.158–165 (2003)
2. Debevec, P., Hawkins, T., Tchou, C., Duiker, H.-P., Sarokin, W., Sagar, M.: Acquiring the reflectance field of a human face. In: Proc. SIGGRAPH, pp.145–156 (2000)
3. Manakoy, A., Restrepo, J.F., Klehm, O., Hegedus, R., Eisemann, E., Seidel, H.-P., Ihrke, I.: A reconfigurable camera add-on for high dynamic range, multispectral, polarization, and light-field imaging. ACM Trans. Graph. **32**(4) (2013); Proc. SIGGRAPH
4. Park, J.-I., Lee, M.-H., Grossberg, M.D., Nayar, S.K.: Multi spectral imaging using multiplexed illumination. In: Proc. ICCV (2007)
5. Tominaga, S., Nishioka, D., Horiuchi, T.: An integrated spectral imaging system for producing color images of static and moving objects. Color Research and Application (Early View, April 2014)
6. Tominaga, S., Horiuchi, T.: Spectral Imaging by Synchronizing Capture and Illumination. JOSA A **29**(9), 1764–1775 (2012)

Color Sensation and Perception

Collection, Analysis and Representation of Memory Color Information

G.M. Atiqur Rahaman[1]([✉]), Md. Abul Hasnat[2], and Rahul Mourya[2]

[1] Color in Informatics and Media Technology (CIMET), Khulna, Bangladesh
gmatiqur@gmail.com
[2] University Jean Monnet, 42100 Saint-Étienne, France
{mhasnat,mourya.rahul1981}@gmail.com
http://www.master-erasmusmundus-color.eu

Abstract. Memory color plays an important role in the perceptual process. The aim of this research is to collect, analyze and represent memory color data for certain natural scenes objects: sky, grass and tree leaves. To emphasize reliable data collection, we consider several sources: (a) psychophysical experiment; (b) multispectral image; (c) standard image database and (d) random image collection. Moreover, we consider different daylight conditions and locations. We perform an in-depth analysis of the collected information in the CIE-xy chromaticity space and present the natural scene objects as a memory color ellipse or polygon. Finally, we demonstrate a potential use of the collected information for natural image segmentation and enhancement.

Keywords: Memory Color · Natural Scene Objects

1 Introduction

Memory colors are those colors which are recalled in association with familiar objects in long-term memory Bartleson [1960]. They have influence on the color appearance of objects, and hence play an important role on comparison and decision process. The naturalness of the images in the visuo-cognitive processing depends on the closeness of match between the representation of the image and memory Janssen [2001]. Natural objects like sky, grass etc. has the naturalness property and good candidate of objects containing memory color. These objects should be considered within the context of the entire image. Moreover, since memory colors are those that people often see in life, remember them and can tell when they look right, these objects must have very small gamut. Therefore, it is necessary to define a certain range of values for these objects. This research is motivated by such observations and hence contributes to collect reliable memory color information of certain natural scene objects and represent them in a standard form.

Heretofore, the concept of memory color has been widely studied by the scientific communities from different perspectives Bartleson [1960]; Pérez Carpinell et al. [1998]; Vurro et al. [2013]; Xue et al. [2014]. In image

A. Trémeau et al. (Eds.): CCIW 2015, LNCS 9016, pp. 93–103, 2015.
DOI: 10.1007/978-3-319-15979-9_9

processing, it has been successfully adopted in numerous tasks Boust et al. [2006]; Xue et al. [2014], e.g., image quality evaluation, matching, segmentation and enhancement. For image enhancement, an expert first segments it into regions of interest. A set of these regions correspond to the natural objects. Then s/he changes the colors of these objects such that they match with the color that s/he recalls from memory. Likewise, naive observers use memory colors to judge an image for preference. It is found that, an image is preferred if the colors of the scene objects match with the colors that are stored in memory Boust et al. [2006]. Memory colors have been used for image enhancement through automatic color constancy. Most digital cameras apply color constancy (white balancing) algorithms to estimate the illumination, which ensures that color casts are compensated and colors (other than the neutrals) appear as correct or pleasing Rahtu et al. [2009]. A dataset was collected for such study Rahtu et al. [2009], which is not publicly available. Moreover, it was collected by maintaining several constrains. Therefore, more interests are grown towards conducting similar research with a dataset obtained from restricted as well as publicly available images. This eventually motivates us to collect memory color data that combines information from different sources and conditions.

In this research, our aim is to: (a) collect reliable memory color data for certain natural scenes objects; (b) analyze the data in a widespread color space and (c) provide a standard representation of the memory color. To this aim, first we collect memory color data from several sources, such as: psychophysical experiments, images from internet and personal collection, standard image dataset and multispectral image. Next, we analyze the data in the CIE xy-chromaticity space by observing the color variations of each object. Finally, we represent the objects as an ellipse or polygon in the color space.

A practical use of memory color is image segmentation and enhancement Xiao-Ning Zhang et al. [2010]; Xue et al. [2014]. We observe that, this can be accomplished by exploiting our analyzed data. Therefore, although it is not our primary interest, yet in this paper we demonstrate such an application to clarify the use of our data. Our segmentation procedure consists of simply verifying the pixels color location w.r.t. the memory color ellipse or polygon. We perform image enhancement with a directional shift of the input color of memory objects towards the preferable region.

In the rest of this paper we discuss data collection strategies in Section 2. Then, we present our analysis and observations in Section 3. We present the data representation method in Section 4. Next, we demonstrate an application in Section 5. Finally, we draw conclusions in Section 6.

2   Memory Color Data Collection

We collect memory color data for three natural objects: sky, grass and tree leaves. Our data collection procedure consists of two main strategies: (1) psychophysical experiment, similar to Bartleson [1960]; Pérez Carpinell et al. [1998] and (2) image based data collection.

2.1 Psychophysical Experiment

The aim of psychophysical experiment is to find out what would be the response of an observer when he/she is asked to choose a particular color corresponding to a certain natural scene object. In general, such experiments are conducted in a control environment and the observer does not have any contextual information, i.e., surrounding objects or a reference object.

Similar to Bartleson [1960], we use the Munsell color chart. The color chart is placed in the light cabinet under different light sources. In order to stabilize the light source, we switch ON the light booth for 2 hours before the experiments. At the beginning, the observer is asked to look at the walls of the cabinet for a certain period of time, so that s/he can adapt with the light source. The geometry used here is 0/45.

We consider 18 observers from different backgrounds, i.e., from different countries, male and female, with/without prior knowledge of color. We ask the following questions: (a) "what is the possible color of an object (sky, grass and tree leaves)" and (b) "what is the most preferable color for that object?". The preferred color is considered as "favorite color". The observers are not allowed to take a reference color. We measure the reflectance spectra for the selected color chips using *Perkin-Elmer Lambda 18 UV/VIS* spectrophotometer (specular excluded), between the wavelength 380 nm - 780 nm in step of 1 nm. From the measured spectra, we calculate the tristimulus values for further analysis.

2.2 Image Based Data Collection

In this strategy, an observer can select the memory color (image pixel) regardless of any controlled environment as well as considering the surrounding objects present in the image. A digital image is displayed to an observer. The task here is to select at least 3 pixels for certain natural object. Moreover, they select at least 1 pixel as preferred ("favorite") color.

We consider images from three different sources: (a) multispectral images; (b) standard image database and (b) random images from internet/personal collection. Table 1 provides a list of the number of images and selected data points for each source and object category.

Table 1. Number of images and selected data points for each memory color objects

	Sky		Grass		Tree leaves	
	images	points	images	points	images	points
Psychological	n/a	48	n/a	44	n/a	60
Spectral	13	384	15	428	20	828
Digital image(internet)	155	307	79	155	75	150
Digital image (standard)	188	200	183	551	110	224
Total data	356	939	277	1178	205	1262
Total after clean up	-	922	-	1138	-	1243

Multispectral Images: We collect 26 spectral reflectance images. These images are in the following wavelength ranges with different spatial resolution: (a) 420 nm to 721 nm at the interval of 7 nm; (b) 400 nm to 720 nm at the interval of 10 nm and (c) 450 nm to 800 nm at the interval of 10 nm. Several images consist of a mixture of rural scenes from the Minho region of Portugal, containing trees leaves, grass, earth and urban scenes. These images were used in the study by Foster et al. Foster et al. [2004]. Other images are obtained from the image collection of the Spectral Color Research Group in the University of Eastern Finland.

Due to several limitations, it was not possible to ensure that the collected spectral images are captured in different daylight conditions. Therefore, we use the SPDs of daylight simulators in order to simulate the effect of different day times. We consider four day light CIE standard illuminants: D50, D55, D65 and D75, which typically represent: Horizon light, Mid-morning/Midafternoon, Noon daylight and North sky daylight.

Standard image database: We emphasize to collect memory color data from the images of a renowned, color research oriented and publicly available database. Such an image database[1] Gehler et al. [2008] was created at Microsoft Research Cambridge for color constancy based research. It consists of 568 images, from which we consider 481 images of outdoor natural scenes. Additionally, we label the images as either mid-day or morning/afternoon images.

Random images: We collect 309 natural objects (sky, grass and tree leaves) specific images from internet and personal collection. The aim of this collection is ensure that the images are from different daylight conditions, places and times. Moreover, such images are taken by arbitrary unknown imaging sensors. We label these images based on different times of a day.

3   Data Analysis and Observations

First, We transform the memory color data from each source into the CIE xy-chromaticity space. Next, we identify and use particular thresholds to remove outliers through the data cleanup process. For each object category, we analyze: (a) variations of chromaticity coordinates for different data sources and (b) directions of shift for different daylight conditions. Finally, we store these data as training data for potential applications. Table 2 provides a list of minimum and maximum coordinates found from each data source and for each object.

psychophysical experiments: Fig. 1 illustrates the memory colors obtained from psychophysical experiments, where green indicates "favorite color". We observe that, the sky color in the chromaticity space justifies the identified region of sky color in the image based data collection. The grass color region in the chromaticity space is not in good agreement with the identified region of grass in other data sources. More specifically, they are within the range of 0.26 to 0.38

---

[1] http://files.is.tue.mpg.de/pgehler/projects/color/index.html

Table 2. Analysis of different datasets for memory color objects

	Min x	Max x	Min y	Max y
Sky				
Psychophysical	0.20	0.32	0.25	0.35
Spectral	0.24	0.32	0.26	0.35
Image (random)	0.21	0.31	0.21	0.34
Image (standard)	0.27	0.35	0.28	0.36
Grass				
Psychophysical	0.26	0.38	0.37	0.56
Spectral	0.30	0.40	0.35	0.47
Image (random)	0.36	0.41	0.47	0.54
Image (standard)	0.34	0.42	0.40	0.54
Tree Leaves				
Psychophysical	0.27	0.36	0.42	0.56
Spectral	0.24	0.41	0.26	0.51
Image (random)	0.35	0.44	0.43	0.56
Image (standard)	0.33	0.43	0.38	0.54

in x-coordinate whereas the range is between 0.30 to 0.42 for other datasets. The tree color shows good correlation with other source of images. Moreover, we notice that the favorite colors chosen by different observers are scattered within the region.

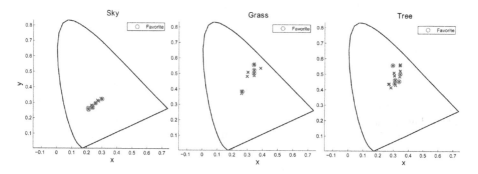

Fig. 1. Illustrations of results from psychophysical experiments. Plots show the CIE-xy coordinates of the natural objects: (from left) of sky, grass and tree leaves.

Spectral Images: Fig. 2 presents the memory color data obtained from the spectral images. Moreover, it illustrates the changes of colors as a function of different illuminations. We see that, due to simulations with different daylight, the memory colors of each object spans wider range in the CIE-xy diagram.

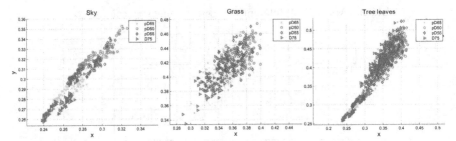

Fig. 2. Illustration of memory colors obtained from spectral images in the CIE-xy chromaticity space. From left, Sky, grass and tree leaf in: D50 (green), D55 (red), D65 (cyan) and D75 (pink).

Standard image database: Fig. 3 illustrates the memory colors obtained from the images of this category. From the analysis of variations, in Fig. 2 and Fig. 3, we found that the sky color regions in the chromaticity space justify the identified region from spectral image. Similar analysis on other objects reveals that, although grass and leaves colors have overlapping with colors data from different sources, yet there are some regions which mismatch.

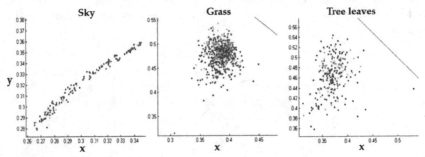

Fig. 3. Illustration of memory colors in the CIE-xy chromaticity space, obtained from standard image database Gehler et al. [2008]. In the plots, blue color indicates mid-day and green color indicates objects memory color in morning/afternoon.

Random image collection: Fig. 4 shows the memory color of objects from the random image collection. This analysis revealed that sky color at the mid-day shift diagonally from the yellow color region. This is because of the dominance of yellow color in the morning / afternoon. Grass and tree-leaves colors show very little amount of shift. Grass colors shift diagonally downwards and from tree-leaves colors no conclusion is possible to make. We can use this shifting directional information during enhancement.

Next, we analyze the data jointly from different sources. We observe that the combined data consists of few outliers. Based on observations, we define thresholds for each memory object to clean up the data. We determine these

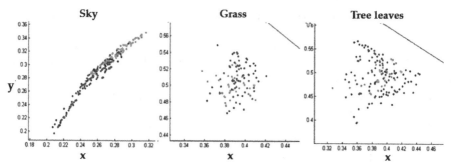

Fig. 4. Illustration of memory colors in the CIE-xy chromaticity space, obtained from randomly collected images. In the plots, blue color indicates mid-day and green color indicates objects memory color in morning/afternoon.

thresholds empirically by examining the Euclidean distances between each data point and the mean of all data. First, we remove the 5% - 10% most distant points from the entire data. Then, as the threshold values, see Table 3, we keep the minimum and maximum coordinates of the remaining data.

Table 3. Thresholds (chromaticity values) for memory color objects

	Min x	Max x	Min y	Max y
Sky	0.21	0.345	0.205	0.356
Grass	0.30	0.42	0.35	0.56
Tree leaves	0.24	0.435	0.262	0.562

In the chromaticity space, because of the changes in daylight situations the same object color may shift in any direction from a particular point. To accurately locate such shifts in color, it is necessary to identify the direction of changes. For this reason, based on the data collected from multispectral images, we calculate and study the angle of changes in different daylight conditions. Table 4 gives the analysis of the angular changes under different illuminations.

Table 4. Intra variation of Angles of colors in different illumination (The unit is in degree between two corresponding colors).

	Sky				Grass				Tree Leaves			
	Max	Min	Avg	SD	Max	Min	Avg	SD	Max	Min	Avg	SD
D65	48.17	46.00	47.36	0.56	52.25	46.99	49.77	1.08	53.18	46.19	49.44	1.66
D50	48.66	46.02	47.61	0.66	51.61	46.23	49.04	1.12	52.39	45.71	48.95	1.39
D55	48.54	46.08	47.58	0.61	51.90	46.57	49.37	1.10	52.71	45.95	49.19	1.47
D75	47.84	45.81	47.06	0.53	52.42	47.22	49.99	1.07	53.59	46.14	49.53	1.84

4   Memory Color Representations

In order to exploit the collected data for practical tasks, it is necessary
to establish a meaningful form to represent them. Following existing work
Xiao-Ning Zhang et al. [2010], we use the notion of ellipse and polygon to represent memory color data. Particularly, the ellipse and polygon are used for all
memory colors, whereas, only the polygon is used to represent the favorite color.
Total numbers of favorite points are around 10% of the total number of considered data points. Fig. 5 illustrates the obtained ellipses and polygons for the
memory color data obtained in Section 2.

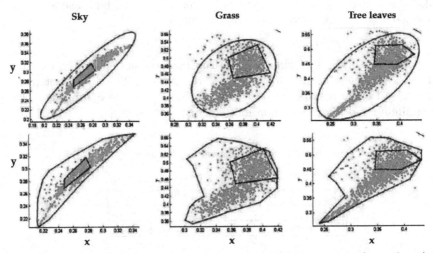

Fig. 5. Illustrations of Memory color ellipses (first row) and polygons (second row) for
the entire data collected for different natural objects. The favorite color polygons are
shown w.r.t. both ellipses and polygons.

First, we define memory color region in the CIE xy-chromaticity space using
an ellipse. From the xy-coordinates, an ellipse is defined using least squares
criterion as:

$$ax^2 + bxy + cy^2 + dx + ey = f \tag{1}$$

We observe that, an ellipse fitted with Eq. (1) tends to exclude many data
points which belong to the memory color of certain objects. Moreover, it often
encompasses unwanted regions. To handle such cases we manually correct the
semi-major axis, semi-minor axis and the center of ellipse. The correction is done
with the principle of minimizing false rejection and false selection. The first row
of Fig. 5 illustrates the ellipses after correction. We see that they cover most of
the regions while excluding few color points.

Experimentally (see Fig. 7(a)) we observed that, memory color ellipse, even
after manual correction, may lead to segmentation fault due to false consideration of some unwanted region. In order to eliminate this problem, we propose

the use of polygon rather than ellipse. The polygons are defined based on manual observation in the chromaticity space. The second row of Fig. 5 illustrates the polygons. Fig. 7(a) shows that, such polygons can successfully handle false selection and rejection.

We define favorite color polygon from the favorite memory color data. In Fig. 5, it is the most interior and smaller polygon. We observe that favorite color polygon is well suited inside the memory ellipse and polygon. Similar to Xiao-Ning Zhang et al. [2010], we will use the it for image enhancement.

5   Application: Image Segmentation and Enhancement

For image enhancement, first we employ a well-known color constancy algorithm called gray-world algorithm Gehler et al. [2008]. Next, we convert the white balanced image from RGB space to xyY space. After that, we apply segmentation based on the defined ellipse/polygon in order to obtain the region of interest (ROI). Any pixel is added to the ROI if it belongs to the ellipse/polygon. Finally, we shift the chromaticity coordinates of the segmented pixels based on its relative distance and subtended angle to the center of favorite color polygon. The distance according to which the data should be shifted depends on two parameters: the distance and the angle of the point in relation to the center of the rectangle Xiao-Ning Zhang et al. [2010].

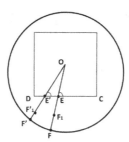

Fig. 6. Color shifting distance in the enhancement process

Fig. 6 illustrates the color shifting method. Point F is the candidate to shift towards the memory color rectangle. According to the rule: $OE : EF = EF^1 : F^1F$, the colors which are further away from the center should be enhanced more than the closer ones. Let us observe points F' and F. Even though the distance from the center to the colors are same, F' is closer to the DC boundary, and therefore should be enhanced less than F. To satisfy this rule, we must consider the angle from the rectangle boundary to the color point. The pixels within the memory rectangle should remain the same. If d is the distance from the center of the rectangle to the color F (let $d = OF$), then the distance from the center to the enhanced point $F^1(d^1 = OF^1)$ should be:

$$d^1 = \frac{h}{sin(\theta)} \left(2 - \frac{h}{d\,sin(\theta)} \right) \qquad (2)$$

where, h is the distance from the center to the middle of the rectangle edge (i.e., O to DC). Finally, we convert shifted pixels from xyY to RGB space.

Fig. 7(a) illustrates the results of segmentation using ellipse/polygon. In the segmented image, the colored portions are the regions where enhancement will be applied. We observe undesirable result in middle column as the pixels belong to the cloud are segmented as sky. This indicates that, segmentation with ellipse produces incorrect segmentation (false selection). On the other hand, based on the result in the last column, we see that memory color polygon performs better.

(a)

(b)

Fig. 7. (a) Result of segmentation: (left) original image, (middle) segmented image generated by memory ellipse, (right) segmented image generated by memory polygon. (b) Results of enhancement of images with sky. Left column shows the original image and right column shows the enhanced image.

Fig. 7(b) illustrates the results of image enhancement. Note that, the proposed method only enhances a particular segment of the image that consist of certain natural object. We observe that, such an enhancement increases the contrast between the memory color objects and other objects of the image. Therefore, it is necessary to perform global enhancement to preserve the coherency of colors, which we consider as a potential future work. Additionally, we observe that: (a) performance of enhancement depends on the accuracy of segmentation and (b) amount of enhancement depends on the area as well as location of polygon in the chromaticity space.

6   Conclusions

The fundamental contribution of this research is to perform acquisition and analysis of memory color information for several objects commonly appears in natural scenes. Therefore, we consider different data sources and devices to collect memory color information. We study the collected data and provide in-depth analysis to ensure reliability and better understanding. We represent object specific data as an ellipse or polygon. As a potential use, we demonstrate applications in image segmentation and enhancement. Results show that, the collected data is reliable and hence can be used for different image processing tasks which concern about the natural scenes objects. In future, this fundamental research can be enhanced by providing different forms of representation of the collected memory color data, e.g., probabilistic representation of the decision boundary of memory color regions in the color spaces. Moreover, we can investigate different color spaces and evaluate them. For the application, we can focus on developing more robust methods and compare them with existing methods.

Acknowledgments. This work was part of annual CIMET project contest. Special thanks to University of Eastern Finland, Jean Monnet University, University of Granada, and Gjovik University College.

References

Bartleson, C.J.: Memory colors of familiar objects. JOSA **50**(1), 73–77 (1960)

Boust, C., Brettel, H., Viénot, F., Alquié, G., Berche, S.: Color enhancement of digital images by experts and preference judgments by observers. Journal of Imaging Science and Technology **50**(1), 1–11 (2006)

Foster, D.H., Nascimento, S., Amano, K.: Information limits on neural identification of colored surfaces in natural scenes. Visual Neuroscience **21**(03), 331–336 (2004)

Gehler, P.V., Rother, C., Blake, A., Minka, T., Sharp, T.: Bayesian color constancy revisited. In: IEEE Int. Conf. on Computer Vision and Pattern Recognition, pp. 1–8. IEEE (2008)

Janssen, R.: Computational image quality, vol. 101. SPIE Press (2001)

Pérez Carpinell, J., de Fez, M.D., Baldoví, R., Soriano, J.C., et al.: Familiar objects and memory color (1998)

Rahtu, E., Nikkanen, J., Kannala, J., Lepistö, L., Heikkilä, J.: Applying visual object categorization and memory colors for automatic color constancy. In: Int. Conf. on Image Analysis and Processing, pp. 873–882 (2009)

Vurro, M., Ling, Y., Hurlbert, A.C.: Memory color of natural familiar objects: Effects of surface texture and 3-d shape. Journal of Vision **13**(7), 20 (2013)

Xiao-Ning Zhang, Z., Jiang, J., Liang, Z.H., Chun-Liang Liu, L.: Skin color enhancement based on favorite skin color in hsv color space. IEEE Trans. on Consumer Electronics **56**(3), 1789–1793 (2010)

Xue, S., Tan, M., McNamara, A., Dorsey, J., Rushmeier, H.: Exploring the use of memory colors for image enhancement. In: IS&T/SPIE Electronic Imaging, pp. 901411–901411 (2014)

The Display Gamut Available to Simulate Colors Perceived by Anomalous Trichromats

João M.M. Linhares[1(✉)], Jorge L.A. Santos[2], Vasco M.N. de Almeida[2],
Catarina A.R. João[1], Sérgio M.C. Nascimento[1]

[1] Center of Physics, Campus Gualtar, University of Minho, 4710-057 Braga, Portugal
{jlinhares,smcn}@fisica.uminho.pt, car.joao89@gmail.com
[2] Department of Physics, University of Beira Interior, 6201-001 Covilhã, Portugal
j.l.a.santos@gmail.com, vasco@ubi.pt

Abstract. The aim of this work was to investigate the effect on a display gamut of varying the optical density and the position of the maximum sensitivity of the cones spectra of anomalous trichromatic observers. The anomalous cone spectral sensitivities were estimated for a set of varying optical density and maximum sensitivity spectra conditions and used to compute the display color gamut. The computed display gamut simulated for normal observers the chromatic diversity perceived by anomalous observers. It was found that even small variations on the optical density and on the position of the maximum sensitivity spectra have an impact on the simulations of the display gamut for anomalous observers. It was also found that simulations for deuteroanomalous observers are the ones with greater impact if the estimation of the corresponding color display gamut is not carefully adjusted for the observer.

Keywords: Anomalous color vision · Color gamut · Color deficient

1 Introduction

The chromatic diversity experienced by normal color vision observers encloses millions of individually discernible colors [1]. These cones are sensitive to the long, middle and small regions of the visible spectrum and are denominated L, M and S-cones, respectively [2]. Anomalous trichromats observers still retain the functional use of the three color sensors, but their spectral sensitivity by the means of a pigment that is photosensitive to visible light is different from the normal color vision observer on the M and L cones [3], [4] and are named deuteroanomalous and protoanomalous, respectively. The differences in the spectral sensitivity of anomalous observers will impair their color vision [5], [6] and might limit their ability to perform some tasks [7]. This limitation is found to be the confusion of some colors that are identified as different by normal color vision observers with a direct impact on color vision perception [8], [9].

The simulation of anomalous color vision as perceived by normal observers is then of valuable use when trying to ascertain anomalous colored vision perception, as by doing so improvements to their color vision might be attempted [10], [11].

© Springer International Publishing Switzerland 2015
A. Trémeau et al. (Eds.): CCIW 2015, LNCS 9016, pp. 104–110, 2015.
DOI: 10.1007/978-3-319-15979-9_10

This simulation is very dependent on the spectral sensitivity of the anomalous cones, the concentration of photopigment available at each individual class of cones (or their optical density) and ocular media transparency [3], [8], [12]. Small variations on each of these quantities will have an impact on anomalous color vision, which might compromise proper color vision assessment by the means of computer color vision tests [13].

The purpose of this work is to study how variations on the optical density and spectral sensitivity of anomalous cones impact the display color gamut simulated for normal observers as a perception of anomalous observers color vison. Simulations of anomalous color vision were computed by fixating the anomalous spectral shift and by independently varying the M or L cones optical density or by fixating the optical density of the M and L cones and varying their spectral position. In each case the simulation of the display color gamut was estimated and its area in CIE 1976 UCS [14] computed as a measurement of the chromatic impact in anomalous color vision. The results obtained here seem to show that each condition variation affects at least 20% on the simulated gamut, amount that can be around 70% in some extreme conditions.

2   Methods

2.1   General Estimation of the Anomalous Cone Spectral Sensitivity Curve

The method used to estimate the anomalous cone sensitivities to simulate for normal observers the colors perceived by anomalous observers was the one described elsewhere [3]: a normal cone spectral sensitivity curve estimated at the cornea [2] was used as template. Average normal observer lens and macular pigment absorption spectra [3] were used to estimate the spectral sensitivity at the retina [15]. The cone photopigment optical density was then corrected for self-screening assuming the original maximum optical (OD_{max}) and converted into wavenumber to ensure that the wavelength shift was shape independent [16]. The shift was then produced as desired. To reconstruct the anomalous spectral sensitivity curve at the cornea the reversed process was used: the shifted spectrum was converted into wavelength, corrected for self screening and for lens and macular pigment absorption. All computations were done in quantal. Whenever conversion from energy to quantal was needed energy data was divided by its corresponding wavelength.

2.2   Estimating Protoanomalous Spectral Sensitivity Curve

Three assumptions were made to estimate the protoanomalous (L') spectral sensitivity curve:

1. M cone was used as template and MOD_{max} was used to compensate for self screening;
2. After shifting the M cone spectral sensitivity spectra towards longer wavelengths the self screening was compensated using the normal LOD_{max} to obtain anomalous L cone sensitivity spectra or L';

3. The amplitude of the L' cone spectral sensitivity was assumed to be equal to the normal L cone.

Using these three assumptions, the L' anomalous cone spectral sensitivity was estimated by:

(a) Fixating the spectral shift in 10 nm and the MOD_{max} to 0.3 and vary the LOD_{max} from 0.3 to 0.5 in 0.01 steps;
(b) Fixating the spectral shift in 10 nm and the LOD_{max} to 0.4 and vary the MOD_{max} from 0.2 to 0.4 in 0.01 steps;
(c) Fixating the LOD_{max} to 0.4 and the MOD_{max} to 0.3 and vary the spectral shift towards longer wavelength from 5 to 15 nm in 0.5 nm steps;

2.3   Estimating Deuteroanomalous Spectral Sensitivity Curve

Three assumptions were made to estimate the deuteroanomalous (M') spectral sensitivity curve:

4. L cone was used as template and LOD_{max} was used to compensate for self screening;
5. After shifting the L cone spectral sensitivity spectra towards shorter wavelengths the self screening was compensated using the normal MOD_{max} to obtain anomalous M cone sensitivity spectra or M';
6. The amplitude of the M' cone spectral sensitivity was assumed to be equal to the normal M cone.

Using these three assumptions, the M' anomalous cone spectral sensitivity was estimated by:

(d) Fixating the spectral shift in 6 nm and the MOD_{max} to 0.3 and vary the LOD_{max} from 0.3 to 0.5 in 0.01 steps;
(e) Fixating the spectral shift in 6 nm and the LOD_{max} to 0.4 and vary the MOD_{max} from 0.2 to 0.4 in 0.01 steps;
(f) Fixating the LOD_{max} to 0.4 and the MOD_{max} to 0.3 and vary the spectral shift towards shorter wavelength from 2 to 10 nm in 0.5 nm steps;

2.4   Estimating the Display Color Gamut

The three phosphors of a CRT monitor (Sony Trinitron GDM-F520, Sony Corp., Japan) were measured using a calibrated telespectroradiometer (PR-650 SpectraScan Colorimeter; Photo Research, Chatsworth, CA). The stimulus was presented in the display by using a video display card (ViSaGe Visual Stimulus Generator; Cambridge Research Systems, Rochester, Kent, UK) to power each phosphor individually at its maximum intensity. The measured spectral radiance was then converted into CIE 1976 UCS chromaticity coordinates [14] assuming each cone sensitivity spectra estimated in (a) to (f). The CIE 1931 standard observer was assumed on all estimations [14].

The CIE 1976 UCS chromaticity coordinates were then used to estimate the triangular color gamut. The area occupied by it was estimated by using a convex hull algorithm available in MatLab (MathWorks, Inc., Natick, MA, United States of America) which is based on the Qhull algorithm [17]. The estimated area was then normalized to its maximum to estimate the variations on the color gamut across the (a) to (f) conditions.

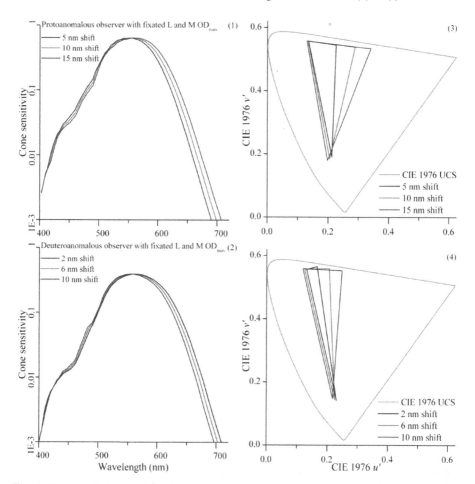

Fig. 1. Protoanomalous and deuteroanomalous spectral sensitivity curves obtained assuming the conditions described in (c) as (1) and in (f) as (2), respectively. (3) and (4) represent the corresponding display color gamut assuming the same conditions. For easier reading only the extreme (blue and black lines) and the middle (red line) of the conditions tested are represented.

3   Results

Figure 1 represents as an example of the estimated spectral sensitivity curves the protoanomalous (1) and deuteroanomalous (2) spectral sensitivity curves obtained assuming the conditions described in (c) and (f), respectively. Also represented are the corresponding display color gamut for protoanomalous (3) and deuteroanomalous (4) observers. For clarity only the extreme and middle conditions are represented. Actual estimations were computed from 5 nm to 15 nm in 0.5 nm steps for protoanomalous and from 2 nm to 10 nm in 0.5 nm steps for deuteroanomalous.

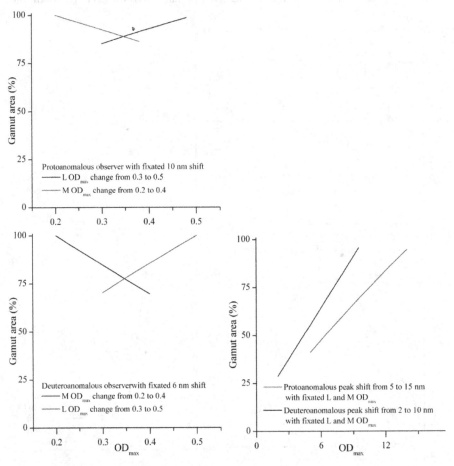

Fig. 2. Top panel represents the variations on computer color gamut area for a protoanomalous observer, assuming conditions (a) as a black line and (b) as a red line. Bottom left panel represents the same variations for the deuteroanomalous, assuming conditions (d) as a red line and (e) as a black line. Bottom right panel shows both observers and same variations as previously described varying only the peak sensitivity of the anomalous cone, assuming conditions (c) as a red line and (f) as a black line.

Figure 2 represents the estimated variations in display color gamut area for all the conditions tested from (a) to (f). The top panel represents the protoanomalous observer with fixed shifted sensitivity peak at 10 nm and independent variations on the LOD_{max} (black line) and MOD_{max} (red line), normalized to its maximum. It was found that the maximum variation of the display color gamut between extreme conditions was of 15% in both cases. Bottom left panel represents the deuteroanomalous observer with fixed shifted peak sensitivity at 6 nm and independent variations on the MOD_{max} (black line) and LOD_{max} (red line), normalized to its maximum. It was found that the maximum variation between extreme conditions was of 30% in both cases.

The bottom right panel represents the protoanomalous (black line) and deuteroanomalous (red line) observers with fixed MOD_{max} and LOD_{max} and varying the shifted peak sensitivity as described in condition (c) and (f), respectively. It was found that the maximum variation between the extreme conditions was of 59% for the protoanomalous observer and of 71% for the deuteroanomalous observer.

4   Discussion and Conclusions

As observed elsewhere [8], [12], varying the optical densities or the position of the maximum spectral sensitivity of the anomalous cone can impact the perceived color vision simulations. The results presented here show that such findings can be express in terms of a display color gamut and estimated in terms of its occupied area. The same magnitude of variations on LOD_{max} or MOD_{max} seems to affect more deuteroanomalous rather than protoanomalous observers. Despite these variations the major effect comes from varying the peak of maximum spectral sensitivity, affecting more the deuteroanomalous observers. Such effects on deuteroanomalous observers might be explained by the higher proximity of the normal L cone and the anomalous M' cone (only 6 nm apart, in average) than in protoanomalous observers where the normal M cone and the anomalous L' cone are separated by 10 nm in average. All computations assumed that the estimated display gamut represented for a normal observer the color gamut perceived by the anomalous observer.

The data presented here are consistent with those presented elsewhere [12] with chromatic diversity increasing with increase OD_{max} variations and decreasing with increasing OD_{max} in protoanomalous and deuteranomalous observers, repectively.

These results seem to indicate that the simulation of deuteroanomalous observers color vision might have a greater impact if the tested assumptions are not carefully adjusted.

Acknowledgments. This work was supported by the Centro de Física of Minho University, by FEDER through the COMPETE Program and by the Portuguese Foundation for Science and Technology (FCT) in the framework of the project PTDC/MHC-PCN/4731/2012.

References

1. Linhares, J.M., Pinto, P.D., Nascimento, S.M.: The number of discernible colors in natural scenes. J. Opt. Soc. Am. A Opt. Image Sci. Vis. **25**(12), 2918–2924 (2008)
2. Wyszecki, G., Stiles, W.S.: Color Science: Concepts and Methods, Quantitative Data and Formulae. 2nd edn. John Wiley & Sons, New York (1982)

3. DeMarco, P., Pokorny, J., Smith, V.C.: Full-Spectrum Cone Sensitivity Functions for X-Chromosome-Linked Anomalous Trichromates **9**(9), 1465–1476 (1992)
4. Merbs, S.L., Nathans, J.: Absorption spectra of the hybrid pigments responsible for anomalous color vision. Science (80-.) **258**(5081), 464–466 (1992)
5. Perales, E., Martínez-Verdú, F.M., Linhares, J.M.M., Nascimento, S.M.C.: Number of discernible colors for color-deficient observers estimated from the MacAdam limits. J. Opt. Soc. Am. A **27**(10), 2106 (2010)
6. Linhares, J.M.M., Felgueiras, P.E.R., Pinto, P.D., Nascimento, S.M.C.: Colour rendering of indoor lighting with CIE illuminants and white LEDs for normal and colour deficient observers. Ophthalmic Physiol. Opt. **30**(5), 618–625 (2010)
7. Cole, B.L.: The handicap of abnormal colour vision. Clin. Exp. Optom. **87**(4–5), 258–275 (2004)
8. Webster, M.A., Juricevic, I., McDermott, K.C.: Simulations of adaptation and color appearance in observers with varying spectral sensitivity. Ophthalmic Physiol. Opt. **30**(5), 602–610 (2010)
9. Baraas, R.C., Foster, D.H., Amano, K., Nascimento, S.M.C.: Anomalous trichromats' judgments of surface color in natural scenes under different daylights. Vis. Neurosci. **23**(3–4), 629–635 (2006)
10. Kovacs, G., Kucsera, I., Abraham, G., Wenzel, K.: Enhancing color representation for anomalous trichromats on CRT monitors. Color Res. Appl. **26**, S273–S276 (2001)
11. Machado, G.M., Oliveira, M.M., Fernandes, L.A.F.: A Physiologically-based Model for Simulation of Color Vision Deficiency. IEEE Trans. Vis. Comput. Graph. **15**(6), 1291–1298 (2009)
12. Thomas, P.B.M., Formankiewicz, M.A., Mollon, J.D.: The effect of photopigment optical density on the color vision of the anomalous trichromat. Vision Res. **51**(20), 2224–2233 (2011)
13. Barbur, J.L., Rodriguez-Carmona, M., Harlow, J.A., Mancuso, K., Neitz, J., Neitz, M.: A study of unusual Rayleigh matches in deutan deficiency. Vis. Neurosci. **25**(3), 507–516 (2008)
14. CIE, Colorimetry, CIE Publ. 15:2004. CIE, Viena (2004)
15. Brainard, D.H., Stockman, A.: Colorimetry. In: Bass, M., DeCusatis, C., Enoch, J., Lakshminarayanan, V., Li, G., MacDonald, C., Mahajan, V., Van Stryland, E. (eds.) Handbook of Optics, Volume III: Vision and Vision Optics, 3rd edn, p. 10.1. The McGraw-Hill Companies, New York (2010)
16. Knowles, A., Dartnall, H.J.A.: The characterization of visual pigments by absorption spectroscopy. In: Davson, H. (ed.) The Eye, 2nd edn, vol. 2B. Academic Press, Michigan (1997)
17. Barber, C.B., Dobkin, D.P., Huhdanpaa, H.: The Quickhull Algorithm for Convex Hulls. ACM Trans. Math. Softw. **22**(4), 469–483 (1996)

Visual Search for Normal Color and Dichromatic Observers Using a Unique Distracter Color

Jorge L.A. Santos[1]([✉]), Vasco M.N. de Almeida[1], Catarina A.R. João[2],
João M.M. Linhares[2], and Sérgio M.C. Nascimento[2]

[1] Department of Physics, University of Beira Interior, 6201-001 Covilhã, Portugal
j.l.a.santos@gmail.com, vasco@ubi.pt
[2] Centre of Physics, Campus de Gualtar, University of Minho,
4710-057 Braga, Portugal
car.joao89@gmail.com,
{jlinhares,smcn}@fisica.uminho.pt

Abstract. It is well known that color coding facilitates search and identification in real-life tasks. The aim of this work was to compare reaction times for normal color and dichromatic observers in a visual search
experiment. A unique distracter color was used to avoid abnormal color
vision vulnerability to background complexity. Reaction times for normal color observers and dichromats were estimated for $2°$ central vision
at 48 directions around a white point in CIE $L^*a^*b^*$ color space for
systematic examination on the mechanisms of dichromatic color perception. The results show that mean search times for dichromats were twice
larger compared to the normal color observers and for all directions.
The difference between the copunctual confusion lines and the confusion
direction measure experimentally was $5.5°$ for protanopes and $7.5°$ for
deuteranopes.

Keywords: Visual search · Dichromatic vision · Color vision tests ·
Color deficiencies

1 Introduction

Color is a relational attribute of objects that facilitates search and identification
tasks [1][2]. This attribute is explored in the natural environment by plants and
animals as well by humans in urban environment such as transports, medical
diagnosis or commercial purposes. Observers with abnormal color vision may
perform many of these tasks poorly. Particularly, the dichromatic population
that comprise about 2% of the male population [3], seems to have longer search
times and the target color object was less salient to them compared with normal
color observers [4]. Although this is an important result no systematic examination was performed for dichromatic observers around a white point.

It has also been reported that reaction time depends on the color difference
between a target and a distracter color. That is, the reaction time increases for

© Springer International Publishing Switzerland 2015
A. Trémeau et al. (Eds.): CCIW 2015, LNCS 9016, pp. 111–117, 2015.
DOI: 10.1007/978-3-319-15979-9_11

small color differences, but for large color differences response time was constant [5]. Two distracters color are typically used [6], being the target color in between the distracters at the middle chromatic distance. Although this is a convenient configuration the number of distracters is a significant factor in search time whereas the color deficient observers are more vulnerable to increased background clutter [4]. Therefore, in experiment 1, we tested a visual search paradigm with a unique distracter color in order to determine (1) how critically the chromatic separation between the target color and the unique distracter color influence reaction time and (2) to characterize the response direction produced by the visual search paradigm.

Finally, in experiment 2 we used the visual search paradigm for systematic reaction time examination of normal and dichromatic observers for 48 positions around a white point in the CIE $L^*a^*b^*$ color space.

2   Methods

2.1   Stimuli

Stimulus was a target color with a diamond like shape and 150 color distracters (50 circles, 50 triangles and 50 squares) on a gray background as shown in Figure 1. The centre of the monitor was market with a plus sign and constitutes the fixation point. The target was always displayed 2° around the centre of the monitor in one of eight possible positions (up, down, left, right, up-left, up-right, down-left, down-right) whereas distracters were randomly distributed over 391 positions across the scene. The background subtended a visual angle of 6.7° × 8.5° and both target and distracters subtended a visual angle of 0.2°. This configuration resembles that of Cole et al. 2004 [4].

The target color was uniquely color coded, i.e. none of the distracters was the same color as the target. All distracters had the same hue and one of five luminance levels (9.5, 11.4, 13.2, 15.1 and 17.0 cd/m^2) attributed randomly. The background had chromaticity (0.31, 0.316) expressed in CIE 1931 (x, y) diagram and luminance 13.2 cd/m^2. The luminance of the target and the mean luminance of the distracters were identical to that of the background. The color of the target and distracters were always $\Delta E_{ab} = 20$ units from the background color represented in Figure 2 at coordinates (0,0) assuming the CIE $L^*a^*b^*$ color space.

In experiment 1 the color of the target and distracters varied along 24 positions centered on the color of the background and the hue angle between target and distracters was +60°, -60°, +90°, -90°, +120° or -120°. In experiment 2 we duplicated the number of positions corresponding to a hue-angle variation of 7.5° and the target color was always at a hue angle of +60° relative to the distracter color. Both experiments enable two opposite colors to be collinear to the deutan confusion line and almost collinear to the protan confusion line.

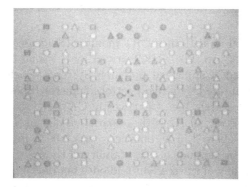

Fig. 1. Stimulus of the visual search paradigm viewed from observers point of view. The background had a mean chromaticity equivalent to illuminant C (CIE 1931 x=0.31, y=0.316) and subtended a visual angle of 6.7° × 8.5° provided by the monitor screen. The color target was always a diamond located 2° around the centre of the monitor (plus sign) and in one of eight cardinal positions. The distracters were 50 circles, 50 triangles and 50 squares randomly distributed over 391 positions across the scene. Both target and distracters subtended a visual angle of 0.2°. None of the distracters had the same color as the target and all distracters had the same hue and one of five levels of luminance in the range 9.5-17cd/m^2. The luminance for the target, background and mean of the distracters was 13.2 cd/m^2 .

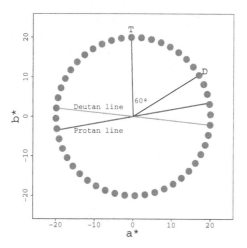

Fig. 2. The 48 testing directions around the background color used in experiment 2. It shows an example of a target color (T) at the fixed hue angle of +60° relative to the distracter color (D). In experiment 1 only 24 directions were tested. The two collinear colors to the deutan confusion line and the two almost collinear colors to the protan confusion line were present on both experiments.

2.2   Apparatus

Stimuli were displayed on a 19-inch CRT monitor (Samsung Sync-Master 750p, Samsung Electronics Corp. Ltd, RPC) driven by a Visual Stimulus Generator VSG2/3 graphics card (Cambridge Research Systems, Rochester, Kent, UK). The monitor was calibrated by a telespectroradiometer (SpectraScan Colorimeter PR-650; Photo Research, Inc., Chatsworth, CA). The stimuli were displayed with a refresh rate set at 80 Hz with a spatial resolution of 1024×768 pixels. The maximum error allowed in chromaticity was 0.0035 in the CIE (x, y) diagram and 0.4 cd/m^2 in luminance. The stability of the color and luminance was checked in the beginning of the sessions and once per day. The reaction time was measured by means of a custom-made response box with precision of 2 ms.

2.3   Procedure

In each trial, observers saw the stimulus monocularly after a 3 min adaptation to the background color. Observers were instructed to find a diamond-shaped target among the circles, triangles and squares, in one of eight possible cardinal positions, and signal its presence as quick as possible by pressing the response box. The stimulus was immediately replaced by the uniform background color after target-detection response or if there was no response after a 1 sec interval for experiment 1 or after a 3 sec interval for experiment 2. If there was a response observers were asked to indicate on a numeric keyboard the cardinal position of the diamond-shape target. If observers press the response box unintentionally they were asked to press the central key on the numeric keyboard. This error and any keyboard mismatch or no response after a 3 sec interval were not accounted as a response but repeated once again at the same session. The experiments were carried out in a dark room.

In experiment 1 the target color was shown counterclockwise compared to the distracter color (Figure 1) for three hue angles (+60° , +90° and +120°) and also for the clockwise direction (-60° , -90° and -120°). There were two sessions and 6x24 trials were randomized over session. For experiment 2 only the +60° combination were used. Each session consisted of 144 trials and a sequence of three different sessions was generated so that all observers saw the same sequence. The trials were randomized over session.

2.4   Observers

Five normal color observers participated in experiment 1. In experiment 2 there were thirteen observers; six had normal color vision, two were deuteranopes and five were protanopes. Color vision was assessed using the Ishihara plates, the City University Color Vision Test (Keeler Ltd) and the Nagel Anomaloscope (Oculus Heidelberg Multi Color). All subjects had monocular visual acuity of at least logMAR 0.00 with correction if needed. Two of the authors (J.S. and V.A.) served as observers and had prior experience in visual search experiments, all other observers were naïve.

3   Results

The results for experiment 1 (Figure 3) represents the reaction time as a function of the response direction. The response direction, calculated as:

$$T - \left(\frac{T - D}{2} + 7.5\right), \tag{1}$$

where T is the target-angle and D the distracter-angle, corresponds to the direction that best tune the six target-distracter pairs of colors or any other pair. This response direction fit in between the target-distracter pair and differs from the mean direction by 7.5° clockwise. Reaction time tended to be constant with large color differences ($\pm$ 120°) and increase nonlinearly for small color differences ($\pm$ 60°). The +60° target-distracter pair corresponds to the best amplification.

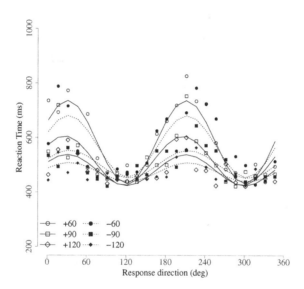

Fig. 3. Results for experiment 1. Represents the variation on reaction time as a function of the direction that best tune any target-distracter pair (response direction). The response direction was calculated as $T - ((T - D)/2 + 7.5)$, where T is the target-angle and D the distracter-angle. The plot shows the results of six target-distracter pairs for five normal color observers. Symbols represent the mean reaction time and the lines the interpolation sino functions of the data.

Figure 4 shows the results of experiment 2 for normal color and dichromatic observers for 48 positions and the +60° target-distracter pair. On the left side the reaction time for six normal color, two deuteranopes and five protanopes are expressed as a function of the response direction for the 48 directions. The interpolation line corresponds to the sino function that best fit the data. Error

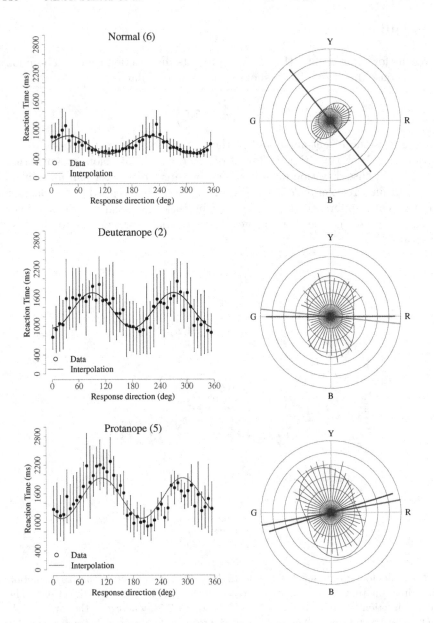

Fig. 4. Results for experiment 2. On the left side are represented the data for six normal color, two deuteranopes and five protanopes for 48 directions using a +60° target-distracter pair. The interpolation line corresponds to the sino function that best fit the data. Error bars represent standard deviation across trials. On the right side the mean data and the interpolation line for the 48 directions were plotted in polar coordinates, signaling the CIE $L^*a^*b^*$ color space directions. The confusion line for deuteranopes (green line) and protanopes (red line) are also showed. The thick-black line corresponds to the confusion direction.

bars represent standard deviation across trials. On the right side the mean data and the interpolation line were plotted in polar coordinates, signaling the CIE $L^*a^*b^*$ color space directions. Each circle corresponds to a 500 ms increment. The confusion line for deuteranopes (green line) and protanopes (red line) are also shown. The thick-black line, collinear to the minimum response direction, corresponds to the confusion direction. That is, color pairs along or parallel to this line show the highest reaction time.

4   Conclusions

It has been reported that the number of distracter colors is a significant factor for search time being the color deficient observers more vulnerable to background complexity [4]. A visual search paradigm using a unique distracter color was first tested to characterize the response direction (experiment 1) and then used for systematic examination on the mechanisms of dichromatic color perception (experiment 2).

The response direction for this unique-distracter paradigm fit in between the target-distracter pairs and differs from the mean direction by 7.5° clockwise. The results also show that decreasing the color difference between target and distracter amplifies the reaction time signal. This result agree to Nagy (1990) observation.

Mean search times for dichromats were twice larger (1.92 for deuteranopes and 2.16 for protanopes) compared to normal color observers and for all directions. Protanopes performed poorly on the yellow-green direction comparatively to the opposite blue-red direction. If the pop-out occurred in the initial 500 ms interval only the normal color observers could detected it on the yellow-green and blue-red directions. Finally, the results show that for both dichromats the difference between the conpuctual confusion lines and the confusion direction measure experimentally was 7.5° for deuteranopes and 5.5° for protanopes.

Acknowledgments. This work was supported by the Departamento de Física of University of Beira interior, by the Centro de Física of Minho University, by FEDER through the COMPETE Program and by the Portuguese Foundation for Science and Technology (FCT) in the framework of the project PTDC/MHC-PCN/4731/2012.

References

1. Christ, R.E.: Review and analysis of color coding research for visual displays. Human Factors **17**, 542–570 (1975)
2. Macdonald, C.A., Cole, B.L.: Evaluating the role of color in flight information cockpit display. Ergonomics **31**(1), 13–37 (1988)
3. Birch, J.: Worldwide prevalence of red-green color deficiency. Journal of the Optical Society of America A **29**(3), 313–320 (2012)
4. Cole, B.L., Maddocks, J.D., Sharpe, K.: Visual search and the conspicuity of colored targets for color vision normal and color vision deficient observers. Clinical and Experimental Optometry **87**(4–5), 294–304 (2004)
5. Nagy, A.L., Sanchez, R.R.: Critical color differences determined with a visual search task. Journal of the Optical Society of America A **7**(7), 1209–1217 (1990)
6. D'Zamura, M.: Color in visual search. Vision Research **31**(6), 951–966 (1991)

First Stage of a Human Visual System Simulator: The Retina

Pablo Martínez-Cañada[1]([✉]), Christian Morillas[1], Juan Luis Nieves[2],
Begoña Pino[1], and Francisco Pelayo[1]

[1] Department of Computer Architecture and Technology,
CITIC, University of Granada, Granada, Spain
{pablomc,cmg,bpino,fpelayo}@ugr.es
[2] Color Imaging Lab, Department of Optics, University of Granada, Granada, Spain
jnieves@ugr.es

Abstract. We propose a configurable simulation platform that reproduces the analog neural behavior of different models of the Human Visual System at the early stages. Our software can simulate efficiently many of the biological mechanisms found in retina cells, such as chromatic opponency in the red-green and blue-yellow pathways, signal gathering through chemical synapses and gap junctions or variations in the neuron density and the receptive field size with eccentricity. Based on an image-processing approach, simulated neurons can perform spatiotemporal and color processing of the input visual stimuli generating the visual maps of every intermediate stage, which correspond to membrane potentials and synaptic currents. An interface with neural network simulators has been implemented, which allows to reproduce the spiking output of some specific cells, such as ganglion cells, and integrate the platform with models of higher brain areas. Simulations of different retina models related to the color opponent mechanisms, obtained from electro-physiological experiments, show the capability of the platform to reproduce their neural response.

Keywords: Retina simulator · Human visual system · Color opponency · Neural network · Spikes

1 Introduction

The first stages of the Human Visual System (HVS), from the retina up to the primary visual cortex, have been extensively studied and there exist numerous models that characterize their anatomy and most of their biophysical functions. Considering the retina, for example, it is possible to find models able to reproduce a specific physiological experiment in great detail [3,6,33,36] and models that aim to mimic the retina processing as a whole [4,11,17,20,21,27,28,39]. Computations performed by these models reproduce those retina behaviors that they have been intentionally designed for, but lack the configurability to modify their simulation circuitry and adapt to new experiments.

© Springer International Publishing Switzerland 2015
A. Trémeau et al. (Eds.): CCIW 2015, LNCS 9016, pp. 118–127, 2015.
DOI: 10.1007/978-3-319-15979-9_12

Among all retina simulators that include all retina stages, Virtual Retina [39] is probably the most complete and detailed one, which is able to reproduce the biological complexity while maintaining the efficient filtering scheme of functional models. One of the contributions of Virtual Retina is the shunting feedback mechanism via amacrine cells towards bipolar cells, also called fast adaptation layer, which allows to reproduce the contrast gain control performed by the retina. At small contrasts, the system has a quasi-linear transformation function but at higher contrasts the retina starts responding sub-linearly and the gain in the bipolar transformation curve is lowered, saturating the output.

We find fewer references of retina simulators that include color processing. Color components are often disregarded in most of retina models, e.g. Virtual Retina, and when they are considered the model simply matches RGB image components with the three types of cones. However, there are remarkable exceptions such as the multi-stage color model by De Valois[11] that includes a quite detailed study of color mechanisms present in the retina, including for instance luminance and color separation of the input visual stimuli by adding the opponent responses of midget bipolar cells. This model also considers random peripheral connectivity for midget bipolar cells, proposing that both type of cones, L and M, connect to the surround of the receptive field and this fact could be enough to generate a cone-opponent signal. Other authors have also implemented the chromatic opponency, red-green and blue-yellow, based on random peripheral connectivity and similar density schema of cones in the fovea [26,29,40] but considering more than one type of cone in the center of the receptive field.

Neural network simulators, on the other hand, describe the low-level biophysics of large and heterogeneous networks of neurons. The user can create neurons individually, or in layers, and then establish connections among them. These simulators have been widely used to simulate, for example, models of the visual cortex. Some of the best known neural network simulators are Neuron[22], STEPS[37], NEST[18], PyNN[9] and Topographica[5]. However, these simulators are computationally time consuming and in most of cases the user needs a background knowledge in Neuroscience.

The platform we propose is halfway between these two approaches and combines the efficient filtering scheme of retina simulators based on image-processing techniques and some biological concepts and implementations considered in neural network simulators. In agreement with other authors [19], we consider that there are sufficient examples of single cell types that serve quite different roles in retina processing to motivate the generalization of basic retinal circuits. Moreover, many retina models are composed of similar processing modules that only change their connection scheme. The platform we describe in this paper is a general-purpose simulation environment that adapts to different retina models and provides a set of elementary simulation modules. The software can be easily used as an efficient benchmark to simulate and understand the visual processing at low-level.

The rest of the paper is organized as follows. In section 2 we describe the biophysical functions of retina cells that have been implemented in the platform.

A general overview of the software is included in section 3. Section 4 explains some of the simulations conducted to evaluate the platform and in section 5 we discuss the conclusions and future work.

2   Anatomy and Physiology of the Retina

In the retina, neurons are arranged in layers that contain cells of the same type. In the brain, most neurons fire action potentials, or spikes, which are electrical impulses well suited to relay the neural signal over long distances. By contrast, most retinal cells form organized maps, with only local interactions between neighboring cells that modify their membrane potential. Neighboring cells are then linked together through two types of synapses: gap junctions (also called electrical synapses) and chemical synapses.

In the simulator, non-linear temporal models can be defined based on single-compartment equations. The basic equation that explains the temporal evolution of a single-compartment model is [10]:

$$C_m \frac{dV(t)}{dt} = \sum_i I_i(t) + \sum_j g_j(E_j(t) - V(t))$$

where the index i indicates the input ionic channel, C_m is the membrane capacitance, V the membrane potential, g_j is the conductance of the channel, E_j the reversal potential of the channel and the term $\sum_i I_i$ denotes external input currents to the neuron. Both the input currents to the neuron and its ionic conductances can be modified by other neurons to model different temporal neural responses.

For some type of cells, the membrane potential integration from controlled physiological experiments can be approximated by linear models. A linear approximation of this neural response of a cell, $L(t)$, can be defined based on the linear kernel $K(x, y, \tau)$ [10,38]:

$$L(t) = \int_0^\infty d\tau \int_{(x,y)\epsilon RF} K(x, y, \tau)s(x_0 - x, y_0 - y, t - \tau)dxdy$$

where $s(x, y, t)$ is the visual stimulus and RF the receptive field of the cell. The neural response of the cell depends linearly on all past values of the input stimulus located in the cells receptive field RF. This integral corresponds to the well-defined convolution operation:

$$L(t) = (s * K)(x_0, y_0, \tau)$$

For some neurons $K(x, y, \tau)$ can be broken down as a product of two functions, one that accounts for the spatial receptive field and the other one for the temporal receptive field:

$$K(x, y, \tau) = K_s(x, y)K_t(\tau)$$

The linear temporal receptive field can be simulated by exponential and gamma filters that model effects such as the membrane signal integration and synaptic transmission. For the spatial receptive field we have considered a set of spatial filters that are based on Gaussian functions, similarly to the kernels used in the receptive field model proposed by Rodieck [30] and Enroth-Cugell and Robson [15]. These filters model spatial integration from chemical synapses in the receptive field and also gap junctions. The three kernels included in the simulation platform are: Gaussian, approximation of a Gaussian and sum of two Gaussians. These three kernels have been implemented based on the recursive approach by Deriche [12–14, 32, 34].

The software also models the retina morphological and physiological variations associated with eccentricity. It is possible to simulate the spread of neuron dendrites with eccentricity and its consequent increase of the receptive field size. We can also configure the spatial distribution of cells according to predefined density functions and probabilistic connections among neurons. Experiments that simulate inter-cell variability and loss of spatial resolution across the human visual field can be reproduced using the topological functions provided by the simulation platform.

Regarding the transformation of the input visual stimuli to the cone responses we use the Hunt-Pointer-Estevez (HPE) matrix [16] to get the different L-, M-, and S-cone values.

3   Overview of the Platform

The basic structure implemented in the platform is a neural layer of cells of the same type, such as horizontal or bipolar cells present in the retina. Spatiotemporal equations of neural layers are updated using an image-based processing approach that benefits from the fact that cells in the retina are arranged in planar maps. A time-driven simulation core is responsible for modifying the membrane potential and synaptic currents associated to each neuron in every discrete time step. When interfacing the platform with models of higher brain areas the neural network simulator integrates our software efficiently and the retina module can be easily loaded in the neural network script. A scheme of the platform connected to a neural network simulator can be seen in figure 1.

The software, which is implemented in C++, has been optimized to run on CPU-based architectures. Space-variant filters are based on the Deriche's recursive approach [12–14, 32, 34]. The main advantage of these filters is that the number of operations per pixel is constant and does not depend on the size of the kernel. Moreover, kernel coefficients can be modified at every pixel to simulate a foveated retina [32]. The performance of the spatial filtering has been significantly improved in a multi-core processor that takes advantage of the fact that every row and every column of the image are processed independently according to the Deriche's recursive algorithm and can be executed in different threads.

Temporal equations are also updated recursively. Linear filter implementation, i.e. exponential and gamma functions, has been adapted from the IIR

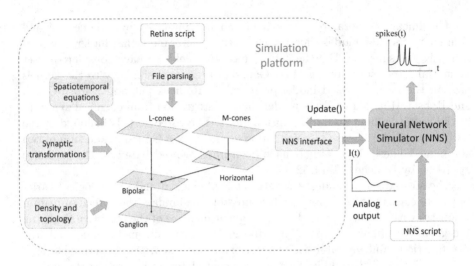

Fig. 1. Scheme of the simulation platform connected to a neural network simulator. The analog outputs of the platform correspond to the ganglion synaptic currents, which are processed by the neural network simulator to produce the spiking output. The neural network simulator drives the simulation time and synchronizes the update process of spatiotemporal equations in the retina model. In the figure we show simultaneously two possible retina configurations where the only difference is the red arrow that links L-cones and horizontal cells. For example, when this link is considered the surround of the receptive field, via horizontal cells, is fed by both M- and L-cones. Other different retina architectures can be easily configured by creating new neural layers and modifying the connection scheme among them.

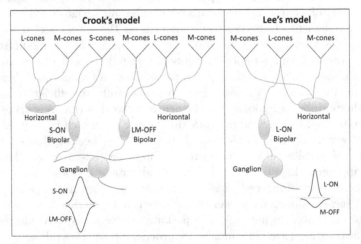

Fig. 2. Outline of two of the retinal circuits simulated by the platform. These retina models have been proposed by Crook et al. [7] and Lee et al. [25] to explain the physiological behavior observed in the blue-yellow and red-green pathways, respectively. The structure of the ganglion receptive field is depicted at the bottom of each circuit.

(Infinite Impulse Response) implementation of Virtual Retina [39] and single-compartment equations are integrated by the so-called Euler method [10]. Provided that the temporal step is sufficiently small, repeated application of these updating methods provides an accurate way of determining the membrane potential.

The platform has been tested under a Linux operating system and connected to the NEST simulator. The processed output of our software can be also adapted to feed other computer vision applications that require a retina input. The source code of this simulator will be open source, following the roadmap of the Human Brain Project [1], and available for download from [2].

4   Evaluation

A set of electrophysiological experiments that reproduce the red-green and blue-yellow opponent pathways in the retina have been simulated to evaluate the capability of the platform to adapt to different retina models. We compare our software with other retina simulators in terms of configurability and scalability. To the best of our knowledge, this is the first simulator that can reproduce retinal circuits as different as those shown in figure 2.

We have simulated two different retina models of the red-green pathway, proposed by Lee et al. [25] and Crook et al. [8] respectively, and one model of the blue-yellow pathway, whose retina circuitry was proposed by Crook et al. [7]. Simulated models are tuned by exhaustive search of parameters that best fit the available published data. There are two different theories explaining the physiological recordings obtained in the red-green pathway: the cone-type selective surround [23–25,31] and the random-wiring or mixed surround [8,35]. While supporters of the cone-type selective surround argue that there is a single cone that feeds the periphery of the receptive field, some research groups proposed that both type of cones, L and M, connect to the surround and this fact could be enough to generate a cone-opponent signal.

With the mixed surround model, a bandpass tuning curve is obtained for a cone-isolating grating targeting the center cone class (see blue graph in figure 2). With the cone-selective surround circuit, the platform reproduces the low-pass shape of the contrast sensitivity function for a cone-isolating grating targeting the center cone class alone (red graph in figure 3). In this figure, the response of the Lee's model for the M-cone isolating grating is also plotted in green to compare the different high-frequency cutoffs of the center, connected to a L-cone, and the periphery, connected to a M-cone, of an L-ON receptive field. Considering there is a 180 deg out of phase between the center and the periphery, which is not represented in this figure, the resulting spatial filtering profile of this cell resembles the typical DoG model.

Some examples of intermediate images produced by the platform and the spiking output generated by the neural network simulator are shown in figures 4 and 5, respectively. A retina density scheme has been configured in the simulation of figure 4 so that the receptive field size of cells is increased with eccentricity.

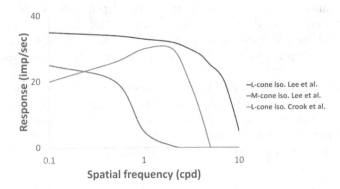

Fig. 3. Contrast sensitivity functions computed from simulation of the retina models proposed for the red-green pathway by Lee et al. [25] and Crook et al. [8]. With the mixed surround model, a bandpass tuning curve is obtained for a cone-isolating grating targeting the center cone class (blue graph). With the cone-selective surround circuit, the platform reproduces the low-pass shape of the contrast sensitivity function for a cone-isolating grating targeting the center cone class alone (red graph). The absolute response of the Lee's model for the M-cone isolating grating is also plotted in green to compare the different high-frequency cutoffs of the center, connected to a L-cone, and the periphery, connected to a M-cone, of an L-ON receptive field.

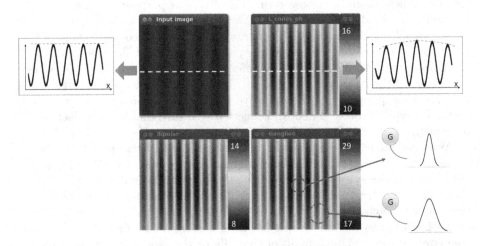

Fig. 4. Example of intermediate outputs generated by the software for a L-cone isolating grating of 5 cpd. The simulated model corresponds to the Lee's retina architecture. It is shown: the input image, membrane potential of L-cones and bipolar cells and input synaptic current of ganglion cells. A retina density scheme has been configured in the simulation so that the receptive field size of cells is increased with eccentricity. This phenomenon produces a decrease of sensitivity in the peripheral area of the simulated retina compared to the center. The horizontal intensity profile of the input image is compared with the profile of the L-cones to further explain this phenomenon.

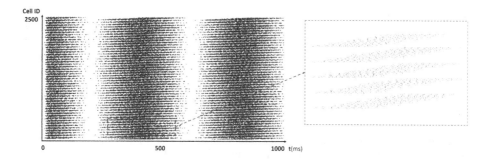

Fig. 5. Raster plot of the spiking outputs generated by NEST [18] for a population of 2500 ganglion cells. The simulation time considered is 1000 ms and the spatial frequency of the input pattern is 0.5 cpd. Every blue spot corresponds to the time a neuron fire a spike. Cell IDs are numbered by rows so that the first 25 cell IDs correspond to cells situated in the top first 25-pixel row. A zoomed area of the raster plot is shown on the right to better visualize the spiking pattern resulting from the input grating.

This phenomenon produces a decrease of sensitivity in the peripheral area of the simulated retina compared to the center.

5   Conclusions and Future Work

A general-purpose simulation environment of the first stages in the visual system is presented. The main contribution is that it can reproduce efficiently the analog neural response of different retina models by modifying not only the model parameters but also its architecture and interconnections of neural layers. The software can be easily used as an efficient benchmark to simulate and understand the visual processing at low-level. Our software can simulate many of the biological mechanisms found in retina cells, such as signal gathering through chemical synapses and gap junctions or variations in the neuron density and the receptive field size with eccentricity. Based on an image-processing approach, simulated neurons perform spatiotemporal and color processing of the input visual stimuli generating the visual maps of every intermediate stage, which correspond to membrane potentials and synaptic currents. An interface with neural network simulators has been implemented, which allows to reproduce the spiking output of some specific cells, such as ganglion cells, and integrate the platform with models of higher brain areas.

The platform has been evaluated based on simulations of different retina models that reproduce the red-green and blue-yellow opponency obtained in electrophysiological experiments. The neural behavior of three retina architectures has been reproduced, the cone-type selective surround and the mixed surround of the red-green pathway and the coextensive receptive field in the blue-yellow pathway, approximating the experimental curves. Simulations of other retina models, concerning contrast and mean luminance adaptation mechanisms in the retina, are being configured to complement the evaluation of the platform.

Acknowledgments. This work has been supported by Erasmus Mundus Master CIMET (Color in Informatics and Media Technology), Human Brain Project (SP11 - Future Neuroscience), Project TIN2012-32039 funded by the Spanish Government and the European Regional Development Fund (ERDF), and the Spanish Government PhD scholarship FPU13/01487.

References

1. Human Brain Project. https://www.humanbrainproject.eu/ (Visited 2014)
2. Source code. http://www.ugr.es/~pablomc/ (Visited 2014)
3. Amthor, F.R., Grzywacz, N.M.: Nonlinearity of the inhibition underlying retinal directional selectivity. Visual neuroscience **6**(03), 197–206 (1991)
4. Andreou, A.G., Boahen, K.A.: A contrast sensitive silicon retina with reciprocal synapses. Advances in Neural Information Processing Systems (NIPS) **4**, 764–772 (1991)
5. Bednar, J.A., Choe, Y., De Paula, J., Miikkulainen, R., Provost, J., Tversky, T.: Modeling cortical maps with topographica. Neurocomputing **58**, 1129–1135 (2004)
6. Berry, M.J., Brivanlou, I.H., Jordan, T.A., Meister, M.: Anticipation of moving stimuli by the retina. Nature **398**(6725), 334–338 (1999)
7. Crook, J.D., Davenport, C.M., Peterson, B.B., Packer, O.S., Detwiler, P.B., Dacey, D.M.: Parallel on and off cone bipolar inputs establish spatially coextensive receptive field structure of blue-yellow ganglion cells in primate retina. The Journal of Neuroscience **29**(26), 8372–8387 (2009)
8. Crook, J.D., Manookin, M.B., Packer, O.S., Dacey, D.M.: Horizontal cell feedback without cone type-selective inhibition mediates red-green color opponency in midget ganglion cells of the primate retina. The Journal of Neuroscience **31**(5), 1762–1772 (2011)
9. Davison, A.P., Brüderle, D., Eppler, J., Kremkow, J., Muller, E., Pecevski, D., Perrinet, L., Yger, P.: Pynn: a common interface for neuronal network simulators. Frontiers in neuroinformatics **2** (2008)
10. Dayan, P., Abbott, L.F.: Theoretical neuroscience: computational and mathematical modeling of neural systems. Journal of Cognitive Neuroscience **15**(1), 154–155 (2003)
11. De Valois, R.L., De Valois, K.K.: A multi-stage color model. Vision research **33**(8), 1053–1065 (1993)
12. Deriche, R.: Using canny's criteria to derive a recursively implemented optimal edge detector. International journal of computer vision **1**(2), 167–187 (1987)
13. Deriche, R.: Fast algorithms for low-level vision. IEEE Transactions on Pattern Analysis and Machine Intelligence **12**(1), 78–87 (1990)
14. Deriche, R.: Recursively implementating the gaussian and its derivatives (1993)
15. Enroth-Cugell, C., Robson, J.G.: The contrast sensitivity of retinal ganglion cells of the cat. The Journal of physiology **187**(3), 517–552 (1966)
16. Estévez, O.: On the fundamental data-base of normal and dichromatic colour vision. PhD thesis, University of Amsterdam (1979)
17. Contreras, E.G.: Algorithms for colour image processing based on neurological models. PhD thesis, Universidad del País Vasco (2012)
18. Gewaltig, M.-O., Diesmann, M.: Nest (neural simulation tool). Scholarpedia **2**(4), 1430 (2007)
19. Gollisch, T., Meister, M.: Eye smarter than scientists believed: neural computations in circuits of the retina. Neuron **65**(2), 150–164 (2010)

20. Hérault, J.: A model of colour processing in the retina of vertebrates: From photore-ceptors to colour opposition and colour constancy phenomena. Neurocomputing **12**(2), 113–129 (1996)
21. Hérault, J., Durette, B.: Modeling visual perception for image processing. In: Computational and Ambient Intelligence, pp. 662–675. Springer (2007)
22. Hines, M.L., Carnevale, N.T.: The neuron simulation environment. Neural computation **9**(6), 1179–1209 (1997)
23. Lee, B.B., Dacey, D.M., Smith, V.C., Pokorny, J.: Horizontal cells reveal cone type-specific adaptation in primate retina. Proceedings of the National Academy of Sciences **96**(25), 14611–14616 (1999)
24. Lee, B.B., Kremers, J., Yeh, T.: Receptive fields of primate retinal ganglion cells studied with a novel technique. Visual neuroscience **15**(01), 161–175 (1998)
25. Lee, B.B., Shapley, R.M., Hawken, M.J., Sun, H.: Spatial distributions of cone inputs to cells of the parvocellular pathway investigated with cone-isolating gratings. JOSA **29**(2), A223–A232 (2012)
26. Lennie, P., Haake, P.W., Williams, D.R.: The design of chromatically opponent receptive fields. Computational models of visual processing, pp. 71–82 (1991)
27. Mead, C.: Neuromorphic electronic systems. Proceedings of the IEEE **78**(10), 1629–1636 (1990)
28. Morillas, C.A., Romero, S.F., Martínez, A., Pelayo, F.J., Ros, E., Fernández, E.: A design framework to model retinas. Biosystems **87**(2), 156–163 (2007)
29. Paulus, W., KrÖger-Paulus, A.: A new concept of retinal colour coding. Vision research **23**(5), 529–540 (1983)
30. Rodieck, R.W.: Quantitative analysis of cat retinal ganglion cell response to visual stimuli. Vision research **5**(12), 583–601 (1965)
31. Solomon, S.G., Lee, B.B., White, A.J.R., Rüttiger, L.: Martin, P.R: Chromatic organization of ganglion cell receptive fields in the peripheral retina. The. Journal of neuroscience **25**(18), 4527–4539 (2005)
32. Tan, S., Dale, J.L., Johnston, A.: Performance of three recursive algorithms for fast space-variant gaussian filtering. Real-Time Imaging **9**(3), 215–228 (2003)
33. Torre, V., Poggio, T.: A synaptic mechanism possibly underlying directional selectivity to motion. Proceedings of the Royal Society of London. Series B. Biological Sciences **202**(1148), 409–416 (1978)
34. Triggs, B., Sdika, M.: Boundary conditions for young-van vliet recursive filtering. IEEE Transactions on Signal Processing **54**(6), 2365–2367 (2006)
35. Verweij, J., Hornstein, E.P., Schnapf, J.L.: Surround antagonism in macaque cone photoreceptors. The Journal of neuroscience **23**(32), 10249–10257 (2003)
36. Wilke, S.D., Thiel, A., Eurich, C.W., Greschner, M., Bongard, M., AmmermuEller, J., Schwegler, H.: Population coding of motion patterns in the early visual system. Journal of Comparative Physiology **187**(7), 549–558 (2001)
37. Wils, S., De Schutter, E.: Steps: modeling and simulating complex reaction-diffusion systems with python. Frontiers in neuroinformatics **3** (2009)
38. Wohrer, A.: Model and large-scale simulator of a biological retina, with contrast gain control. PhD thesis, Nice (2008)
39. Wohrer, A., Kornprobst, P.: Virtual retina: a biological retina model and simulator, with contrast gain control. Journal of computational neuroscience **26**(2), 219–249 (2009)
40. Young, R.A., Marrocco, R.T.: Predictions about chromatic receptive fields assuming random cone connections. Journal of theoretical biology **141**(1), 23–40 (1989)

Color Image Processing

The Color Logarithmic Image Processing (CoLIP) Antagonist Space and Chromaticity Diagram

Yann Gavet[1,2]($\boxtimes$), Johan Debayle[1,2], and Jean-Charles Pinoli[1,2]

[1] École des Mines, Saint-Étienne, France
[2] LGF, UMR CNRS 5307, Lyon, France
yann.gavet@mines-stetienne.fr

Abstract. The CoLIP framework defines a vectorial space for color images. It is in accordance with the theories of visual perception (Weber, Fechner) as well as Hering's trichromacy theory. It is mathematically well defined and computationally usable. This article recalls the fundamentals of the LIP framework for graytone images, and introduces the elementary operations of the vectorial structure for color images. It illutrates the representation of the chromaticity diagram with color modification application, namely white balance correction and color transfer. The results show that the hull of the diagram are not modified, but the colors are.

Keywords: Color logarithmic image processing · Chromaticity diagram · Image processing

1 Introduction

Regarding the fact that the current color spaces (e.g., RGB, CIE XYZ, CIE $L^*a^*b^*$, CIECAM02) do not follow an additive law, and therefore fail to obey the linear concept that is of a very high theoretical and practical interest in mathematics and their applications, the Color Logarithmic Image Processing (CoLIP) framework was developped, in accordance with the main laws and characteristics of the human color visual perception.

The trichromacy theory [13] states that humans have three different receptors sensitive to color stimuli. Indeed, the color photoreceptors in the retina, namely the cones, are sensitive to 3 different wavelength ranges: long, medium and short wavelengths, and thus classified into 3 types of cones: L, M and S, respectively.

The CoLIP theory is based on the Logarithmic Image Processing (LIP) theory that was developed for the representation and processing of images valued in a bounded intensity range [6]. As for the LIP theory [8], the CoLIP theory is physically and psychophysically well justified since it is consistent with the multiplicative image formation model and is consistent with several laws and characteristics of human brightness perception (e.g., Weber's law, Fechner's law, saturation effect, brightness range inversion). The Weber's law [12], and its generalization with Fechner's law [2], are translated into a logarithmic relationship

© Springer International Publishing Switzerland 2015
A. Trémeau et al. (Eds.): CCIW 2015, LNCS 9016, pp. 131–138, 2015.
DOI: 10.1007/978-3-319-15979-9_13

between the perceived brightness versus the stimulus. For each channel LMS, a Weber's fraction does exist, yielding a LMS Fechner's law, respectively [9].

Another important theory is called opponent-process theory. Hering [5], and later Svaetichin [10] noticed that particular colors like reddish-green or yellowish-blue would never be observed. Schematically, the color informations are coded in opponent red-green (denoted rg) and yellow-blue (denoted yb) channels to improve the efficiency of the transmission (reducing the noise) and to decorrelate the LMS channels [1].

2   LIP Theory

The LIP theory (Logarithmic Image processing) has been introduced in the middle of the 1980s [8]. It defines an algebraic framework that allows operations on images in a bounded range [6]. This model is mathematically well defined as well as physically consistent with the transmitted light imaging process.

2.1   Gray Tone Functions

In the LIP theory, a graytone function f is associated to an intensity image F. f is defined on a spatial support $D \subset \mathbb{R}^2$ and has its values in the real-number range $[0; M_0[$, with M_0 being a strictly positive real number. In the context of transmitted light imaging, the value 0 corresponds to the total transparency and M_0 to the total opacity. Thus, the gray tone function f is defined, for F_{max} being the saturating light intensity level (glare limit), by:

$$f = M_0 \left(1 - \frac{F}{F_{max}}\right). \tag{1}$$

2.2   The Vectorial Structure

The vectorial space S of gray tone functions is algebraically and topologically isomorphic to the classical vector space of real-valued functions, defined through the following isomorphism φ and the inverse isomorphism φ^{-1}:

$$\varphi(f) = -M_0 \ln\left(1 - \frac{f}{M_0}\right), f = \varphi^{-1}(\varphi(f)) = M_0\left(1 - \exp\left(-\frac{\varphi(f)}{M_0}\right)\right) \tag{2}$$

This isomorphism φ allows the introduction of notions and structures outcoming from Functional Analysis, like the Euclidean norm:

$$\forall f \in S, \ \| f \|_\Delta = |\varphi(f)|_\mathbb{R},$$

with $|\cdot|_\mathbb{R}$ being the usual absolute value.

Then, the following operations of addition, scalar multiplication, opposite and subtraction are defined:

$$\forall f, g \in S, \ f \mathbin{\triangle\!\!\!\triangle} g = f + g - \frac{fg}{M_0}, \tag{3}$$

$$\forall f \in S, \forall \lambda \in \mathbb{R}, \ \lambda \mathbin{\triangle\!\!\!\triangle} f = M_0 - M_0 \left(1 - \frac{f}{M_0}\right)^{\lambda}, \tag{4}$$

$$\forall f \in S, \ \mathbin{\triangle\!\!\!\triangle} f = \frac{-M_0 f}{M_0 - f}, \tag{5}$$

$$\forall f, g \in S, \ f \mathbin{\triangle\!\!\!\triangle} g = M_0 \frac{f - g}{M_0 - g}. \tag{6}$$

The definition of the opposite operation $\mathbin{\triangle\!\!\!\triangle} f$ extends the gray tone range to the unbounded real-number range $]-\infty; M_0[$.

3   CoLIP Theory

The previous section has introduced the LIP theory for graytone images. This section presents the color space CoLIP, previously defined in [3,4]. It models the different stages of the human color vision, and also defines a vector space for color images.

The starting point for all CoLIP operations is the LMS color space [1]. The numerical applications (conversions from the different color spaces) are performed using the OptProp toolbox[1].

3.1   From Cone Intensities to Achromatic and Chromatic Tones

In the CoLIP framework, the chromatic tones are defined from the cone intensities L, M and S, as:

$$\forall c \in \{l, m, s\}, C \in \{L, M, S\}, c = M_0 \left(1 - \frac{C}{C_0}\right), \tag{7}$$

with C_0 is the maximal transmitted intensity level. M_0 is arbitrarily chosen at normalized value 100. Notice that $C \in]0; C_0]$ and $c \in [0; M_0[$.

The logarithmic response of the cones, as in the LIP theory, is modeled through the isomorphism φ.

$$\text{For } c \in \{l, m, s\}, \ \tilde{c} = \varphi(c) = -M_0 \ln \left(1 - \frac{c}{M_0}\right) \tag{8}$$

$(\tilde{l}, \tilde{m}, \tilde{s})$ are called the logarithmic chromatic tones.

To follow the opponent-process theory of Hering, the three logarithmic color channels $(\tilde{l}, \tilde{m}, \tilde{s})$ are represented by a logarithmic achromatic tone $\tilde{a}$, and two

---

[1] By Jerker Wågberg, *More Research* and *DPC*, www.more.se

logarithmic chromatic tones, $\tilde{rg}$ and $\tilde{yb}$, where $\tilde{rg}$ opposes red and green, and $\tilde{yb}$ opposes yellow and blue. The conversion is obtained by the Eq. 9. The antagonist transformation matrix P is defined as follows according to the CIECAM02 specifications [1]. The achromatic channel is computed considering a ratio 40:20:1 in red, green and blue sensibility of the eye [11].

$$
\begin{pmatrix} \tilde{a} \\ \tilde{rg} \\ \tilde{yb} \end{pmatrix} = P \times \begin{pmatrix} \tilde{l} \\ \tilde{m} \\ \tilde{s} \end{pmatrix}, \text{ with } P = \begin{pmatrix} 40/61 & 20/61 & 1/61 \\ 1 & -12/11 & 1/11 \\ 1/9 & 1/9 & -2/9 \end{pmatrix}. \tag{9}
$$

3.2   The Trichromatic Antagonist Vectorial Structure

A color tone function, denoted f, is defined on a compact set D, with values in $]-\infty; M_0[^3$, by:

$$
x \in D, \ F(x) = \begin{pmatrix} L(x) \\ M(x) \\ S(x) \end{pmatrix} \mapsto f(x) = \begin{pmatrix} a_f(x) \\ rg_f(x) \\ yb_f(x) \end{pmatrix}. \tag{10}
$$

Thus, the operations of addition, scalar multiplication and subtraction can be defined in Eq. 11, and 12.

$$
f \triangle g = \begin{pmatrix} a_f \triangle a_g \\ rg_f \triangle rg_g \\ yb_f \triangle yb_g \end{pmatrix}, \ \lambda \triangle f = \begin{pmatrix} \lambda \triangle a_f \\ \lambda \triangle rg_f \\ \lambda \triangle yb_f \end{pmatrix}, \tag{11}
$$

$$
\triangle g = \begin{pmatrix} \triangle a_g \\ \triangle rg_g \\ \triangle yb_g \end{pmatrix}, \ f \triangle g = \begin{pmatrix} a_f \triangle a_g \\ rg_f \triangle rg_g \\ yb_f \triangle yb_g \end{pmatrix}. \tag{12}
$$

The set I of color tone functions defined on D and valued in $]-\infty; M_0[^3$, with the operations of multiplication $\triangle$ and internal addition $\triangle$ is a real vector space. With the logarithmic color tone functions, $\tilde{f} = \varphi(f)$, the classical operations are used $(+, \times, -)$.

3.3   Bounded Vector Space

The vector space I defines a framework for manipulating color tone functions with values in $]-\infty; M_0[^3$. The opponent channels rg and yb are thus not symmetric, which can cause problems for computational manipulation and storage, or for representation. To handle this, it is proposed to introduce the three channels $\hat{f} = (\hat{a}, \hat{rg}, \hat{yb})$ defined by:

$$
\hat{a} = a \tag{13}
$$

$$
\hat{rg} = \begin{cases} rg & \text{if } rg \geq 0 \\ -\triangle rg & \text{if } rg < 0 \end{cases} \tag{14}
$$

$$
\hat{yb} = \begin{cases} yb & \text{if } yb \geq 0 \\ -\triangle yb & \text{if } yb < 0 \end{cases} \tag{15}
$$

This representation is illustrated in the next sections.

3.4 Summary

The different conversion operations are presented in the following diagram:

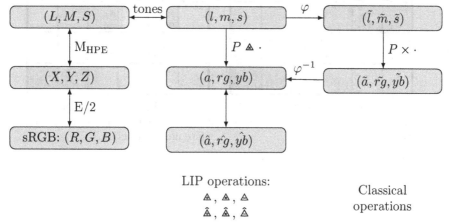

Now that the formal definitions are introduced, the next section will show the connections with the psychophysical theories.

4 Applications

The chromaticity diagram is the representation of colors in a given space, for example (x, y), and in the case of the CoLIP space, $(\hat{rg}, \hat{yb})$. The purple line is a virtual straight line that links extreme values of the spectrum in (x, y). The Maxwell triangle is the representation of all RGB colors in this space (it has a shape of a triangle in (x, y)). The following applications will focus on the effect on the chromaticity diagram.

4.1 White Balance Correction

The proposed white balance correction method derives from the Von Kries adaptation model [1,7]. If L, M and S represent the cone responses, and L', M' and S' represent the adapted cone responses, this model can be written as $L' = \frac{L}{L_{\text{White}}}$, $M' = \frac{M}{M_{\text{White}}}$, $S' = \frac{S}{S_{\text{White}}}$.

The Figure 1 presents the effects of the correction in the chromaticity diagram. The new white appears at coordinates $(0,0)$, all colors appear more blue and brighter. This operation is not a translation in the $(\hat{rg}, \hat{yb})$ subspace.

4.2 Color Transfer

Color transfer is another application of white balance correction. Let us consider two images f_1 and f_2. The following notation is introduced, for a given collection

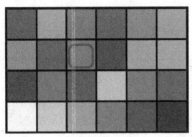 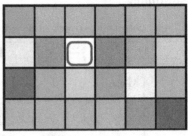

(a) MacBeth colorchecker. The chosen color is delineated with a red
square.

(b) White balance correction for one
color. The red square designates the
white after correction.

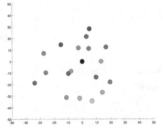 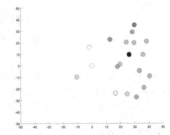

(c) Chromaticity diagram of the
MacBeth colorchecker. All achromatic tones (gray values from white
to black) appear at coordinates
$(0,0)$.

(d) Chromaticity diagram of the
MacBeth colorchecker after white
balance correction.

Fig. 1: White balance correction with a manual selection of the White, with $\hat{rg}$
in absissa and $\hat{yb}$). in ordinates.

of values c: $\mu(c)$ is the mean of c, and $\sigma(c)$ is the standard deviation of c. For a
color image in the CoLIP space,

$$\mu(f) = \begin{pmatrix} \mu(a) \\ \mu(rg) \\ \mu(yb) \end{pmatrix} \text{ and } \sigma(f) = \begin{pmatrix} \sigma(a) \\ \sigma(rg) \\ \sigma(yb) \end{pmatrix} \qquad (16)$$

The transfer of colors of image f_1 into image f_2 corresponds to the Eq. 17,
that gives the resulting image f_{new}. This formula centers and normalizes the
distribution of colors in the original image f_1, and applies the same distribution
as in image f_2 to the new image f_{new}.

$$f_{\text{new}} = \left(\frac{\sigma(f_1)}{\sigma(f_2)} \triangle (f_2 \triangle \mu(f_2)) \right) \triangle \mu(f_1) \qquad (17)$$

The Figure 2 shows the results of the transfer of the colors of two paintings
(from VanGogh and Monet) into the painting of Guillaumin. The hull of the

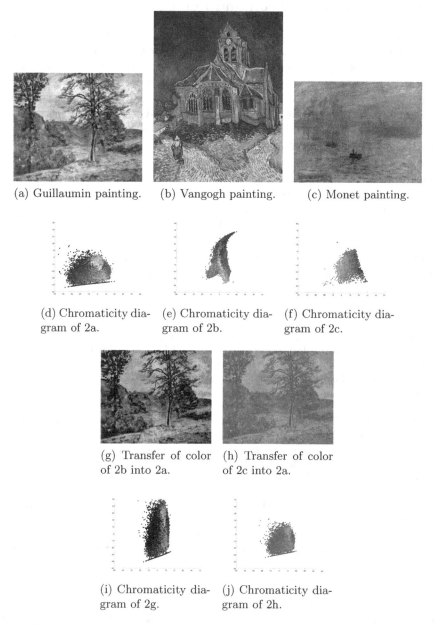

(a) Guillaumin painting.   (b) Vangogh painting.   (c) Monet painting.

(d) Chromaticity dia-   (e) Chromaticity dia-   (f) Chromaticity diagram of 2a.   gram of 2b.   gram of 2c.

(g) Transfer of color   (h) Transfer of color
of 2b into 2a.   of 2c into 2a.

(i) Chromaticity dia-   (j) Chromaticity diagram of 2g.   gram of 2h.

Fig. 2: Color transfer of different paintings and the representation of the colors
in the $(\hat{rg}, \hat{yb})$ space.

color diagrams in $(\hat{rg}, \hat{yb})$ are similar to the original one, but the colors are now
similar to the transfered paintings ones.

5   Concluding Discussion and Perspectives

This article has introduced the CoLIP framework and the representation of the colors of images in the form of a chromaticity diagram in the $(\hat{rg}, \hat{yb})$ space. The effects of basic operations like white balance correction or color transfer are proposed and illustrated, showing that the hull of the diagram is conserved, and the new colors are applied. The CoLIP framework presents two connections with the human visual perception system: it follows the Weber/Fechner law with its logarithmic model, and it also takes into account the opponent-process theory from Hering. Some other color spaces try have psychophysical justifications. For example, the $L^*a^*b^*$ space represents the opponent process with a^* (red-green opposition) and b^* (yellow-blue opposition), and the non linearity follows more or less the Stevens law (power law). In the case of the YC_bC_r color space, the non linearity coming from the gamma correction can be seen as a Stevens law, but the opponent-process theory is not included in this model.

The perspectives in the field of the CoLIP framework are to define color attributes like hue, saturation, and more mathematically, develop a distance between colors and define CoLIP mathematical morphology operators.

References

1. Fairchild, M.D.: Color appearance models. Wiley (2013)
2. Fechner, G.T.: Elemente der Psychophysik. Breitkopf und Härtel, Leipzig (1860)
3. Gouinaud, H., Gavet, Y., Debayle, J., Pinoli, J.C.: Color correction in the framework of color logarithmic image processing. In: Proceedings of the 7th IEEE International Symposium on Image and Signal Processing and Analysis (ISISPA), Dubrovnik, Croatia, pp. 129–133 (2011)
4. Gouinaud, H.: Traitement logarithmique d'images couleur. Ph.D. Thesis, École Nationale Supérieure des Mines de Saint-Etienne (2013)
5. Hering, E.: Outlines of a theory of the light sense. Harvard University Press (1964).(Trans. Hurvich, L.M., Jameson, D.)
6. Jourlin, M., Pinoli, J.C.: Logarithmic image processing. Acta Stereologica **6**, 651–656 (1987)
7. von Kries, J.: Die gesichtsempfindungen. Handbuch der physiologie des menschen **3**, 109–282 (1905)
8. Pinoli, J.C.: The logarithmic image processing model: Connections with human brightness perception and contrast estimators. Journal of Mathematical Imaging and Vision **7**(4), 341–358 (1997)
9. Stockman, A., Mollon, J.: The spectral sensitivities of the middle-and long-wavelength cones: an extension of the two-colour threshold technique of ws stiles. Perception **15**, 729–754 (1986)
10. Svaetichin, G.: Spectral response curves from single cones. Acta Physiol Scand Suppl. **39**(134), 17–46 (1956)
11. Vos, J., Walraven, P.: On the derivation of the foveal receptor primaries. Vision Research **11**(8), 799–818 (1971)
12. Weber, E.: Der Tastsinn und das Gemeingefühl. Handwörterbuch der Physiologie **3**(2), 481–588 (1846)
13. Young, T.: The bakerian lecture: On the theory of light and colours. Philosophical transactions of the Royal Society of London, pp. 12–48 (1802)

Does Color Influence Image Complexity Perception?

Gianluigi Ciocca[1,3], Silvia Corchs[1,3], Francesca Gasparini[1,3(✉)],
Emanuela Bricolo[2,3], and Riccardo Tebano[2]

[1] Dipartimento di Informatica, Sistemistica e Comunicazione,
University of Milano-Bicocca, Viale Sarca 336, 20126 Milano, Italy
{ciocca,corchs,gasparini}@disco.unimib.it
[2] Department of Psychology, University of Milano-Bicocca, Via Dell' Innovazione 10,
20126 Milano, Italy
emanuela.bricolo@unimib.it, r.tebano@campus.unimib.it
[3] NeuroMi - Milan Center for Neuroscience, Milan, Italy

Abstract. In this paper we investigate if color influences the perception of image complexity. To this end we perform two different types of psycho-physical experiments on color and grayscale images. In the first experiment, images are ranked based on their complexity (image ranking), while in the second experiment the complexity of each image is assessed on a continuous scale (image scaling). Moreover, we investigate if ten image features, that measure colors as well as other spatial properties of the images, correlate with the collected subjective data. The performance of these correlations are evaluated in terms of Pearson correlation coefficients and Spearman rank-order correlation coefficients. We observe that for each type of experiment, subjective scores for color images are highly correlated with those of the corresponding grayscale versions suggesting that color is not a relevant attribute in evaluating image complexity. Moreover none of the tested simple image features seem to be adapt to predict the image complexity according to the human judgments.

Keywords: Image complexity · Psycho-physical experiment · Color image features

1 Introduction

There exist in the literature many different definitions of image complexity. For example, it can be analyzed by using mathematical treatments based on Kolmogorov complexity theory [1]. Snodgrass et al. [2] refer to the visual complexity as the amount of detail or intricacy in an image. Birkhoff [3] relates the image complexity to visual aesthetics. Researchers from various fields have conducted psycho-physical experiments to study the subjective perception of visual complexity and some studies exist where experimental estimation of image complexity is correlated to objective measures. The state of the art studies differ in the

© Springer International Publishing Switzerland 2015
A. Trémeau et al. (Eds.): CCIW 2015, LNCS 9016, pp. 139–148, 2015.
DOI: 10.1007/978-3-319-15979-9_14

kind of stimuli used during the experimental sessions and on the type of objective measures used to correlate the subjective scores. Chikhman et al. [4] use Chinese hieroglyphs and outline images of well known common objects as stimuli sets. On the other side, experiments exist that address the image complexity of real world scenes, like the study by Oliva et al. [5]. Recently, Purchase et al. [6] use sixty images, including landscapes, domestic objects and city scenes, as stimuli. Further efforts attempt to describe the image complexity using different mathematical models like fuzzy approaches [7,8], information-theoretic approaches [9] and independent component analysis [10]. Rosenholtz et al. [11] associate the concept of complexity to that of visual clutter. They have tested three measures of visual clutter: Feature Congestion (FC), Subband Entropy (SE) and the edge density measure used to predict subjective judgments of image complexity by Mack and Oliva [12].

Image complexity can be useful in many different domains. It finds application to context-based image retrieval [10], icons and symbol search, particularly relevant in human computer interaction [13,14], and computer graphics, where a better understanding of visual complexity can aid in the development of more advanced rendering algorithms [15]. Other fields of application are image recognition [16], watermarking [17], compression [18], and image quality [19,20]. The image complexity concept is also used by neuroscientists, interested in the mechanisms of object recognition, learning and memory [21].

Aim of this paper is to investigate the role of color when evaluating image complexity. To this end, two types of experimental setups have been performed on a set of 29 color images and on the set of the corresponding grayscale images. These are real-world images, belonging to the image quality database LIVE [22]. Setup 1 is a ranking experiment, where observers rank the 29 images in increasing order of complexity. Setup 2 is a scaling experiment, where observers judge the image complexity on a continuous scale [0-100]. We point out that no definition of *image complexity* is provided to the observers during the experimental sessions. We investigate the effect of color on the perception of image complexity comparing the subjective results obtained with color and grayscale sets of images for both experimental setups. Moreover, we also consider ten image features as complexity measure candidates, and we evaluate their correlation with subjective data. The performance of these correlations are evaluated in terms of the linear Pearson Correlation Coefficient (PCC) and the Spearman Rank Order Correlation Coefficient (SROCC).

2   Color versus Grayscale: Subjective Data

The 29 images belonging to the LIVE database [22] have been used as stimuli for estimating subjective perception of image complexity. They have been chosen to sample different contents both in terms of low level features (frequencies, colors) and higher ones (face, buildings, close-up, outdoor, landscape). Their thumbnail color versions are shown in Figure1, and the corresponding greyscale versions are shown in Figure 2.

Fig. 1. Thumbnails of the color images used as stimuli in the psycho-physical experiments

Fig. 2. Thumbnails of the grayscale images used as stimuli in the psycho-physical experiments

2.1   Experimental Setup 1: Image Ranking

A group of 76 observers with normal or corrected-to-normal visual acuity and normal color vision took part in this psycho-physical experiment. Ishihara color test plates printed on paper have been preliminarily presented to the observers for detecting color vision deficiency. The images in the LIVE database were professionally printed on a high quality paper to create the cards for the psycho-physical experiment. The cards with the color images were given to 37 observers. Cards with the same greyscale images from the LIVE database were given to the remaining 39 observers. Observers could look at all the stimuli simultaneously for an unlimited time. The task of the observer was to arrange the images in order of increasing complexity. No definitions of complexity were imposed to the observers. The final rank of each image was obtained ranking the average of the positions assigned by the observers (from 1 the simplest image to 29 the most complex one).

2.2 Experimental Setup 2: Image Scaling

A group of 31 observers with normal or corrected-to-normal visual acuity and normal color vision took part in the psycho-physical experiment. A single stimulus method was adopted, where all the images are individually shown. No specific task was provided, just assessing the image complexity of each image using a scale in the range [0-100]. 14 observers evaluated the 29 color images, while the remaining 17 observers judged the grayscale counterparts. The images were shown on a web-based interface in a random order, different for each subject. The subjects reported their complexity judgments by dragging a slider onto a continuous scale. The position of the slider is automatically reset after each evaluation. A grayscale chart was shown to calibrate the brightness and the contrast of the monitor. Ishihara color test have been preliminarily presented to the observers for estimating color vision deficiency.

Seven training images were presented to the observers prior to the 29 test ones. These images have been used to train the subjects about the range of complexity to be evaluated. The corresponding data has been discarded and not considered as experimental result.

We have applied Z-score and outliers detection to obtain the final Mean Opinion Scores (MOS) of each image. The raw complexity score r_{ij} for the i-th subject ($i = 1, ...14$ in case of color images or $i = 1, ...17$ in case of grayscale images) and j-th image ($j = 1, ...29$) was converted into Z scores:

$$z_{ij} = \frac{r_{ij} - \bar{r}_i}{\sigma_i} \tag{1}$$

where $\bar{r}_i$ is the average of the complexity scores over all images ranked by the subject, and σ_i is the standard deviation. The Z scores were then averaged across subjects after the removal of the outlier scores. A score for an image was considered to be an outlier, and thus removed from the average computation, if it was outside an interval of width two standard deviations about the average score for that image.

3 Color versus Grayscale: Assessing Image Complexity

The following features have been considered as candidate complexity measures:

- **F1** Contrast, extracted applying the MATLAB function *graycoprops* to the gray-level co-occurence matrix.
- **F2** Homogeneity, Extracted applying the MATLAB function *graycoprops* to the gray-level co-occurence matrix.
- **F3** Edge density [12]: the MATLAB's Canny edge detector is applied to the image to measure the density of edge pixels.
- **F4** Feature Congestion [11]: its implementation involves: (1) computation of local measures (color, orientation, and luminance contrast) covariance at multiple scales and computing the volume of the local covariance ellipsoid, (2) combine clutter across scale and feature types, (3) pooling over space to get a single measure.

- **F5** Subband Entropy [11]: it is based on the notion of clutter as related to the efficiency with which the image can be encoded and inversely related to the amount of redundancy and grouping in the image.
- **F6** Compression Ratio of the image JPEG compressed with Q factor = 100.
- **F7** Number of Regions, calculated using the mean shift algorithm [23].
- **F8** Colorfulness [24]: linear combination of the mean and standard deviation of the pixel cloud in the color plane of CIELab.
- **F9** Number of colors [26]: number of distinct color in the image.
- **F10** Color harmony [25][26]: it is based on the perceived harmony of color combinations.

The first three features, labeled $F1$, $F2$, $F3$ work on grayscale images, features from $F4$ to $F7$ are mainly developed for color images but they are also meaningful for grayscale images while $F8$, $F9$, and $F10$ are meaningful only for color images.

These features are correlated with the subjective data obtained in the psychophysical experiments. In the case of the ranking experiment we are interested in assessing if the features are able to replicate the subjective ranks. In the case of the scaling experiment the aim is to assess the ability of the features to predict the MOS. For the latter case a proper logistic regression is used as follows.

Denoting by y_j the MOS of the $j - th$ image and by x_j the corresponding objective feature value, the logistic transformation reads:

$$f(x_j) = \frac{\alpha}{1 + e^{\beta(x_j - \gamma)}} + \delta \tag{2}$$

where the parameters α, β, γ and δ are chosen to minimize the mean square error between the MOS $\{y_j\}$ and the predicted values $\{f(x_j)\}$.

4   Experimental Results

We initially investigate if color influences the perception of image complexity by analyzing the subjective data collected within each experimental setup. To this end we consider the raw data for both the experimental setups. In case of ranking experiment, we consider as raw data the average of the positions assigned by the observers. In case of scaling experiment, the raw data are the mean of the scores. The raw data collected for the grayscale images are correlated with those collected for the corresponding color images within each type of experiment. In Figure 3 on the left, the raw data of the ranking experiment are considered: the raw data of the 29 grayscale images are plotted with respect to the corresponding data of color images. In Figure 3 on the right, the raw data of the scaling experiment of the 29 grayscale images are plotted with respect to the raw data of the corresponding color versions. To measure the linear correlation between grayscale and color data for each experimental setup we evaluate the PCC, while to quantify their rank-order correlation we use the SROCC. In Table 1 these coefficients are reported for the two experimental setups.

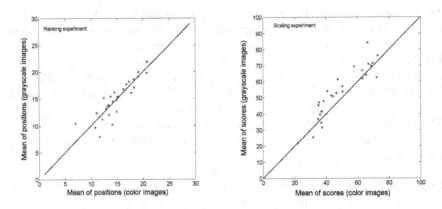

Fig. 3. Correlation between grayscale and color image data. Left: results from ranking experiment. Right: results from scaling experiment.

Table 1. Correlation coefficients between grayscale and color data for each experimental setup

Setup	PCC	SROCC
Ranking	0.877	0.903
Scaling	0.914	0.926

Subjective evaluations of color and grayscale images are highly correlated within each experimental setups. In particular in the case of scaling experiment these results suggest that the perception of image complexity is not significantly influenced by color. To have further insight into this issue, we evaluate the correlation between subjective and objective data. As objective data we adopted the ten features listed in Section 3. The last three features can not be evaluated for grayscale images as they are designed to measure color properties only.

In the case of the ranking experiment we consider the performance of the features in predicting the subjective rank. The results are presented using the SROCC and reported in Table 2 first row for the color images, second row for the grayscale images.

In the case of the scaling experiment we consider the performance of the features in predicting the MOS, using a proper logistic regression. The results are presented in terms of PCC and SROCC and reported in Tables 3 and 4.

In general we can notice that in the case of ranking experiment all the features evaluated on grayscale images better predict the subjective ranks than the corresponding ones on color images. Instead, in the case of scaling experiment all

Table 2. SROCC of the ten features in the ranking experiment

SROCC	F1	F2	F3	F4	F5	F6	F7	F8	F9	F10
Color	0.649	0.600	0.587	0.600	0.497	0.568	0.544	0.076	0.380	0.308
Grayscale	0.763	0.726	0.755	0.759	0.655	0.727	0.675	-	-	-

Table 3. PCC of the 10 features in the scaling experiment

PCC	F1	F2	F3	F4	F5	F6	F7	F8	F9	F10
Color	0.751	0.656	0.740	0.622	0.604	0.683	0.583	0.211	0.321	0.128
Grayscale	0.696	0.736	0.740	0.628	0.762	0.777	0.427	-	-	-

Table 4. SROCC of the 10 features in the scaling experiment

SROCC	F1	F2	F3	F4	F5	F6	F7	F8	F9	F10
Color	0.759	0.721	0.734	0.692	0.624	0.738	0.582	0.030	0.247	0.188
Grayscale	0.721	0.738	0.746	0.669	0.709	0.740	0.500	-	-	-

Fig. 4. Images in the first four rank positions (low complexity) in the ranking experiment for color and grayscale images

Fig. 5. Images in the last four rank positions (high complexity) in the ranking experiment for color and grayscale images

the features perform similarly for both color and grayscale data. This behavior is related to the higher correlation between color and grayscale data in the scaling experiment than in the ranking one (see Figure 3). The three color features $F8$, $F9$, and $F10$ are not appropriate to correlate subjective color data. This analysis suggests that the perception of image complexity is slightly influenced by color especially in the second experimental setup. The four lowest and four highest complexity images for both color and grayscale datasets and for both experimental setups are shown in Figures 4-7.

Fig. 6. Images with the four lowest MOS (low complexity) in the scaling experiment for color and grayscale images

Fig. 7. Images with the four highest MOS (high complexity) in the scaling experiment for color and grayscale images

5   Conclusions

In this work we have shown that there is a significant correlation between psycho-physical data on color and grayscale images when observers are asked to evaluate image complexity. This suggests that color does not influence significantly the perception of image complexity. Moreover, features that are developed only to measure color properties seem not to be suitable to correlate with the psycho-physical data. We recall that we have here considered real world images, where the lightness component provides enough information about the image content. Other kind of experiments, for example using images of color patches could yield different conclusions, as the grayscale images could be less meaningful. As a future work we plan to extend the psycho-physical experiments both in number of observers and in number of images. However psycho-physical experiments with a huge amount of images are a difficult task. In fact images should be divided into different groups to be judged by different groups of observers and the final data should be properly aligned. Furthermore we plan to investigate if a proper combination of metrics that takes into account simultaneously spatial, frequency and color image characteristics can better predict subjective evaluations.

References

1. Kolmogorov, A.N.: Three approaches to the quantitative definition of information. Problems of Information Transmission **1**(1), 1–7 (1965)
2. Snodgrass, J.G., Vanderwart, M.: A standardized set of 260 pictures: norms for name agreement, image agreement, familiarity, and visual complexity. Journal of Experimental Psychology: Human Learning and Memory **6**(2), 174 (1980)
3. Birkhoff, G.D.: Collected mathematical papers (1950)
4. Chikhman, V., Bondarko, V., Danilova, M., Goluzina, A., Shelepin, Y.: Complexity of images: Experimental and computational estimates compared. Perception **41**, 631–647 (2012)
5. Oliva, A., Mack, M.L., Shrestha, M.: Identifying the perceptual dimensions of visual complexity of scenes. In: Proc. 26th Annual Meeting of the Cognitive Science Society (2004)
6. Purchase, H.C., Freeman, E., Hamer, J.: Predicting visual complexity. In: Proceedings of the 3rd International Conference on Appearance, Edinburgh, UK, pp. 62–65 (2012)
7. Mario, I., Chacon, M., Alma, D., Corral, S.: Image complexity measure: a human criterion free approach. In: Annual Meeting of the North American Fuzzy Information Processing Society, NAFIPS 2005, pp 241–246. IEEE (2005)
8. Cardaci, M., Di Gesú, V., Petrou, M., Tabacchi, M.E.: On the evaluation of images complexity: a fuzzy approach. In: Bloch, I., Petrosino, A., Tettamanzi, A.G.B. (eds.) WILF 2005. LNCS (LNAI), vol. 3849, pp. 305–311. Springer, Heidelberg (2006)
9. Rigau, J., Feixas, M., Sbert, M.: An information-theoretic framework for image complexity. In: Proceedings of the First Eurographics Conference on Computational Aesthetics in Graphics, Visualization and Imaging, pp. 177–184. Eurographics Association (2005)
10. Perkiö, J., Hyvärinen, A.: Modelling image complexity by independent component analysis, with application to content-based image retrieval. In: Alippi, C., Polycarpou, M., Panayiotou, C., Ellinas, G. (eds.) ICANN 2009, Part II. LNCS, vol. 5769, pp. 704–714. Springer, Heidelberg (2009)
11. Rosenholtz, R., Li, Y., Nakano, L.: Measuring visual clutter. Journal of Vision **7**(2), 17 (2007)
12. Mack, M.L., Oliva, A.: Computational estimation of visual complexity. In: The 12th Annual Object, Perception, Attention, and Memory Conference (2004)
13. Reppa, I., Playfoot, D., McDougall, S.J.P.: Visual aesthetic appeal speeds processing of complex but not simple icons. In: Proceedings of the Human Factors and Ergonomics Society Annual Meeting, vol. 52, pp. 1155–1159. SAGE Publications (2008)
14. Forsythe, A.: Visual complexity: is that all there is? In: Harris, D. (ed.) EPCE 2009. LNCS, vol. 5639, pp. 158–166. Springer, Heidelberg (2009)
15. Ramanarayanan, G., Bala, K., Ferwerda, J.A., Walter, B.: Dimensionality of visual complexity in computer graphics scenes. In: Electronic Imaging 2008, pp. 68060E–68060E. International Society for Optics and Photonics (2008)
16. Peters, R.A., Strickland, R.N.: Image complexity metrics for automatic target recognizers. In: Automatic Target Recognizer System and Technology Conference, pp. 1–17 (1990)
17. Yaghmaee, F., Jamzad, M.: Estimating watermarking capacity in gray scale images based on image complexity. EURASIP Journal on Advances in Signal Processing **2010**, 8 (2010)

18. Yu, H., Winkler, S.: Image complexity and spatial information. In: 2013 Fifth International Workshop on Quality of Multimedia Experience (QoMEX), pp. 12–17. IEEE (2013)
19. Corchs, S., Gasparini, F., Schettini, R.: Grouping strategies to improve the correlation between subjective and objective image quality data. In: Image Quality and System Performance X, IS&T/SPIE Electronic Imaging, p. 86530D(1–8). SPIE (2013)
20. Bianco, S., Ciocca, G., Marini, F., Schettini, R.: Image quality assessment by preprocessing and full reference model combination. In: Image Quality and System Performance VI, vol. 7242, p. 72420O. SPIE (2009)
21. Donderi, D.C.: Psychological Bulletin. Visual complexity: a review **132**(1), 73 (2006)
22. Sheik, H., Wang, Z., Cormakc, L., Bovik, A.: LIVE Image Quality Assessment Database Release 2. http://live.ece.utexas.edu/research/quality
23. Comaniciu, D., Meer, P.: Mean shift: A robust approach toward feature space analysis and the edge detection algorithm. IEEE Transactions on Pattern Analysis and Machine Intelligence **24**, 603–619 (2002)
24. Hasler, D., Suesstrunk, S.E.: Measuring colorfulness in natural images. Electronic Imaging **2003**, 87–95 (2003)
25. Solli, M., Lenz, R.: Color harmony for image indexing. In: IEEE 12th International Conference on Computer Vision Workshops, pp. 1885–1892 (2009)
26. Artese, M.T., Ciocca, G., Gagliardi, I.: Good 50x70 Project: A portal for Cultural And Social Campaigns. In: IS&T Archiving 2014 Conference, Final Program and Proceedings, pp. 213–218 (2014)

Adaptive Filters for Color Images: Median Filtering and Its Extensions

Andreas Kleefeld[1], Michael Breuß[1]([⊠]), Martin Welk[3],
and Bernhard Burgeth[2]

[1] Faculty of Mathematics, Natural Sciences and Computer Science,
Brandenburg Technical University Cottbus-Senftenberg, 03046 Cottbus, Germany
{kleefeld,breuss}@tu-cottbus.de
[2] Department of Mathematics and Computer Science,
Saarland University, 66123 Saarbrücken, Germany
burgeth@math.uni-sb.de
[3] Biomedical Image Analysis Division, Department of Biomedical Computer Science
and Mechatronics, University for Medical Informatics and Technology (UMIT),
Eduard-Wallnöfer-Zentrum 1, 6060 Hall/Tyrol, Austria
martin.welk@umit.at

Abstract. In this paper we are concerned with robust structure-preserving denoising filters for color images. We build on a recently proposed transformation from the RGB color space to the space of symmetric 2×2 matrices that has already been used to transfer morphological dilation and erosion concepts from matrix-valued data to color images. We investigate the applicability of this framework to the construction of color-valued median filters. Additionally, we introduce spatial adaptivity into our approach by morphological amoebas that offer excellent capabilities for structure-preserving filtering. Furthermore, we define color-valued amoeba M-smoothers as a generalization of the median-based concepts. Our experiments confirm that all these methods work well with color images. They demonstrate the potential of our approach to define color processing tools based on matrix field techniques.

Keywords: Matrix field · Color image · Median filter · M-smoother · Amoeba filter

1 Introduction

Thanks to modern technology, digital color images have become a ubiquitous element of our every-day life, creating an ever-increasing demand for efficient algorithms to process color image data. With noise being one of the most widespread sources of image degradation, denoising is a crucial task of image processing. Despite decades of research, it continues to pose new challenges, not least due to the ongoing spread of imaging into new application fields with unfavorable acquisition conditions with higher noise levels and an increasing diversity of noise sources. For example, low-light photography by mobile phones combined with

© Springer International Publishing Switzerland 2015
A. Trémeau et al. (Eds.): CCIW 2015, LNCS 9016, pp. 149–158, 2015.
DOI: 10.1007/978-3-319-15979-9_15

compression for low-rate data transfer may lead to mixtures of significant sensor noise with scattered light and compression noise. To cope with such application contexts requires robust and structure-preserving denoising approaches. Whereas the present work does not aim at giving a fully developed algorithm for a specific application problem, it intends to contribute to the development of robust denoising algorithms. Our approach combines a suitable choice of color space with multi-channel median filtering on adaptive neighborhoods. The median filter component is later generalized by so-called M-smoothers. In the following, we therefore provide some background on these four concepts.

Color Spaces. Since the output of most digital image sensors consists of red, green, and blue intensity values, the corresponding RGB color space is often used to perform color image processing. Targeting at the enhancement of images for human observers, it makes sense, however, to adopt a color space that reflects better the sensitivity and contrast perception of the human visual system. In the latter, the excitations of retina cones, which are close to an RGB model, undergo several transformation steps before they become color impressions, giving rise to several color spaces that relate to different steps in this chain. From this realm, the hue-chroma-luminance (HCL) lends itself as a good compromise for image denoising because it is on one hand close enough to the RGB input and thereby to the physical noise process, whilst at the same time it reflects reasonably the perceptual metric of human color vision.

Color image processing is embedded in the context of multi-channel image processing, which includes e.g. processing of tensor fields [11] as well. An interesting link between the concepts developed there and color image processing results from the structure of the HCL, HSV and similar color spaces. The latter model the gamut of colors as a cone or bi-cone with a luminance or brightness value as axial dimension. Likewise, symmetric positive definite matrices as are used to represent diffusion tensors form a cone whose axial dimension represents an overall intensity. In [4] this relation has been fruitfully exploited to transfer multi-channel morphology concepts from tensor data to color image processing.

Median Filtering. For gray-scale images, a time-proven method for robust denoising is median filtering [10], which establishes a filtered image by assigning to each pixel the median of gray values from the input image within a neighborhood of that pixel. Neighborhoods for all pixels are generated by shifting a fixed-shape mask across the image. The process can be iterated, by computing a first filtered image from the input, a second filtered image from the first one, and so on. This procedure can cope with heavy-tailed noise distributions such as salt-and-pepper noise, whilst preserving important image features like edges that are crucial for human interpretation of images.

Attempts to transfer median filtering to multi-channel contexts like color images have therefore been made as early as 1990 [2]. The notion of vector median introduced there selects as median of a finite set of vectors always one of the input vectors. While this is advantageous in terms of algorithmic complexity, it leads to discontinuous dependence of output data from input data, and applied to color images, to noticeable color artifacts, as demonstrated in [8]. Indeed, a median concept that drops the restriction to select one of the input values has already been proposed several decades before by Weiszfeld [12]. Following these, the median of data points in a metric space is the point in the same space that minimizes the sum of distances to the input values. This notion of median has been applied to color images in [8] via the RGB color space. The same approach has been introduced to tensor field processing in [15].

Adaptive Neighborhoods. For each pixel, the median filtering procedure involves two steps: a sliding-window *selection* step, and the *aggregation* of selected input values via the median. To increase the sensitivity to important image structures, the selection step can be modified by using spatially adaptive neighborhoods. One representative of these are *morphological amoebas* as introduced by Lerallut et al. [5], see also the further analysis in [13,14]. In this approach, spatial distance in the image plane is combined with contrast into an image-adaptive metric. On the basis of this metric, adaptive neighborhoods called amoebas are established and used to replace the sliding window in median filtering in order to perform adaptive filtering.

M-Smoothers. Combining the sliding-window selection step with different aggregation operators leads to other well-known image filters, such as average filter (with aggregation by mean value), morphological dilation and erosion (with maximum or minimum). A general class of position estimators for univariate distributions are M-estimators, which include median and mean value as special cases [7]. In combination with the sliding-window procedure they give rise to image filters called *M-smoothers* [9].

Our Contributions. In this paper, we combine the ideas reviewed in the preceding paragraphs in several ways. First, we use the color-tensor link from [4] to transfer the median filtering idea of [15] to color images and compare the resulting version of a color median filter with the RGB-based approach from [8]. This is further combined with the amoeba approach [5] for spatial adaptive filtering to yield a color amoeba median filter with enhanced structure preservation. Second, we transfer the tensor-valued M-smoothers studied in [15] to color images and combine them with the amoeba approach.

2 Color Images and Matrix Fields

In this section, we briefly recall the conversion of RGB-images to matrix fields as introduced in [4]. Given an RGB-image we transform it in two steps into a matrix field $\mathbf{F}$ of equal dimensions, i.e. we assign each pixel of the image a symmetric 2×2 matrix.

In the first step, we transform the color values of the image from the RGB representation to the HCL color space. We assume that red, green and blue intensities are normalized to $[0, 1]$. For a pixel with red, green and blue intensities r, g, b, resp., we obtain its hue h, chroma c and luminance l via $M = \max\{r, g, b\}$, $m = \min\{r, g, b\}$, $c = M - m$, $l = \frac{1}{2}(M + m)$, and $h = \frac{1}{6}(g - b)/M$ modulo 1 if

$M = r$, $h = \frac{1}{6}(b-r)/M + \frac{1}{3}$ if $M = g$, $h = \frac{1}{6}(r-g)/M + \frac{2}{3}$ if $M = b$, compare [1, Algorithm 8.6.3]. Replacing further the luminance l with $\tilde{l} := 2l - 1$, and interpreting c, $2\pi h$, and $\tilde{l}$ as radial, angular and axial coordinates, resp., of a cylindrical coordinate system, we have so far a bijection from the unit cube of triples (r, g, b) onto a solid bi-cone, see Figure 1. Its base is the unit disc in the plane $\tilde{l} = 0$, while its tips correspond to $\tilde{l} = \pm 1$ on the $\tilde{l}$-axis. The bi-cone is then transformed from cylindrical to Cartesian coordinates via $x = c\cos(2\pi h)$, $y = c\sin(2\pi h)$, $z = \tilde{l}$.

The second step takes the Cartesian coordinate triples (x, y, z) and maps them to symmetric matrices $A \in \mathrm{Sym}(2)$ via

$$A = \frac{\sqrt{2}}{2}\begin{pmatrix} z - y & x \\ x & z + y \end{pmatrix}, \qquad (1)$$

compare [4]. Note that the mapping $\Psi : \mathbb{R}^3 \to \mathrm{Sym}(2)$ defined by (1) is bijective and even an isometry from the Euclidean space $\mathbb{R}^3$ to the space $\mathrm{Sym}(2)$ with the metric defined by the Frobenius norm $\|\cdot\|_{\mathrm{F}}$, $d(A, B) := \|A - B\|_{\mathrm{F}}$. Denoting by $\mathcal{M} \subset \mathrm{Sym}(2)$ the set of all matrices A which correspond to points of the bi-cone, we have therefore a bijection between the RGB color space and the bi-cone $\mathcal{M}$ in

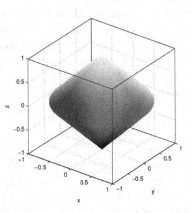

Fig. 1. Color bi-cone, figure adapted from [3]

$\mathrm{Sym}(2)$. The inverse transform from matrices to RGB triples is obtained in a straightforward way, compare [4].

To illustrate the conversion of color values, we state RGB, Cartesian bi-cone and symmetric matrix representations of exemplary colors in Table 1.

3   Constructing Amoebas

In this section, we explain how to construct an adaptive, pixel-wise varying filtering domain, *amoeba* for short, for a given matrix field **F**. In doing this we

Table 1. Colors and their RGB, Cartesian bi-cone and matrix representations

Color	Black	Red	Green	Blue
(r, g, b)	$(0, 0, 0)$	$(1, 0, 0)$	$(0, 1, 0)$	$(0, 0, 1)$
(x, y, z)	$(0, 0, -1)$	$(1, 0, 0)$	$(-1/2, \sqrt{3}/2, 0)$	$(-1/2, -\sqrt{3}/2, 0)$
A	$-\frac{\sqrt{2}}{2}\begin{pmatrix} 1 & 0 \\ 0 & 1 \end{pmatrix}$	$\frac{\sqrt{2}}{2}\begin{pmatrix} 0 & 1 \\ 1 & 0 \end{pmatrix}$	$-\frac{1}{4}\begin{pmatrix} \sqrt{6} & \sqrt{2} \\ \sqrt{2} & -\sqrt{6} \end{pmatrix}$	$-\frac{1}{4}\begin{pmatrix} -\sqrt{6} & \sqrt{2} \\ \sqrt{2} & \sqrt{6} \end{pmatrix}$
Color	Yellow	Magenta	Cyan	White
(r, g, b)	$(1, 1, 0)$	$(1, 0, 1)$	$(0, 1, 1)$	$(1, 1, 1)$
(x, y, z)	$(1/2, \sqrt{3}/2, 0)$	$(1/2, -\sqrt{3}/2, 0)$	$(-1, 0, 0)$	$(0, 0, 1)$
A	$\frac{1}{4}\begin{pmatrix} -\sqrt{6} & \sqrt{2} \\ \sqrt{2} & \sqrt{6} \end{pmatrix}$	$\frac{1}{4}\begin{pmatrix} \sqrt{6} & \sqrt{2} \\ \sqrt{2} & -\sqrt{6} \end{pmatrix}$	$-\frac{\sqrt{2}}{2}\begin{pmatrix} 0 & 1 \\ 1 & 0 \end{pmatrix}$	$\frac{\sqrt{2}}{2}\begin{pmatrix} 1 & 0 \\ 0 & 1 \end{pmatrix}$

extend the approach of Lerallut et al. in a straightforward fashion: In [5], color channels have been considered separately for amoeba construction.

Let (x_i, y_i) be the coordinates of the i-th pixel of an image with gray-value f_i. For a given pixel i_0 with coordinates (x_{i_0}, y_{i_0}) the amoeba is constructed as follows. As a first step, we only consider pixels i^* that are located in a prescribed maximal Euclidean distance ϱ of pixel i_0 which limits the maximal size of the amoeba. As a second step, we take these pre-selected pixels and consider paths $(i_0, i_1, \ldots, i_k \equiv i^*)$ which connect i_0 with i^* allowing only pixels that are neighbors to enter P. We determine the *shortest path* P among all those possibilies using the *amoeba distance* $L(P)$, a combination of spatial and tonal distances, defined by

$$L(P) = \sum_{m=0}^{k-1} 1 + \sigma \sum_{m=0}^{k-1} \left| f_{i_{m+1}} - f_{i_m} \right|, \qquad (2)$$

where $\sigma > 0$ is a given parameter that penalizes large deviations in gray-valued data. If $L(P) \leq \varrho$ for P holds, then pixel i^* is a member of the amoeba.

Because the amoeba distance includes a tonal distance, the amoeba has the ability to grow around structures given by large tonal differences, compare the sketches in Figure 2: A filter applied over fixed masks takes into account all values as e.g. here both white and gray region, while an amoeba may grow around corners as indicated.

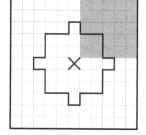

Note that modifications of this approach are possible and have been done by Welk et al. [14]. Precisely, they considered 8-point instead of 4-point neighbors as we do in this work, and different distance measures. To efficiently implement the amoeba computation we use the fast marching method similarly as in [13,14].

Since we deal with matrix fields, we have to consider an amoeba distance defined for matrices. A natural extension of (2) is

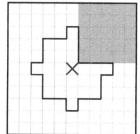

$$L(P) = \sum_{m=0}^{k-1} 1 + \sigma \sum_{m=0}^{k-1} \left\| F_{i_{m+1}} - F_{i_m} \right\|_F \qquad (3)$$

where F_i is the symmetric matrix of size 2×2 at the coordinate (x_i, y_i). Here, $\|\cdot\|_F$ denotes the Frobenius norm, which we employ in all computations. Of course, also other norms like e.g. the nuclear norm

Fig. 2. Masks centered at marked pixels. **Top.** Spatially fixed window. **Bottom.** Amoeba domain.

[6, p. 615] are possible, however, one should not employ different norm definitions for amoeba distance and the filtering methods described in the following.

4 Median Filtering and Its Generalizations

Given a color image, we first convert it to a matrix field as described in Section 2. Then amoebas are constructed via the procedure given in Section 3 for all pixels.

For an amoeba as an adaptive structuring element, it is possible to extract the matrices $A_1, \ldots, A_n$ that participate in it.

Median Filters. The Frobenius matrix median M of this set of symmetric 2×2 matrices is given by

$$M := \mathrm{med}_F(A_1, \ldots, A_n) := \arg\min_{X \in \mathrm{Sym}(2)} \sum_{i=1}^{n} \|X - A_i\|_F \qquad (4)$$

compare for example [15]. Note that the matrices $A_1, \ldots, A_n$ represent points in a solid bi-cone defining a convex set. The resulting median is located in the convex hull of this set and hence, the median operation never leads to RGB color values outside the unit cube, see [15, Proposition 2]). To calculate the median numerically one may reformulate the problem as a convex minimization problem; compare [15, Section 3.2.1] for the reformulation and a discussion.

Given a matrix field $\mathbf{F}^{(0)} := \mathbf{F}$, an amoeba median filter works now as follows. For each matrix in the matrix field, one computes the amoeba, selects the set of matrices $A_1, \ldots, A_n$, and computes the Frobenius matrix median. The resulting matrix is stored in the matrix field $\mathbf{F}^{(1)}$.

An *iterated amoeba median filter* (IAMF) applies this procedure iteratively p times yielding matrix fields $\mathbf{F}^{(0)}, \ldots, \mathbf{F}^{(p)}$. At the end, the resulting matrix field $\mathbf{F}^{(p)}$ is converted back to a RGB image. In the subsequent section we report the experimental results when this procedure is applied to various color test images.

M-Smoothers. Next, we consider a generalization of the median filter that can be traced back to Barral Souto [7] by modifying (4) as

$$M_p := \arg\min_{X \in \mathrm{Sym}(2)} \sum_{i=1}^{n} \|X - A_i\|_F^p \qquad (5)$$

where we assume $p \geq 1$ to ensure uniqueness of the minimizer, cf. [13, pp.20–21]). The symmetric matrix M_p is called a *matrix-valued M-smoother*. For $p = 1$ we recover the median, for $p = 2$ we obtain the arithmetic mean, and for the limiting case $p \to \infty$ the mid-range. Using amoebas and calculating the M-estimators iteratively leads to an *iterated amoeba M-smoothers* (IAMS).

5   Experiments

The structure of our experimental section is as follows. First we confirm that the use of our new color scheme for both amoeba construction and filtering gives better results than simpler amoeba-based methods employed in a similar style as by Lerallut et al. [5] where experiments were designed to give a proof of concept. Then we show an experiment demonstrating benefits of amoeba structuring elements over fixed filtering masks. This is followed by a comparison of our new set-up for median filtering with a recent method for median computation working with RGB data, namely the method of Spence and Fancourt [8]. Finally, we present some results of our new amoeba-based M-smoothers.

Comparison with a Simple Amoeba-Based Median Filter. The purpose of this experiment is to demonstrate that the use of amoebas alone without a proper median computation cannot give high-quality results.

To this end we take up a test image used in [5], see Figure 3. The image in the middle is obtained by a simple, amoeba-based iterated median filtering. Here the median is determined channel-wise in RGB, iterating three times amoeba construction and median filtering analogously to IAMF. This is compared with three iterations IAMF by our method, see the image on the right hand side.

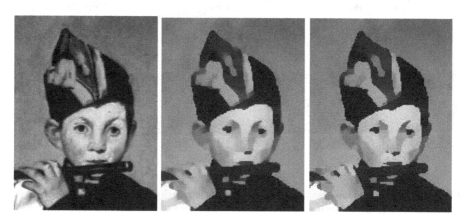

Fig. 3. IAMF versus amoeba-based simple median computation, amoeba parameters are $\varrho = 5$ and $\sigma = 5$. **Left.** Input image, size 131×173. **Middle.** Result for amoebas and channel-wise median filter. **Right.** Result of IAMF with three iterations.

Our method yields reasonable colors after filtering, while the simple channel-based median exhibits the expected problems of color distortions, e.g. have a look at the left part of the nose or at green spots around the eyes and at the transition of hat to background. Let us also note that the expected edge-preserving properties of the amoebas are clearly observable when using a proper median as performed by our method.

Comparison of Amoebas with Fixed Filtering Masks. The purpose of this experiment is to verify that the edge-preserving properties of median amoeba filters that can be observed for gray-valued images [5,13] are carried over to filtering of color images. Because of the well-known difficulties in dealing with color vectors we do not expect that this is self-evident.

In order to illuminate the mentioned effect we employ a low resolution test image of size 64×64, see Figure 4. In the first row we demonstrate the edge-preserving capability of the amoebas and show that our color scheme for median filtering gives reasonable results. The shape of the peppers is well-preserved while regions of similar color are more uniform after IAMF, in contrast to plain median filtering which shows expected rounding effects of image structures. By the second row we demonstrate that our method is capable of delivering reasonable shape information if the input is perturbed by noise. Note that the stipe

Fig. 4. Amoebas versus fixed filtering mask with iterated median filter. **Left column.** Input images, original (top) and with added Gaussian noise in each channel (bottom). **Middle column.** Iterated median filtering with our color scheme for 3×3 masks and three iterations. **Right column.** IAMF with $\sigma = 5$, $\varrho = 3$ and three iterations.

of the thin pepper is not well preserved in the filtering process. The filtering of this kind of thin, oblique structures can be improved by using 8-neighborhoods instead of 4-neighborhoods in the amoeba construction; however, we leave this algorithmical improvement to future research. Note also that we employed $\varrho = 3$ in this test instead of $\varrho = 5$ in Fig. 3, since the resolution of the input image in Fig. 4 is much lower and the parameter ϱ controls the maximal size of the structuring element.

Comparison to RGB-Based Color Median Approach. The aim of this experiment is to show that our median filter based on our specific color representation yields competitive results compared to a RGB-based method for median filtering, namely the approach of Spence and Fancourt [8].

The Figure 5 shows results for the *Hamburg* test image. We filter the image with IAMF with parameters $\varrho = 5$, $\sigma = 5$ and perform three iterations. Let us note that in order to achieve directly comparable results, we adjust the parameter σ by the factor $\sqrt{4/3}$ when using the method of Spence and Fancourt. This factor can be derived by considering the distances between black and white in RGB space and our color space, respectively. As can be expected from the similarity of the methods, the results of our approach and that from [8] are largely comparable.

Fig. 5. Comparison of IAMF with 5 iterations, $\varrho = 5$, $\sigma = 5$, for different color median filters. **Left.** Input image, size 213×213. **Middle.** Method of Spence and Fancourt. **Right.** Our color scheme.

Iterated Amoeba M-Smoothers. For demonstrating the flexibility of our framework we present in Figure 6 results for IAMS with several values for p, see (5). The results show that image simplification can be achieved by our method without color distortions. Results with fixed structuring elements are equally possible but not very illustrative here. We observe the expected increased smoothing effect when letting p grow combined with the edge-preserving mechanism of the amoebas.

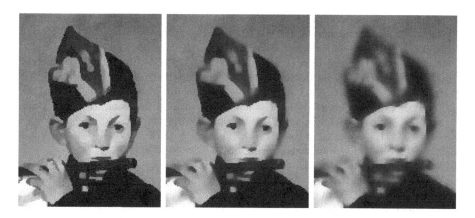

Fig. 6. Matrix-valued M-smoothers with exponent p and 5 iterations. **Left.** IAMS with $p = 1$ identical to IAMF. **Middle.** IAMS with $p = 2$, i.e. the image shows an amoeba-based arithmetic mean. **Right column.** IAMS with $p = 5$.

6   Conclusion

In this paper we have extended the work from [3] on using matrix fields for the processing of color images. We have introduced a color median filter concept based on this approach and used it in connection with morphological amoebas for robust, structure-preserving image denoising. We have also formulated a more general filter class of color amoeba M-smoothers. Our experiments demonstrate the viability and versatility of the approach. Ongoing work is directed at generalizations to further image filters and applications for color image processing. For future work we aim to make our algorithm more efficient and to exploit theoretical connections of our approach to bilateral filtering and related concepts.

References

1. Agoston, M.K.: Computer Graphics and Geometric Modeling: Implementation and Algorithms. Springer, London (2005)
2. Astola, J., Haavisto, P., Neuvo, Y.: Vector median filters. Proceedings of the IEEE **78**(4), 678–689 (1990)
3. Burgeth, B., Kleefeld, A.: An approach to color-morphology based on Einstein addition and Loewner order. Pattern Recognition Letters **47**, 29–39 (2014)
4. Burgeth, B., Kleefeld, A.: Order based morphology for color images via matrix fields. In: Burgeth, B., Vilanova, A., Westin, C.-F. (eds.) Visualization and Processing of Tensor Fields and Higher Order Descriptors for Multi-Valued Data. Springer, Berlin (2014)
5. Lerallut, R., Decencière, E., Meyer, F.: Image processing using morphological amoebas. In: Ronse, C., Najman, L., Decencière, E. (eds.) Mathematical Morphology: 40 Years On Computational Imaging and Vision, vol. 30, pp. 13–22. Springer, Dordrecht (2005)
6. Schatten, R., von Neumann, J.: The cross-space of linear transformations. II. Annals of Mathematics **47**(3), 608–630 (1946)
7. Souto, J.B.: El modo y otras medias, casos particulares de una misma expresión matemática. Technical Report 3, Cuadernos de Trabajo, Instituto de Biometría, Universidad Nacional de Buenos Aires, Argentina (1938)
8. Spence, C., Fancourt, C.L.: An iterative method for vector median filtering. In: Proceedings of the International Conference on Image Processing, ICIP 2007, San Antonio, Texas, USA, September 16–19, pp. 265–268 (2007)
9. Torroba, P.L., Cap, N.L., Rabal, H.J., Furlan, W.D.: Fractional order mean in image processing. Optical Engineering **33**(2), 528–534 (1994)
10. Tukey, J.W.: Exploratory Data Analysis. Addison-Wesley, Menlo Park (1971)
11. Weickert, J., Hagen, H. (eds.): Visualization and Processing of Tensor Fields. Springer, Berlin (2006)
12. Weiszfeld, E.: Sur le point pour lequel la somme des distances de n points donnés est minimum. Tôhoku Mathematics Journal **43**, 355–386 (1937)
13. Welk, M., Breuß, M.: Morphological amoebas and partial differential equations. In: Hawkes, P. (ed.) Advances in Imaging and Electron Physics, vol. 185, pp. 139–212. Academic Press, Elsevier Inc. (2014)
14. Welk, M., Breuß, M., Vogel, O.: Morphological amoebas are self-snakes. Journal of Mathematical Imaging and Vision **39**, 87–99 (2011)
15. Welk, M., Weickert, J., Becker, F., Schnörr, C., Feddern, C., Burgeth, B.: Median and related local filters for tensor-valued images. Signal Processing **87**, 291–308 (2007)

Spectral Imaging

Can Linear Data Projection Improve Hyperspectral Face Recognition?

Simone Bianco[✉]

University of Milano-Bicocca, 20126 Milano, Italy
`simone.bianco@disco.unimib.it`

Abstract. This paper investigates if the performance of hyperspectral face recognition algorithms can be improved by considering 1D projections of the whole spectral data along the spectral dimension. Three different projections are investigated: single spectral band selection, non-negative spectral band combination, and unbounded spectral band combination. Experiments are performed on a standard hyperspectral dataset and the obtained results outperform seven existing hyperspectral face recognition algorithms.

1 Introduction

Since intra-person differences are often larger than inter-person ones in presence of variations in viewing point and illumination conditions, face recognition is still a challenging problem.

Most of the current research is based on features extracted from grayscale or RGB images, which are usually acquired in the visible spectrum [1,2].

With the aim of increasing the dimensions in face images, many researchers have considered the use of hyperspectral imaging [3–7]. Hyperspectral imaging can increase facial discrimination by capturing more biometric measurements such as the spectral response of faces. A hyperspectral image is a data cube with two spatial dimensions and one spectral dimension. It is captured by a hyperspectral camera which operates in multiple narrow bands and densely samples the radiance information in both space and wavelength, producing a radiance spectra at every pixel.

In addition to face appearance, spectral measurements in multiple wavelengths can also measure subsurface tissue features [4] which may be significantly different for each person.

Although the high dimensionality of hyperspectral data is a desirable feature for separating the different identities, at the same time it poses new challenges such as inter-band misalignments and low signal to noise ratio (SNR) in certain spectral bands.

Due to the high dimensionality of hyperspectral data, discriminative feature extraction for face recognition is more challenging than 2D images. The different approaches for dimensionality reduction and feature extraction range from the sub-sampling of the hyperspectral data [4,5,7] to the more promising approaches which use whole-band features [3,8].

© Springer International Publishing Switzerland 2015
A. Trémeau et al. (Eds.): CCIW 2015, LNCS 9016, pp. 161–170, 2015.
DOI: 10.1007/978-3-319-15979-9_16

Starting from the best hyperspectral method in the state of the art [8], this paper investigates if the use of linear projections along the spectral dimension can improve face recognition performance with respect to the use of the full hyperspectral data.

The experiments are performed on the PolyU Hyperspectral [3,9] standard hyperspectral face database. The results are compared with seven existing hyper-spectral face recognition algorithms.

2   Baseline Method

The proposed method builds on the method of Uzair et al. [8], which has three main steps respectively related to the normalization of illumination variations, feature extraction and classification.

The first step consists in filtering the individual bands with a circular (8,1) neighborhood LBP [12] filter to normalize for the illumination variations.

The second step is the feature extraction step which is based on a three-dimensional Discrete Cosine Transform (3D-DCT). The Discrete Cosine Transform (DCT) [13] decomposes a discrete signal into linear combination of independent cosine basis functions. DCT tends to generate a representation in which the low-frequency coefficients encode most of the signal information. A compact representation can be obtained by selecting as features only the low-frequency coefficients. The 3D-DCT of a hyperspectral cube $H(x, y, \lambda)$ with size $N_1 \times N_2 \times N_3$ is given by

$$F(u, v, w) = \Omega_1(u)\Omega_2(v)\Omega_3(w) \sum_{x=0}^{N_1-1} \sum_{y=0}^{N_2-1} \sum_{\lambda=0}^{N_3-1} H(x, y, \lambda)$$

$$\cos \frac{\pi(2x + 1)u}{2N_1} \cos \frac{\pi(2y + 1)v}{2N_2} \cos \frac{\pi(2\lambda + 1)w}{2N_3} \qquad (1)$$

with $u = \{0, \ldots, N_1 - 1\}$, $v = \{0, \ldots, N_2 - 1\}$, $w = \{0, \ldots, N_3 - 1\}$, and $\Omega_i(\cdot)$ is defined $\sqrt{1/N_i}$ if its argument is zero, and $\sqrt{2/N_i}$ otherwise.

The low frequency coefficients near the origin of $F(u, v, w)$ represent most of the energy of the hyperspectral cube, and therefore the high-frequency coefficients can be discarded. In order to construct the feature vector, in [8] a frequency sub-cube $\Gamma(u, v, w)$ of dimensions $(\alpha \times \beta \times \gamma)$ is sampled by retaining only the low-frequency elements around the origin of $F(u, v, w)$. The sub-cube $\Gamma(u, v, w)$ is then vectorized and normalized to unit magnitude to obtain the final feature vector $f \in \mathbb{R}^d$, where $d = \alpha\beta\gamma$, which is then used for classification.

The last step consists in the use of the Partial Least Squares (PLS) regression [14] for the classification. PLS models the relations between sets of observed variables by means of latent variables. In its general form, PLS creates orthogonal score vectors by maximizing the covariance between different variable sets. The only parameter to be set in PLS is the number of latent variables to use.

3   The Proposed Method

Building on top of the method of Uzair et al. [8], this work wants to understand if the full hyperspectral information is actually needed to improve face recognition accuracy or if a projection of it suffices. The projection is applied directly to the hyperspectral cube $H(x, y, \lambda)$ (i.e. the radiance data), before any step of the method in [8], and depends on the set of weights $W(\lambda_i) = w_i$, $i = 1, \ldots, N_3$:

$$P(x,y) = \sum_{i=1,\ldots,N_3} H(x, y, \lambda_i) W(\lambda_i) \qquad (2)$$

The projection $P(x, y)$ is thus a 2D image, forcing $\gamma = 1$ for the sub-cube size. In this work three different projections are considered. The first one is

$$W_1(\lambda) = \delta_{\lambda_0}(\lambda) = \begin{cases} 1 & \text{if } \lambda = \lambda_0 \\ 0 & \text{otherwise} \end{cases} \qquad (3)$$

and can be seen as a band selection operator, or a pass-band optical filter.

The second projection is

$$W_2(\lambda_i) = w_i, i = 1, \ldots, L \text{ s.t. } \forall w_i : w_i \in \mathbb{R}, 0 \leq w_i \leq 1 \qquad (4)$$

which can be seen as a non-negative linear combination of the different hyperspectral bands. This is an operation analogue to what optical filters do in traditional imaging, and could be done using a monochrome digital camera coupled with a custom designed filter.

The third projection is an unbounded linear combination of the hyperspectral bands, and can be defined as in equation 4 removing the lower and upper bounds on the filter coefficients w_i, i.e.:

$$W_3(\lambda_i) = w_i, i = 1, \ldots, L \text{ s.t. } \forall w_i : w_i \in \mathbb{R} \qquad (5)$$

This is a generalization of the second one, and is the only one that cannot be realized through an optical filter since it could have negative coefficients as well as $|w_i| > 1$.

The optimal $W_1(\lambda)$ projection is obtained by exhaustive search, while for both $W_2(\lambda)$ and $W_3(\lambda)$ a Particle Swarm Optimization (PSO) [10,11] is used. PSO is a population based stochastic optimization technique. A population of individuals is initialized as random guesses to the problem solutions and a communication structure is also defined, assigning neighbors for each individual to interact with. These individuals are candidate solutions. The particles iteratively evaluate the fitness of the candidate solutions and remember the location where they had their best success. The best solution of each individual is called the particle best or the local best. Each particle makes this information available to its neighbors. Movements through the search space are guided by these successes. The swarm is typically modeled by particles in multidimensional space that have a position and a velocity. These particles move into the search space

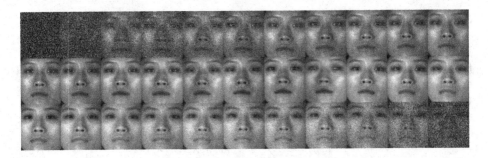

Fig. 1. A hyperspectral face cube from the PolyU-HSFD dataset

and have two essential reasoning capabilities: the memory of their own best position and the knowledge of the global best position (or the best position of their neighbors). Members of a swarm communicate good positions to each other and adjust their own position and velocity based on these good positions.

4   Experiments

4.1   Dataset

The hyperspectral face database used is the Hong Kong Polytechnic University Hyperspectral Face Database(PolyU-HSFD) [3,9]. It consists of hyperspectral image cubes acquired using a CRIs VariSpec Liquid Crystal Tuneable Filter. Each cube contains 33 bands acquired in the 400-720nm spectral range in 10nm steps. The database has been collected over a long period of time and shows significant appearance variations of the subjects (e.g. changes of hair style, skin conditionss, etc.). Signal to noise ratio (SNR) in bands near the blue wavelength is very low, and the database contains inter-band misalignments due to subject movements during the acquisition at the different wavelengths.

The database contains a total of 48 subjects (13 females and 35 males). For each of the first 25 subjects four to seven cubes are available, while the remaining 23 subjects only have one cube each. Following the experimental protocol of [3,7], only the first 25 subjects are used in the experiments. For each subject, two cubes are randomly selected for the gallery and the remaining cubes are used as probes. The random selection is repeated ten times and the results are averaged. As in [3] the eye, nose tip, and mouth corners coordinates were located manually for image registration, and a subregion containing the face was cropped from each band, normalized, and scaled to one quarter size.

An example of the hyperspectral face cubes used is reported in Figure 1, while examples of appearance variations are reported in Figure 2.

4.2   Compared Hyperspectral Face Recognition Algorithms

The seven existing hyperspectral face recognition algorithms used for comparisons include Spectral Signature Matching [4], Spectral Angle Measurement [6],

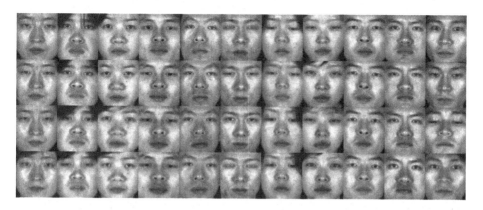

Fig. 2. Examples of appearance variations. The same hyperspectral band correspond-ing to $\lambda_{15} = 540$nm is selected for all subjects.

Spectral Eigenface [5], 2D PCA [3], 3D Gabor Wavelets [7], and 2D and 3D-DCT with PLS regression [8]. The parameters of these algorithms are set as follows. For spectral signature matching algorithm [4], five adjacent square regions of size 17x17 pixels arranged in a cross pattern are used to represent hair, forehead and cheeks. For the lips, square regions of size 9x9 pixels are used . For Spectral Eigenface [5], 99% energy is preserved by retaining 48 PCA basis vectors. For 2D PCA [3], 99% energy is preserved by retaining 27 PCA basis vectors. For the 3D Gabor method, 52 Gabor wavelets are used for feature generation as recom-mended by [7]. For the 2D and 3D-DCT [8] method the parameters are taken as suggested by the authors: $\alpha = \beta = \gamma = 10$ for the sub-cube size to extract the features, and 45 PLS basis.

4.3 Results

The results of the hyperspectral face recognition algorithms compared are reported in terms of average recognition rate in Table 1. The results of Spectral Signature Matching [4], Spectral Angle Measurement [6], Spectral Eigenface [5], 2D PCA [3], 3D Gabor Wavelets [7], and 2D and 3D-DCT with PLS regression [8] are all taken from [8], with the only exception of the 3D-DCT method for which the results using an our implementation are also reported.

It is possible to notice that the proposed method outperforms the best algo-rithm in the state of the art by 4.3% up to 6.11%. The best projections found for $W_1(\lambda)$, $W_2(\lambda)$, and $W_3(\lambda)$ are reported in Figure 3. Interestingly, the band selected by $W_1(\lambda)$ and the bands receiving higher weights by $W_2(\lambda)$ and $W_3(\lambda)$ are localized at the oxyhemoglobin peak absorption valley [3,15].

As already said in Section 3 the projections $W_1(\lambda)$ and $W_2(\lambda)$ could both be realized through an optical filter since they do not have negative coefficients. The projection $W_3(\lambda)$, instead can not be realized through a single optical filter, but exploiting the linearity of equation 2 it could be realized by subtracting two

Table 1. Average recognition rates and standard deviations (%) for ten-fold experiments on the database

Algorithm	Average recognition rate (std)
Spectral Signature [4]	24.63 (3.87)
Spectral Angle [6]	25.49 (4.36)
Spectral Eigenface [5]	70.30 (3.61)
2D PCA [3]	71.11 (3.16)
3D Gabor Wavelets [7]	90.19 (2.09)
2D-DCT + PLS [8]	91.43 (2.10)
3D-DCT + PLS [8]	93.00 (2.27)
3D-DCT + PLS (author's implementation)	93.32 (3.13)
Proposed ($W_1(\lambda)$, single band selection)	97.20 (1.66)
Proposed ($W_2(\lambda)$, non-negative band combination)	98.34 (1.83)
Proposed ($W_3(\lambda)$, unbounded band combination)	**99.11 (1.21)**

different optical filters $W_3^+(\lambda_i)$ and $W_3^-(\lambda_i)$:

$$P(x,y) = \sum_{i=1,\ldots,N_3} H(x,y,\lambda_i)W_3^+(\lambda_i) - \sum_{i=1,\ldots,N_3} H(x,y,\lambda_i)W_3^-(\lambda_i) \quad (6)$$

where

$$W_3^+(\lambda_i) = \begin{cases} W_3(\lambda_i) & \text{if } w_i > 0 \\ 0 & \text{otherwise} \end{cases} \quad (7)$$

and

$$W_3^-(\lambda_i) = \begin{cases} -W_3(\lambda_i) & \text{if } w_i < 0 \\ 0 & \text{otherwise} \end{cases} \quad (8)$$

Some examples of the projected output given by applying equation 2 with the optimal $W_1(\lambda)$, $W_2(\lambda)$, and $W_3(\lambda)$ projections are reported in Figure 4.

From the images reported it is possible to see that using the $W_1(\lambda)$ projection results in sharper images, due to the fact that only one spectral band is used. On the contrary, since $W_2(\lambda)$ and $W_3(\lambda)$ use the whole spectra, they make inter-band misalignments evident resulting in more blurred images.

In Figure 5 some examples of errors across the ten-fold experiments when using the $W_3(\lambda)$ projection are reported. The two gallery images are reported for each example together with the probe image and the gallery images of the incorrectly assigned identity.

The sensitivity of the proposed method is analyzed in Figure 6 by plotting equal recognition rate curves as a function of number of PLS basis and sub-cube size ($\alpha = \beta$ and $\gamma = 1$, due to the effect of the projection).

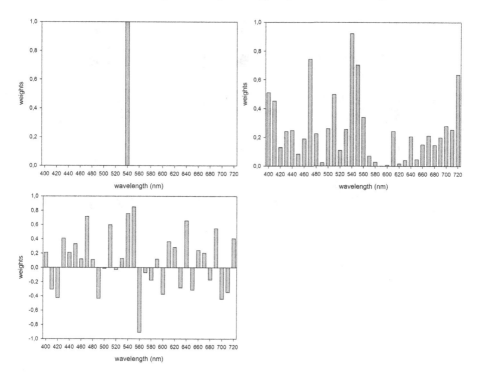

Fig. 3. Best projections found: W_1 (top left), W_2 (top right), and W_3 (bottom left)

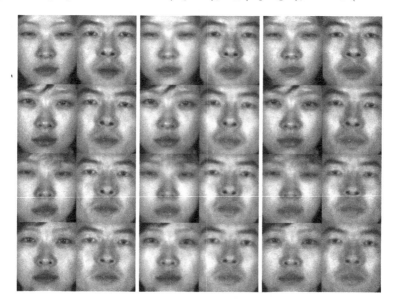

Fig. 4. Examples of the projections obtained by applying the optimal projections found. $W_1(\lambda)$, single band selection (left); $W_2(\lambda)$, non-negative linear combination (middle); $W_3(\lambda)$ and unbounded linear combination (right).

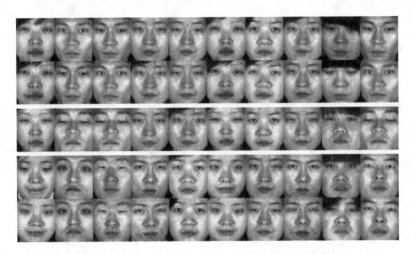

Fig. 5. Examples of errors for the ten-fold experiment using the $W_3(\lambda)$ projection: gallery cubes (top), probes (middle), gallery cubes for the predicted identity (bottom)

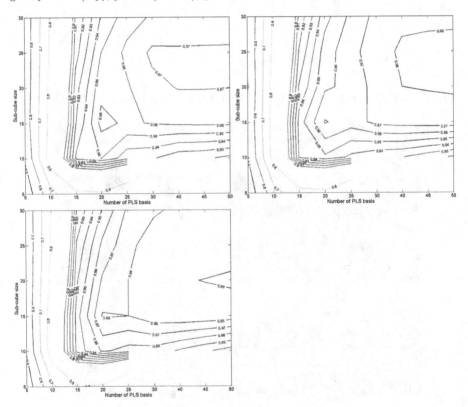

Fig. 6. Equal recognition rate curves as a function of sub-cube size (y-axis) and number of PLS basis (x-axis): single band selection (top left), non-negative linear combination (top right), and unbounded linear combination (bottom left)

5 Conclusion

In this paper it is shown that the performance of hyperspectral face recognition algorithms can be improved by just considering 1D projections along the spectral dimension of the full spectral cube. Three different projections have been investigated: single spectral band selection, non-negative spectral band combination, and unbounded spectral band combination.

Experiments were performed on a standard hyperspectral dataset and the results of the proposed algorithm were compared with seven existing hyperspectral face recognition algorithms. Experimental results showed that the application of the optimal linear projections can improve the performance of the best hyperspectral face recognition algorithm in the state of the art by more than 6%, reaching an average recognition rate on a ten-fold experiment of more than 99%.

As future work it will be investigated the use of linear projections compatible with physically plausible optical filters, by adding smoothness constraint on the projection weights. It will be also studied if multiple linear projections can further improve the recognition rate and which are the best fusion strategies. Furthermore, it will be investigated if the approach proposed in this work can be applied to hyperspectral images recovered from traditional RGB images using spectral recovery techniques [16].

References

1. Zhao, W., Chellappa, R., Phillips, P.J., Rosenfeld, A.: Face recognition: A literature survey. ACM Computing Surveys (CSUR) **35**(4), 399–458 (2003)
2. Li, S.Z., Jain, A.K.: Handbook of face recognition, 2nd edn. Springer (2011)
3. Di, W., Zhang, D., Pan, Q.: Studies on hyperspectral face recognition in visible spectrum with feature band selection. IEEE Transactions on Systems, Man and Cybernetics, Part A: Systems and Humans **40**(6), 1354–1361 (2010)
4. Pan, Z., Healey, G., Prasad, M., Tromberg, B.: Face recognition in hyperspectral images. IEEE Transactions on Pattern Analysis and Machine Intelligence **25**(12), 1552–1560 (2003)
5. Pan, Z., Healey, G., Tromberg, B.: Comparison of spectral-only and spectral/spatial face recognition for personal identity verification. EURASIP Journal on Advances in Signal Processing **8**, 943602 (2009)
6. Robila, S.A.: Toward hyperspectral face recognition. In: Electronic Imaging, International Society for Optics and Photonics, pp. 68120X–68120X (2008)
7. Shen, L., Zheng, S.: Hyperspectral face recognition using 3D gabor wavelets. In: 21st IEEE International Conference on Pattern Recognition (ICPR), pp. 1574–1577 (2012)
8. Uzair, M., Mahmood, A., Mian, A.: Hyperspectral face recognition using 3D-DCT and partial least squares. In: British Machine Vision Conference, pp. 57.1–5-7.10 (2013)
9. PolyU-HSFD. www4.comp.polyu.edu.hk/~biometrics/
10. Kennedy, J., Eberhart, R.: Particle swarm optimization. In: Proceedings of the IEEE International Conference on Neural Networks, vol. 4, pp. 1942–1948 (1995)

11. Bianco, S., Schettini, R.: Two new von Kries based chromatic adaptation transforms found by numerical optimization. Color Research & Application **35**(3), 184–192 (2010)
12. Ahonen, T., Hadid, A., Pietikäinen, M.: Face recognition with local binary patterns. In: Pajdla, T., Matas, J.G. (eds.) ECCV 2004. LNCS, vol. 3021, pp. 469–481. Springer, Heidelberg (2004)
13. Ahmed, N., Natarajan, T., Rao, K.R.: Discrete cosine transform. IEEE Transactions on Computers **100**(1), 90–93 (1974)
14. Rosipal, R., Krämer, N.: Overview and recent advances in partial least squares. In: Subspace, Latent Structure and Feature Selection, pp. 34–51 (2006)
15. Zijlstra, W.G., Buursma, A., Meeuwsen-Van der Roest, W.P.: Absorption spectra of human fetal and adult oxyhemoglobin, de-oxyhemoglobin, carboxyhemoglobin, and methemoglobin. Clinical Chemistry **37**(9), 1633–1638 (1991)
16. Bianco, S.: Reflectance spectra recovery from tristimulus values by adaptive estimation with metameric shape correction. JOSA A **27**(8), 1868–1877 (2010)

Spectral Impulse Noise Model for Spectral Image Processing

Hilda Deborah[1,2]($\boxtimes$), Noël Richard[1], and Jon Yngve Hardeberg[2]

[1] Laboratory XLIM-SIC UMR CNRS 7252, University of Poitiers, Poitiers, France
hildad@hig.no
[2] The Norwegian Colour & Visual Computing Laboratory,
Gjøvik University College, Gjøvik, Norway

Abstract. The performance of an image processing algorithm can be assessed through its resulting images. However, in order to do so, both ground truth image and noisy target image with known properties are typically required. In the context of hyperspectral image processing, another constraint is introduced, i.e. apart from its mathematical properties, an artificial signal, noise, or variations should be physically correct. Deciding to work in an intermediate level, between real spectral images and mathematical model of noise, we develop an approach for obtaining suitable spectral impulse signals. The model is followed by construction of target images corrupted by impulse signals and these images will later on be used to evaluate the performance of a filtering algorithm.

Keywords: Hyperspectral image · Image processing · Impulse noise

1 Introduction

One way to evaluate the performance of an image processing algorithm is through its resulting images, and thus to employ full-reference image quality assessment (IQA). In order to conduct full-reference IQA, both reference and target images are required. Reference image will be image of an ideal case that is to be achieved by the algorithm. Target image is usually the modification of the reference image by certain criteria that is defined according to its application, e.g. filtering, segmentation, classification, etc. It is therefore by having the target image with known properties that we are able to measure the performance of image processing algorithms, e.g. stability, robustness, etc.

The performance of filtering algorithms are evaluated by means of signal/ image denoising or frequency-band decomposition. However, for nonlinear filters, the relationship between spatial frequency and the parameters of the filters are not straightforward. Therefore, filtering performance is assessed through its performance in denoising task, given a certain noise model. Among the existing noise models, nonlinear impulse noise is most often used [2,5,8] as it models or approximates the malfunctioning pixels in camera sensor, transmission problems over a noisy channel, or faulty memory locations in data storage [6]. Interestingly,

© Springer International Publishing Switzerland 2015
A. Trémeau et al. (Eds.): CCIW 2015, LNCS 9016, pp. 171–180, 2015.
DOI: 10.1007/978-3-319-15979-9_17

Table 1. Notation

$I(x) = S$	Image function at location x, $I(x) \subset \mathbb{R}^n$
$\tilde{I}(x)$	An image disturbed by noise or unwanted variations
S	A spectrum describing image value at $I(x)$, $S = \{s_i,\ i \subset [1, n_c]\}$
n_c	Number of channels
$\overline{S}$	Average spectrum
$\mathfrak{S}$	A set of spectra, $\mathfrak{S} = \{S_i, i \subset [1, n_S]\}$
$\mathfrak{S}_n$	A set of candidate impulse signals
R	Random variable
r	Probability value of a pixel to be corrupted by impulse
T	Probability threshold
$\mathcal{N}$	Impulse signal
$\mathcal{H}(y)$	Heavyside function, $\mathcal{H}(y) = 1,\ \forall y > 0$
$d(S_1, S_2)$	Distance between 2 spectra S_1 and S_2
$\mu_d,\ \sigma_d$	Mean and standard deviation of distance
c	A constant number

even assuming a calibrated imaging system, in spectral image domain impulse noise is said to be ubiquitous [10]. It is therefore necessary to extend the model of impulse noise in the context of spectral image processing, and to do it correctly by taking a careful consideration of the nature of spectral data.

This article is organized as follows. Section 2 describes the existing impulse noise model that is widely used for grayscale and color images extended to spectral images. Furthermore, an extension to spectral images at an intermediate level which embeds mathematical model and real physical properties of noise is proposed. In Section 3 we study the characteristics of several pigment patches that were acquired by a hyperspectral scanner. The patches will then be used construct ground truth and noisy target images that will be used to assess the performance of a filtering algorithm in Section 4. The conclusion of this study is finally drawn in Section 5.

2   Impulse Noise Models

Impulse noise model was initially defined for grayscale image and is characterized by very large positive and negative values corrupting an image value for a short duration; these short-lived noise introduces speckles to an image. Impulse noise will then result in black and white spots in an image, hence the name *salt-and-pepper* noise. This noise model has uniform probability density function, i.e. a random variable R is independent and identically distributed over the image.

2.1   Salt-and-Pepper Noise

By definition there are two different models of salt-and-pepper noise, i.e. fixed and randomized noise signals [7]. In the case of grayscale image, fixed noise signals means that noise signals will be of value 0 or 1, while randomized signals

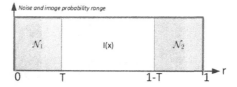

Fig. 1. The probability range of an image value being disturbed by an impulse

means that its value will lie between $[0, 1]$. The randomized approach has been used to extend this noise model to color image domain. In color image, impulse noise is modeled by randomly and independently generating the impulse in each color channel [4,9], causing the occurrences of false colored pixels. In other words, the extension of impulse noise to color image takes a marginal approach. To extend this model to spectral images, we choose to use a fixed signals approach rather than the randomized one. Two spectra $\mathcal{N}_1$ and $\mathcal{N}_2$ that are randomly generated will be used as noise signals corrupting an image value.

$$\mathcal{N}_k = \{s_i = y, i \subset [1, n_c], y \subset [0, 1]\} \tag{1}$$

As mentioned previously, this noise model has a uniform probability density function, see Fig. 1. The probability of having either $\mathcal{N}_1$ or $\mathcal{N}_2$ disturbing an image value is identical, i.e. $T_1 = 1 - T_2 = T$. Consequently, the probability of having an image value corrupted by impulse signals is $2T$. Finally, an image in the presence of impulse noise is classically described as follows:

$$\tilde{I}(x) = I(x) + \mathcal{H}\Big(T - r\Big)\Big(\mathcal{N}_1 - I(x)\Big) + \mathcal{H}\Big(r - 1 + T\Big)\Big(\mathcal{N}_2 - I(x)\Big) \tag{2}$$

2.2 Spectral Impulse Noise

Extending the construction of impulse noise to spectral images, especially hyperspectral image, induces a question whether the model is suitable for these images. Hyperspectral acquisition captures the physical composition of scenes or objects. The imaging system is calibrated and the acquired image is given after several corrections, e.g. radiometric, geometric, etc. Nevertheless, impulse noise is ubiquitous [10]. The origin of impulse signals in hyperspectral images might then be due to physical variations of the object itself or factors that affect photons arriving on the sensor.

Knowing that the impulse signals mostly originate from factors that happen before the sensor, it should rather be considered as spectral variations as opposed to spectral noise. Image examples in Fig. 2 show that variations that appear in uniform regions vary from the initial color by certain hues and magnitudes. With this consideration, we define a spectral impulse noise model that is not only a mathematical model but is also integrating the physical aspects of data by using a dataset of real impulse signals, where the noise signals $\mathcal{N}_1$ and $\mathcal{N}_2$ can be obtained by defining local constraints on the uniform regions.

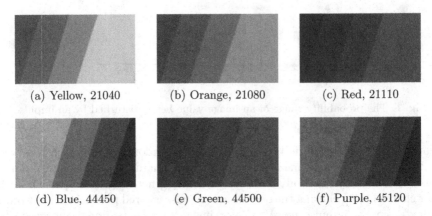

(a) Yellow, 21040   (b) Orange, 21080   (c) Red, 21110

(d) Blue, 44450   (e) Green, 44500   (f) Purple, 45120

Fig. 2. Pigment patches of several different color hues. In addition to having several hues, each of the hues are given in four different saturations.

The construction of dataset of real impulse signals is as follows. Given a uniform region of N_P pixels, in which the uniformity is defined as satisfying certain external criteria, we extract all the spectra within this uniform region forming a set of spectra $\mathfrak{S}$. For a specific uniform region, a subset of furthest spectra from the average spectrum is extracted, see Eq. 5 where c allows to reduce the subset size. Then, the candidate impulse signals are the two furthest signals obtained from within the subset, see Eq. 6.

$$\overline{S} = \frac{1}{N_P} \sum_{i=1}^{N_P} S_i \tag{3}$$

$$\mu_d = \frac{1}{N_P} \sum_{i=1}^{N_P} d(S_i, \overline{S}), \; \sigma_d = \sqrt{\frac{1}{N_P} \sum_{i=1}^{N_P} \left(d(S_i, \overline{S}) - \mu_d \right)^2} \tag{4}$$

$$\mathfrak{S}_n = \{S_i : d(S_i, \overline{S}) \geq (\mu_d + c \cdot \sigma_d), S_i \in \mathfrak{S}\} \tag{5}$$

$$(\mathcal{N}_1, \mathcal{N}_2) = \{ \underset{\forall (S_i, S_j) \in \mathfrak{S}_n^2}{\arg\max} \; d(S_i, S_j)\} \tag{6}$$

3 Experimental Study and Discussion

More than 50 pigment patches of different hues were acquired using a pushbroom hyperspectral scanner HySpex [1]. This hyperspectral scanner provides data with 160 spectral bands in the range of 414.2 to 993.7 nm, in 3.6 nm interval. Some of the acquired images are shown in Fig. 2. In addition to hue variations, each patch comes with four different saturation levels. Spatial regions or pixels having the same hue and saturation level are defined as uniform region; further on, this

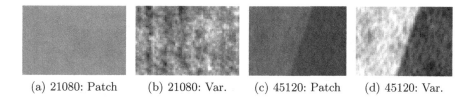

(a) 21080: Patch   (b) 21080: Var.   (c) 45120: Patch   (d) 45120: Var.

Fig. 3. Cutouts of two pigment patches, showing variations in regions that are nevertheless defined as uniform regions

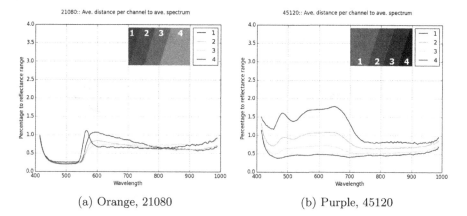

(a) Orange, 21080   (b) Purple, 45120

Fig. 4. Average spectral variations in original image computed channel-by-channel to the average spectrum for each pigment shade

uniform region will be referred to as *pigment shade*. Using the pigment patches we are able to obtain the dataset of impulse signals using the model explained in Section 2.2, as the patches provide us with uniform regions. Two impulse noise spectra $\mathcal{N}_1^k$ and $\mathcal{N}_2^k$ are therefore defined for each uniform region $\mathcal{R}^k$. With this noise generation, we are able to construct both ground truth and noisy target images required by full-reference image quality assessment in order to estimate the performance of spectral image processing algorithms.

3.1   Spectral Variations in Uniform Regions

By saying that each of the pigment shades is a uniform region, we are making a hypothesis that these regions are not textured. And consequently, spectral variations originating from physical composition of the materials, e.g. surface thickness and pigment density variations, are unwanted. The aforementioned variations can be observed in more details for several pigment patches in Fig. 3.

To investigate the distribution of spectral variations that exist in all pigment patches, we compute an average spectrum for each pigment shade giving four

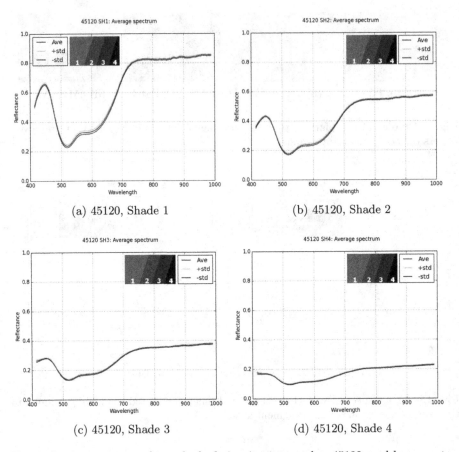

Fig. 5. Average spectrum for each shade in pigment patches 45120, and how spectra within these shades vary around the average spectrum

average spectra for each pigment patch; pixels located around edges are not taken into account. Spectral variations for all pixels in the image are then computed relative to its corresponding average spectrum, in terms of average and standard deviation of channel-by-channel difference. The average difference of several pigment patches to its respective average spectrum is provided in Fig. 4. By the two examples, we can observe that there is a lack of correlation between the magnitude of spectral variations and the spectral structures which correspond to hue and saturation differences. In Fig. 5 we can observe the magnitude of unwanted spectral variations to average spectrum of pigment 45120.

From this observation it can be seen that the magnitude of spectral variations cannot be predicted easily. It is certainly not independent from the choice of color or pigment and does not correlate to saturation; not to mention many other factors that have not been taken into account. Finally this observation lead us to take another hypothesis, i.e. each pigment spectrum has its particular unwanted

Original   Salt-and-pepper   Spectral impulse

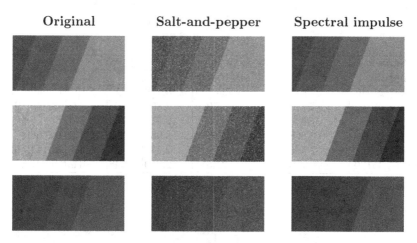

Fig. 6. Color images of several pigment patches acquired using a hyperspectral scanner and its corresponding artificial noisy images that are constructed using two impulse noise models with $T = 0.15$, i.e. salt-and-pepper and spectral impulse noise model.

spectral variations that are different from other spectra. Nevertheless, we can consider that between two spectra, the spectral variations can be interpolated knowing the nature of continuous world.

3.2 Artificially Noisy Pigment Patches

To obtain noisy spectral images required to evaluate the performance of spectral image processing algorithms, those that are with known properties and similar to real spectral images, the dataset of spectral impulse noise is used. We consider the proposed model described in Subsection 2.2 to be generic, although to this point it has only been investigated for water-based pigment that are applied to its substrate by screen-printing.

In Fig. 6 we can see the acquired images of several pigment patches and also its corresponding artificial target images. The target images were constructed using two models, i.e. salt-and-pepper and the proposed spectral impulse noise model, with probability threshold $T = 0.15$. Distortion measures relative to ground truth images are given for each pigment patch in Table 2. This table allows us to compare the distortion level of artificial target images constructed using the two different models. Salt-and-pepper model needs probability threshold $T < 0.05$ to have a similar distortion level to that of the acquired images. However, with such low amount of variations in a target image we will be unable to evaluate filtering performance, as the algorithm will perform the task perfectly. On the other hand with spectral impulse noise model, we can achieve a similar distortion level to that of the original image, i.e. with $T = [0.15, 0.2]$. Eventually by comparing the artificial target to acquired images, we can say that spectral impulse noise model is more realistic than salt-and-pepper.

Table 2. Distortion measures relative to ground truth images. The measures are given for originally acquired images and artificial target images constructed using salt-and-pepper and spectral impulse noise model. Values are given in unit of 10^{-3}.

Pigment patch	Original	Salt & pepper $T = 0.05$	Spectral impulse				
			$T = 0.05$	0.1	0.15	0.2	0.25
Yellow, 21040	7.884	25.814	3.279	6.212	8.885	11.349	13.441
Orange, 21080	7.776	27.076	2.356	4.405	6.338	8.046	9.627
Red, 21110	7.875	24.936	2.514	4.799	6.877	8.759	10.398
Blue, 44450	10.868	21.383	3.983	7.553	10.871	13.766	16.538
Green, 44500	7.565	23.917	2.333	4.467	6.418	8.144	9.745
Purple, 45120	8.789	21.615	2.810	5.348	7.645	9.701	11.667

Original	Impulse T=0.05	Impulse T=0.15

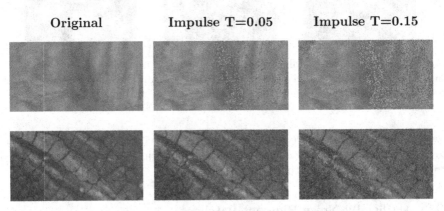

Fig. 7. Two cutouts taken from hyperspectral images of two different paintings. Original images are provided in the leftmost, and followed by the versions corrupted by impulse signals generated using spectral impulse noise model. The probability threshold are $T = 0.05, 0.15$.

3.3   More Examples

The use of the obtained dataset of spectral impulse noise is not limited to images containing uniform regions. In Fig. 7 we show several cutouts taken from hyperspectral images of different paintings. In the case of such images, a pixel that is corrupted by spectral impulse noise will be corrupted by an impulse signal that is taken from the dataset and has the most similarity to the original signal. However, as the number of colors are reduced to patches that are available in our database, a weak density is obtained in spectral space and consequently some color noise are not processed at a sufficient realistic level. Such case is illustrated in the green images shown in Fig. 7.

4   Application for Filtering Assessment

The main objective of this work on spectral noise model construction is to compare the performance of spectral image processing tools under controlled set-

Table 3. Distortion measure of several images before and after filtering process using Vector Median Filter embedding ECS distance. The corrupting impulse signals were generated with spectral impulse noise model and $T = 0.15$.

Pigment patch	Original		Salt & pepper		Spectral impulse	
	Before	After	Before	After	Before	After
Yellow, 21040	7.884	6.786	69.306	2.427	8.885	0.919
Orange, 21080	7.776	6.611	71.901	2.590	6.338	0.709
Red, 21110	7.875	7.028	72.849	1.524	6.877	0.509
Blue, 44450	10.868	7.835	58.291	2.582	10.871	0.522
Green, 44500	7.565	6.271	62.197	1.205	6.418	0.488
Purple, 45120	8.789	6.657	62.428	2.251	7.645	0.621

tings. Therefore in this section, we provide an application of the noise model construction on the assessment of spectral filtering performance. Vector Median Filter (VMF) by Astola et al. [3] is a median filtering algorithm suitable for multivariate data; its performance in the removal of impulse noise has been proven theoretically and numerically. We will use the artificial target images that have been constructed in Section 3.2 as filtering input; the ground truth is averaged image of the corresponding pigment patch.

In Table 3 distortion measures of several images before and after VMF are provided. For the original spectral images, VMF does not result in large modifications. VMF is effective for removing uniformly distributed impulse signals, while the distribution of variations in these images is certainly not uniform, for example see Fig. 3. Thus, VMF is not able to modify further the initial content of the images. When target images are corrupted with salt-and-pepper noise ($T = 0.15$), the initial distortion values are increased with ratio of ≈ 10. Nevertheless, the filtering impact allows to obtain images with reduced distortions compared to their corresponding original images, i.e. ratio of ≈ 20. In the case of the proposed spectral impulse noise model, the initial distortion measure is similar from the original real spectral images and the filtering process is able to reduce it with ratio of ≈ 9. Finally, the proposed spectral impulse noise model modifies the initial local statistics of the images, i.e. 30% of pixels in a local neighborhood are corrupted when $T = 0.15$, and thus simplifies the filtering process of the images as shown by the corresponding distortion measures for the original/ corrupted and filtered images.

5   Conclusion

Having a realistic model of spectral noise is crucial in order to assess the performance of spectral image processing tools. We have shown that theoretical models without inter-channel correlations are not suitable to model spectral noise, as theoretical models provide us with unrealistic aspect and behavior of spectral data. In this work we proposed a suitable spectral noise model using spectral database of uniform color/ pigment patches, which answers the challenge of identifying spectral noise model. This noise construction allows to produce realistic model that is suitable for the assessment of spectral filtering algorithms performances. The limitation of this model is due to the reduced number of uniform color patches that are available in our database. However, by adding more color patches into the database such limit can be overcome and will eventually enable us to produce more complex spectral noise.

Acknowledgments. Authors would like to thank Norsk Elektro Optikk AS (NEO) for providing the hyperspectral scanner HySpex and the hyperspectral images of uniform pigment patches.

References

1. Norsk Elektro Optikk AS: HySpex. http://www.neo.no/hyspex/
2. Alajlan, N., Jernigan, E.: An effective detail preserving filter for impulse noise removal. In: Campilho, A.C., Kamel, M.S. (eds.) ICIAR 2004. LNCS, vol. 3211, pp. 139–146. Springer, Heidelberg (2004)
3. Astola, J., Haavisto, P., Neuvo, Y.: Vector median filters. Proceedings of the IEEE **78**(4), 678–689 (1990)
4. Bar, L., Brook, A., Sochen, N., Kiryati, N.: Color image deblurring with impulsive noise. In: Paragios, N., Faugeras, O., Chan, T., Schnörr, C. (eds.) VLSM 2005. LNCS, vol. 3752, pp. 49–60. Springer, Heidelberg (2005)
5. Celebi, M.E., Kingravi, H.A., Aslandogan, Y.A.: Nonlinear vector filtering for impulsive noise removal from color images. Journal of Electronic Imaging **16**(3), 033008-1–033008-21 (2007)
6. Chan, R., Ho, C.W., Nikolova, M.: Salt-and-pepper noise removal by median-type noise detectors and detail-preserving regularization. IEEE Transactions on Image Processing **14**(10), 1479–1485 (2005)
7. Justusson, B.J.: Median filtering: Statistical properties. Two Dimensional Digital Signal Processing **2**, 161–196 (1981)
8. Kober, V., Mozerov, M., Álvarez-Borrego, J.: Automatic removal of impulse noise from highly corrupted images. In: Sanfeliu, A., Cortés, M.L. (eds.) CIARP 2005. LNCS, vol. 3773, pp. 34–41. Springer, Heidelberg (2005)
9. Nair, M.S., Revathy, K., Tatavarti, R.: Removal of salt-and pepper noise in images: a new decision-based algorithm. In: Proceedings of the International MultiConference of Engineers and Computer Scientists (IMECS) I, pp. 19–21 (2008)
10. Nowicki, K.J., Edwards, C.S., Christensen, P.R.: Removal of salt-and-pepper noise in THEMIS infrared radiance and emissivity spectral data of the martian surface. IEEE-Whispers Transactions (2013, in press)

Evaluation of the Colorimetric Performance of Single-Sensor Image Acquisition Systems Employing Colour and Multispectral Filter Array

Xingbo Wang[1,2]($\boxtimes$), Philip J. Green[1], Jean-Baptiste Thomas[2],
Jon Y. Hardeberg[1], and Pierre Gouton[2]

[1] Norwegian Colour and Visual Computing Laboratory,
Gjøvik University College, 2815 Gjøvik, Norway
xingbo.wang@hig.no
http://www.colourlab.no, http://www.springer.com/lncs
[2] Laboratoire Electronique, Informatique et Image,
Université de Bourgogne, Dijon, France
http://le2i.cnrs.fr

Abstract. Single-sensor colour imaging systems mostly employ a colour filter array (CFA). This enables the acquisition of a colour image by a single sensor at one exposure at the cost of reduced spatial resolution. The idea of CFA fit itself well with multispectral purposes by incorporating more than three types of filters into the array which results in multispectral filter array (MSFA). In comparison with a CFA, an MSFA trades spatial resolution for spectral resolution. A simulation was performed to evaluate the colorimetric performance of such CFA/MSFA imaging systems and investigate the trade-off between spatial resolution and spectral resolution by comparing CFA and MSFA systems utilising various filter characteristics and demosaicking methods including intra- and inter-channel bilinear interpolation as well as discrete wavelet transformed based techniques. In general, 4-band and 8-band MSFAs provide better or comparable performance than the CFA setup in terms of CIEDE2000 and S-CIELAB colour difference. This indicates that MSFA would be favourable for colorimetric purposes.

Keywords: Colorimetric performance · Colour filter array · Multispectral imaging · Single-sensor

1 Introduction

Single-sensor trichromatic imaging systems mostly employ a colour filter array (CFA) in order to sense a portion of the incoming spectra selectively on a pixel-by-pixel basis. An example of CFA that has achieved commercially notable success is known as Bayer filter mosaic consisting of three types of filters, i.e., red,

A. Trémeau et al. (Eds.): CCIW 2015, LNCS 9016, pp. 181–191, 2015.
DOI: 10.1007/978-3-319-15979-9_18

blue and green [2], as shown in Figure 1. Thanks to the spatial and spectral inter-pixel correlation an image may possess, the lost information about the incident stimuli can be estimated through demosaicking. Demosaicking is an operation in the image processing chain carried out on the mosaicked image read from the sensor. Consequently each pixel will comprise three components, thereby recovering a full colour image. The success gained by the CFA based single-sensor colour imaging systems has awakened particular interest from the academia and the industries in generalise this concept to the multispectral domain by integrating more than three types of filters into one filter array, which results in the multispectral filter array (MSFA). Two instances of MSFAs can be seen in Figure 2 and 3.

Fig. 1. Bayer CFA   **Fig. 2.** 4-band MSFA   **Fig. 3.** 8-band MSFA

In general, the development of a MSFA based imaging system involves design of filter transmittances, spatial arrangement of mosaic patterns paired with an associated demosaicking algorithm, and a regression process to recover colorimetric or spectral information.

In recent years, sustained research effort went into designing multispectral filter array (MSFA) [15] and developing associated demosaicking algorithms [1,3, 14,16,17,21,22]. Also widely explored is the influence of filter characteristics on colour/spectrum reproduction [9,19,23,24]. Nevertheless, to our best knowledge, little is known about how filter design and demosaicking algorithms affect the colorimetric performance of a CFA and particularly MSFA image acquisition system.

In comparison with CFAs, MSFAs populate higher number of channels, thus reducing the number of pixels assigned to a certain channel for a given sensor. Obviously this lowers spatial resolution, however MSFA may offer higher spectral resolution. While the former effect generally lowers the colorimetric performance of the system, the latter should improve the accuracy of colour reproduction. It is therefore of particular interest to evaluate the colorimetric performance of such MSFA imaging systems and investigate the trade-off between spatial resolution and spectral resolution by comparing CFA and MSFA systems utilising various filter characteristics and demosaicking methods.

The following sections of the paper are organised as follows. We first present the methods used including the simulated framework illustrated in Section 2.1, the filter design strategy described in Section 2.2, the mosaic generation demonstrated in Section 2.3, the demosaicking algorithms introduced in Section 2.4, the colour and spectral reflectance estimation method for device calibration presented in Section 2.5, the evaluation means explained in Section 2.6 and the experimental conditions listed in Section 2.7. Results are shown in Section 3 that leads to reasonable conclusions drawn in Section 4.

2 Methods

2.1 Simulated Framework

A simulated workflow was constructed so as to conduct the research due to practical difficulties in physical implementation of the MSFAs [12]. As shown in Figure 4, the framework consists of a chain of processing that starts from the hyperspectral images used as virtual optical images. A MSFA mounted sensor is merely a combination of the filter array and the image sensor, and the mosaicked optical image is therefore formed in between. As a result, a hyperspectral image can be considered as a spectrally sampled optical image which will then be spectrally filtered and spatially interleaved by the filter array. In this manner, the process of mosaicking is simulated.

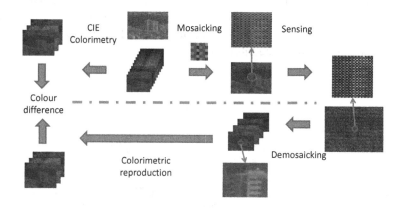

Fig. 4. The experimental framework

Next, an ideal image sensor populating the same number of pixels as the images integrates the incident power at each pixel over the spectrum. Quantum efficiency of the sensor is integrated with the spectral transmittance of filters, so that filter characteristics referred to in this work represent sensor sensitivities. And neither optical crosstalk nor optical/electronic noise is considered in this work.

Mosaic image, namely the sensor output, is actually a digital representation of a spatially or spectrally subsampled and interleaved trichromatic or multispectral image. Therefore, it needs to be interpolated spatially and/or spectrally, in order to recover the information lost in the mosaicking process. In other words, interpolation yields a colour or multispectral image of full spatial resolution.

At this stage, the recovered image is not colorimetrically meaningful as the digital counts have not been assigned any physical meaning. This is addressed by device colour calibration. It first models the device by associating stimuli with known colorimetric characteristics and the corresponding sensor response, and later estimates original colorimetric information of the unknown stimuli from the corresponding sensor response.

CIE tristimulus values are computed before colour difference between the original and reproduced hyperspectral images is calculated.

2.2   Filter Design in MSFA Systems

Among the derivatives of Bayer mosaic, some possess complementary colour filters in comparison to the primary colour filters utilised in the original patent [2].

Literature presents distinct results. It is obvious that complementary colour filters intrinsically bear wider pass-band than their primary counterparts, and it is widely accepted that the former gives rise to better colour reproduction and signal-to-noise ratio in sufficient lighting conditions, whereas the latter offers higher sensitivity as well as resolution [18,19]. Our results, nevertheless, show that appropriate pass-bands outperforms some narrower ones [23,24]. In addition, our previous research on multispectral demosaicking poses the question of filter design in relation to the inter-band correlation [21,22].

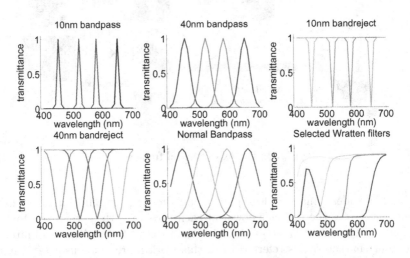

Fig. 5. Transmittances of a 4-band filter set

An instance of 4-band filter set used in this research is depicted in Figure 5. Following the aforementioned findings, we are interested in narrowband and broadband bandpass filters as well as corresponding inverted ones such as band-stop filters. The FWHM (Full Width at Half Maximum) of passband and stop-band have been set to 10 nm and 40 nm respectively. In practice, a passband of 10 nm simulates very narrow bandpass filters like LCTF (Liquid Crystal Tunable Filter), a stopband of 10 nm mimics notch filters relying on destructive inter-ference. Similarly, a passband and a stopband of 40 nm resemble the spectral transmittances of thin-film filters.

In addition to the filters mentioned above, we introduced two more types. One is based on the principle that the transmittances of filters should sample the spectrum evenly with their FWHM. The other is in fact the result produced by a filter selection algorithm [7] that chooses a given number of optimal(or sub-optimal) filters from a set of available candidates that are physically practicable, on the assumption that high spectral performance is yielded by the "brightest" filter that transmits the most light combined with other filters which are orthog-onal to each other in a vector space. Here we employ a set of transmittance data measured from Wratten filters produced by Kodak, as shown in Figure 6.

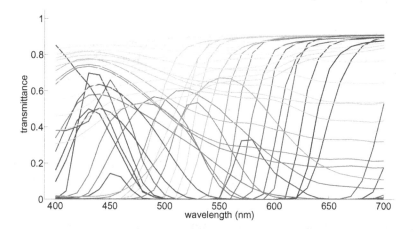

Fig. 6. Transmittances of a set of Wratten filters

2.3   Mosaic Pattern Generation

Filter arrays experimented with in this project were designed with the help of a generic binary tree based generation method of MSFA spatial arrangement start-ing from a chequerboard pattern introduced by Miao *et al.* [15]. By manipulating the pattern through a combination of decomposition and subsampling steps, the method presented may generate MSFAs that satisfy varied design requirements proposed by the authors including probability of appearance, spectral consis-tency and uniform distribution. It is shown, through case studies, that most of the CFAs currently used by the industry can be derived as special cases.

2.4   MSFA Demosaicking

A large number of CFA demosaicking algorithms have been proposed over the decades [13]. In this work, we used intra-channel bilinear interpolation, channel difference bilinear interpolation [11] and discrete wavelet transform (DWT) based demosaicking [5].

Bilinear interpolation makes use of merely intra-pixel correlation and estimates unknown colour components by exploiting the spatial correlation between sampled colours in a certain spectral plane, and function plane by plane.

Channel difference interpolation brings inter-channel correlation into play and interpolates the difference between one colour plane and another [11] on the assumption that hue changes smoothly in images.

DWT transforms an image into various frequency bands, and natural images often possess rather similar high-frequency information among these bands, which provides yet another solution to demosaicking problem. This algorithm has been extended to a 4-band MSFA as reported in the literature [22].

2.5   Device Calibration

Colour calibration is an inverse problem aimed at an estimation of the tristimulus values of the stimuli from the corresponding measurements obtained from sensors. In concrete terms, a colour acquisition process can be described in a linear form as

$$R = QS \tag{1}$$

where R refers to the sensor responses, Q corresponds to system responsivities and S represents the incoming stimuli.

Colour calibration aims at an estimation of S from R. Equation 1 is solvable if Q is known and invertible, however it is not true in the case of colorimetric calibration. Nevertheless it can be estimated by means of training where a collection of training stimuli S_t and corresponding responses R_t are utilised to derive an approximation of Q^{-1}. In this work, we employed the method of linear least squares [8] which attempts to solve (1) by means of pseudoinverse which leads to (2)

$$S' = S_t R_t^+ R \tag{2}$$

where S' is an estimation of S and R_t^+ is a right pseudoinverse of R_t : $R_t^+ = R_t^T (R_t R_t^T)^{-1}$.

2.6   Performance Evaluation

An evaluation of the colorimetric performance of CFA and MSFA based imaging systems can be solved by means of colour difference formula. However, considering that the targets are digital images rather than uniform colour patches, a metric incorporating some low-level HVS features, such as S-CIELAB, might be suitable as well and may provide more information.

CIEDE2000 is the latest colour difference formula developed and recommended by the CIE [4]. It further improves perceptual uniformity in comparison with the CIE94 formula by introducing a few revised compensation terms for lightness, chroma and hue respectively. In addition, there are three corresponding parameters that are usually set to 1:1:1 and can be adjusted according to specific applications. For instance, CIE recommended 2:1:1 for textile industry. In this work, we used 2:2:1 to evaluate image colour difference.

The S-CIELAB metric extends the CIELAB Delta E metric to colour images by adding a spatial pre-processing step to the standard CIE $\Delta E_{a^*b^*}$ metric to account for the spatial-colour sensitivity of the human eye [26]. It measures how accurate the reproduction of a colour is to the original when viewed by a human observer.

2.7   Experimental Conditions

The experiments were conducted in such conditions as follows. Spectral range covers the spectrum between 400 nm and 700 nm with 10 nm interval. CIE D65 was used as the illuminant. Among the 48 hyperspectral images used as virtual scenes, 16 are from Foster database [6] and 32 are from CAVE database [25]. Three types of MSFA were considered, namely 3-band CFA, 4-band and 8-band. For the least-square regression, 170 spectral reflectances of natural objects [20] and the corresponding CIE XYZ tristimulus values were utilised as the training targets. Tristimulus values were calculated with colour-matching functions for the CIE 1931 standard colorimetric observer [10]. For the calculation of S-CIELAB colour difference, the viewing distance was set to 60 cm, and the resolution was set to 95.78 dpi, so as to mimic a 23-inch LCD monitor of 1920×1080 pixels and an aspect ratio of 16:9.

3   Results and Discussion

Results are presented in Figure 7 and 8. It is of great moment to realise that the colour difference shown here reflect the overall performance of the system consisting of filter characteristics, spatial arrangements, demosaicking methods as well as colour estimation techniques. However, a comparative analysis of the results reveal some clues.

From the results we can observe that increased number of bands in general offer lower or comparable colour difference especially when paired with 10 nm and 40 nm bandpass filters and a selected range of Wratten filters. In particular, the 40 nm bandpass filters result in the lowest colour difference among all of the methods and configurations, whereas the 10 nm bandstop filters yield significantly larger errors.

In general, the DWT based demosaicking outperforms the other two where the widths of passband are significantly broader, whereas bilinear interpolation

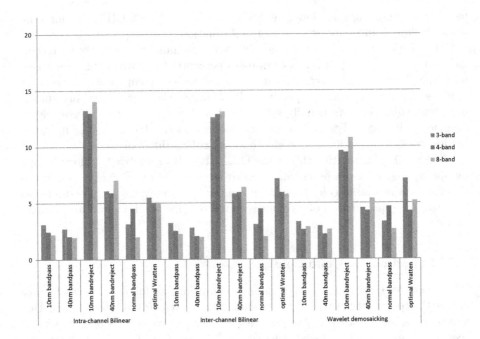

Fig. 7. Average CIEDE2000 colour difference among test images

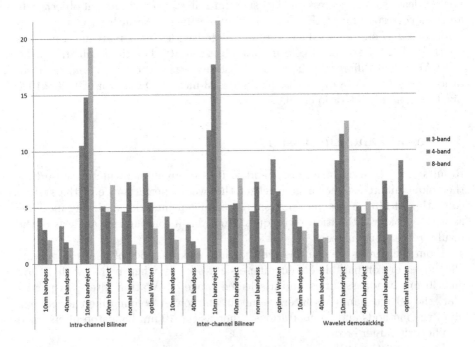

Fig. 8. Average S-CIELAB colour difference among test imags

carried out on channel differences does not perform satisfactorily. This is also related to insufficient high-frequency components in the image databases [22], as inter-channel demosaicking should benefit from inter-channel correlation at high frequencies and broader passbands may boost this correlation.

In most cases S-CIELAB results coincide with CIE DE2000 ones, although the former tends to exaggerate the discrepancy of the results between the CFA and the MSFAs.

4   Conclusion

A simulation was performed to investigate the colorimetric performance of MSFA based image acquisition systems. In total, 48 virtual scenes were captured by the simulated camera for 3-band, 4-band and 8-band MSFAs respectively, each paired with 6 different types of filter characteristics and 3 demosaicking algorithms. Results were all transformed to CIE XYZ tristimulus values and evaluated with CIEDE2000 (2:2:1) and S-CIELAB colour difference. CIEDE2000 and S-CIELAB results coincide in most cases. In general, the 4-band MSFA provides better or comparable performance in comparison with the 3-band setup except the case of 10 nm bandreject and normal bandpass filters. Similarly the 8-band MSFA delivers higher colour accuracy expect the case of 10 nm and 40 nm bandreject filters. Therefore MSFA is generaly helpful for an application where colorimetric reproduction is required.

Moreover, it is obvious to see that spectral characteristics of a filter set not only make a direct impact on the colour reconstruction, but also influence the spectral correlation of the observed image on which some demosaicking methods depend.

Certainly the validity of the results obtained in this work is limited by the realisticness of the simulation. In a real system, the presence of various types of noise will probably impact the results. However, this laid a foundation for the design of a new MSFA sensor planned in 2015 [12].

References

1. Baone, G.A., Qi, H.: Demosaicking methods for multispectral cameras using mosaic focal plane array technology. In: Proc. SPIE, vol. 6062, January 2006
2. Bayer, B.E.: Color imaging array. Patent, uS 3971065 (07 1976)
3. Brauers, J., Aach, T.: A color filter array based multispectral camera. In: Group, G.C. (ed.) 12th Workshop Farbbildverarbeitung. Ilmenau, October 5–6, 2006
4. Colorimetry - Part 6: CIEDE2000 Colour-Difference Formula. No. CIE Draft Standard DS 014–6/E:2012. CIE, Vienna, Austria (2012)
5. Driesen, J., Scheunders, P.: Wavelet-based color filter array demosaicking. In: International Conference on Image Processing (ICIP), vol. 5, pp. 3311–3314. IEEE, October 2004
6. Foster, D.H., Amano, K., Nascimento, S.M.C., Foster, M.J.: Frequency of metamerism in natural scenes. J. Opt. Soc. Am. A **23**(10), 2359–2372 (2006)

7. Hardeberg, J.Y.: Acquisition and Reproduction of Color Images: Colorimetric and Multispectral Approaches. dissertation.com (2001)
8. Hironaga, M., Shimano, N.: Estimating the noise variance in an image acquisition system and its influence on the accuracy of recovered spectral reflectances. Appl. Opt. **49**(31), 6140–6148 (November 2010)
9. Imai, F.H., Rosen, M.R., Berns, R.S.: Comparison of spectrally narrow-band capture versus wide-band with a priori sample analysis for spectral reflectance estimation. In: Proceedings of the IS&T/SID Eighth Color Imaging Conference: Color Science and Engineering Systems, Technologies, and Applications, pp. 234–241. IS&T, Scottsdale, Arizona, November 2000
10. CIE Colorimetry - Part 1: Standard Colorimetric Observers. No. ISO 11664-1:2007(E)/CIE S 014-1/E:2006. ISO, Geneva, Switzerland (2007)
11. Adams, J.E.: Interactions between color plane interpolation and other image processing functions in electronic photography. SPIE **2416**, 144–151 (1995)
12. Lapray, P.J., Wang, X., Thomas, J.B., Gouton, P.: Multispectral filter arrays: Recent advances and practical implementation. Sensors **14**(11), 21626–21659 (2014)
13. Menon, D., Calvagno, G.: Color image demosaicking: An overview. Image Commun. **26**(8–9), 518–533 (October 2011)
14. Miao, L., Qi, H., Ramanath, R.: A generic binary tree-based progressive demosaicking method for multispectral filter array. In: IEEE International Conference on Image Processing, pp. 3221–3224 (October 2006)
15. Miao, L., Qi, H., Snyder, W.E.: A generic method for generating multispectral filter arrays. In: International Conference on Image Processing, vol. 5, pp. 3343–3346, October 2004
16. Monno, Y., Tanaka, M., Okutomi, M.: Multispectral demosaicking using adaptive kernel upsampling. In: 18th IEEE International Conference on Image Processing (ICIP), Brussels, pp. 3157–3160, September 2011
17. Monno, Y., Tanakaa, M., Okutomia, M.: Multispectral demosaicking using guided filter. In: Battiato, S., Rodricks, B.G., Sampat, N., Imai, F.H., Xiao, F. (eds.) Digital Photography VIII. Proc. of SPIE, vol. 8299, Burlingame, California, USA, pp. 82990O–82990O-7, January 2012
18. Panasonic: Primary color and complementary color filters. http://panasonic.jp/support/global/cs/dsc/knowhow/knowhow29.html (retrieved on December 16, 2013)
19. Parulski, K.A.: Color filters and processing alternatives for one-chip cameras. IEEE Transactions on Electron Devices **32**(8), 1381–1389 (1985)
20. Vrhel, M.J., Gershon, R., Iwan, L.S.: Measurement and analysis of object reflectance spectra. Color Research & Application **19**(1), 4–9 (1994)
21. Wang, X., Thomas, J.B., Hardeberg, J.Y., Gouton, P.: Median filtering in multispectral filter array demosaicking. In: Digital Photography IX. Proc. SPIE, vol. 8660
22. Wang, X., Thomas, J.B., Hardeberg, J.Y., Gouton, P.: Discrete wavelet transform based multispectral filter array demosaicking. In: Proc. Colour and Visual Computing Symposium (CVCS), pp. 1–6, September 2013
23. Wang, X., Thomas, J.B., Hardeberg, J.Y., Gouton, P.: A study on the impact of spectral characteristics of filters on multispectral image acquisition. In: Proc. 12th AIC Congress. AIC, July 2013
24. Wang, X., Thomas, J.B., Hardeberg, J.Y., Gouton, P.: Multispectral imaging: narrow or wide band filters? Journal of the International Colour Association **12** (July 2014)

25. Yasuma, F., Mitsunaga, T., Iso, D., Nayar, S.K.: Generalized assorted pixel camera: Post-capture control of resolution, dynamic range and spectrum. Tech. rep., Department of Computer Science, Columbia University CUCS-061-08, November 2008. http://www1.cs.columbia.edu/CAVE/databases/multispectral/
26. Zhang, X., Wandell, B.A.: A spatial extension of cielab for digital color-image reproduction. Journal of the Society for Information Display **5**(1), 61–63 (1997)

Color in Digital Cultural Heritage

High-Resolution Multispectral Scanning for Mesoscopic Investigation of Discoloration of Traditional Japanese Pigments

Jay Arre Toque[1]([✉]), Pengchang Zhang[2], Peng Wang[2], and Ari Ide-Ektessabi[2]

[1] Sabia Inc., Tamatushima-cho, Shimogyo-ku, Kyoto 600-8427, Japan
jayarre81@gmail.com
[2] Graduate School of Engineering,
Kyoto University Katsura Campus, Kyoto, Japan
{pengchang.zhang,wpwp1000}@gmail.com ide.ari.4n@kyoto-u.ac.jp

Abstract. This study describes a non-invasive analytical imaging scanning technique utilizing multispectral images to study discoloration and degradation of pigments used in traditional Japanese artworks. The images have high spatial resolution which can achieve mesoscopic resolution (typically 0.1mm-10mm). Since the images are being scanned line by line instead of being recorded frame by frame, this enables accurate color and spectral recording of the material response from visible and near infrared irradiation. The multispectral images were used to reconstruct color information and spectral reflectance. The mathematical model is based on the Moore-Penrose pseudoinverse. Using mesoscopically resolvable images, it is possible to measure the spectral reflectance of pigments ranging from μm-mm ROI unlike conventional spectrometers that requires big sampling area. The significance of mesoscopically-resolved analysis is demonstrated by investigating the discoloration and degradation of natural and artificial Japanese pigments. The pigments were heated in air at 300°C and sampled every 10 minutes. It was observed that the pigments discolored at seemingly random clusters. The reconstruction of the spectral reflectance at different sizes of ROI reveals strong correlation with background reflection. The size of the initial discoloration sites makes it impossible to measure using conventional spectrometers. It was observed that by using sub-mm ROI, it is possible to observe reflection and absorption patterns in the pigments which does not register with mm-scale ROI. The results have shown that mesoscopically resolvable multispectral images can be used effectively to study degradation and discoloration in pigments.

Keywords: Analytical imaging · Spectral reflectance · Mesoscopic · Multispectral · Japanese pigments

1 Introduction

Noninvasive and nondestructive analysis is important in the field of cultural heritage [1-3]. This is particularly significant since they are irreplaceable treasures which are in the making over centuries and even millennia. As a result, a lot of effort has been

© Springer International Publishing Switzerland 2015
A. Trémeau et al. (Eds.): CCIW 2015, LNCS 9016, pp. 195–207, 2015.
DOI: 10.1007/978-3-319-15979-9_19

given to the preservation, conservation and investigation of these objects. However, there is always conflict between conservators and investigators. On the one hand, conservators wants to preserve the integrity of the object by minimizing its exposure to damaging conditions such as prolonged exposure to uncontrolled humidity and temperature as well as unsafe ambient light. This meant that a lot of these precious artifacts are locked in a safe place never seeing the light of day. On the other hand, investigators could become overzealous in documenting and acquiring as much information as possible without so much regard on the integrity of the object. This is justified by saying that deterioration is inevitable no matter how careful the objects are stored. Objects are still deteriorating even if it is kept in a controlled storage and not exposed to any harmful environment. Therefore this could warrant the argument for recording the state of the object before it is completely destroyed. Both arguments have merits but in the end, these cultural treasures belong to the world; not to the museum that is keeping them or the researchers that study them. Therefore there is need for an accurate but safe technique for investigating cultural treasures.

The most common analytical technique used for investigating cultural heritage is either based on X-ray or infrared radiation [4-13]. Some of the common techniques in art analysis are synchrotron radiation X-ray fluorescence (XRF) [4-7], X-ray absorption fine structure (XAFS) [7], X-ray absorption near edge structure (XANES) [8], x-ray diffraction (XRD) [9-10], particle induced x-ray emission (PIXE) [11], neutron diffraction [10], laser induced breakdown spectroscopy (LIBS) [12], Fourier transform infrared spectroscopy (FTIR) [8], Raman spectroscopy [13] and many more others. Visible light radiation is also used but mostly for qualitative analysis and visualization. However, like other forms of electromagnetic radiation, the interaction of visible light with matter can be quantified. We refer to this as analytical imaging.

Analytical imaging refers to the technique which uses image processing, data mining and pattern recognition to extract useful and relevant information about different properties of a material. This is based on the fact that a material subjected to an incident electromagnetic radiation behaves in a predictable and quantifiable way. The characteristic material response depends on the energy and frequency of the radiation. In the past imaging only refers to the visible region but due to the developments in optical sensors, images can be formed with almost any electromagnetic spectrum. In this study, focus was given to the visible to near infrared range of the electromagnetic spectrum. This radiation spectrum provides useful information about pigment characteristics which are not readily observable in other spectrum [14]. The material response is quantified based on its spectral properties, colorimetric information and spatial features. It is believed that the most important aspect of an imaging system is the acquisition of the images. Especially, in art investigation, it is vital to have not only an accurate digital archive of the artwork but as well as being able to use it for analysis. Without an image that has reliable spectral, spatial and color information, it would remain to be usable only as a visual tool. Therefore there is a great need for the development and implementation of a nondestructive and noninvasive means of analytical imaging which is capable of acquiring uninterpolated high resolution images able to accommodate small- to large-sized objects. The images should have high color reproducibility, reliable spectral information and accurate spatial resolution. This is the reason why the analyses were performed multispectrally with mesoscopic resolutions.

The use of multispectral system for material analysis has been investigated in the past [15-18]; the advances in CMOS and CCD technologies have enabled the production of high quality images with good color reproduction; finally, spectrometer technologies are making strides in producing devices with high spectral resolutions. These three aspects are important in analytical imaging. Although these technologies have been around for quite some time, there are still limitations. As mentioned previously; color reproducibility, spectral accuracy and spatial resolution is important. With the previous multispectral imaging systems, they have high spectral accuracy but lack in good color reproduction and spatial resolution. The advanced imaging devices have high color fidelity but lacks readily usable spectral information. Conventional spectrometers could only produce accurate spectral data. In addition, there is a limitation in the spot size or the region of interest (ROI). Normally, the ROI is in the range of few millimeters to centimeters. This could affect the accuracy of the spectral data when analyzing sub-millimeter spots. This is why a system capable of extracting color and spectral information with mesoscopic resolution is important. Mesoscopic (~0.1mm-10mm) dimension refers to the resolution between macroscopic (>1cm) and microscopic (<100μm) scale.

Mesoscopic imaging has been widely used biology but is still considered in its infancy compared to microscopic and macroscopic techniques [19]. In cultural heritage investigation, it is almost unheard of. However, there are parallels that can be drawn between biological imaging and cultural heritage imaging. In biological imaging, there are living organisms that remain largely inaccessible by current optical imaging methods due to the limitation on depth resolution that can be achieved beyond several microns [20]. Similarly, pigment analysis in cultural heritage requires sub-mm resolution since discoloration and degradation occur on random spots. Without the capability of resolving the images mesoscopically, it is very easy to miss important information. To address this concern, an analytical imaging technique using mesoscopically-resolved images was used to analyze pigment discoloration and degradation patterns on selected Japanese mineral pigments.

The pigments were artificially degraded by heating at high temperatures (~300°C) and observed at short time lapses to investigate the structural, colorimetric and spectral changes *in situ* and noninvasively. The influence of the ROI size on the spectral measurement was discussed as well as its dependence on background reflection. Based on the results, there is a strong argument that high resolution multispectral imaging could be a very useful tool for cultural heritage investigations.

2   Methods and Experiments

2.1   Multispectral Imaging and Spectral Reflectance Reconstruction

The multispectral images were captured with a monochromatic CMOS line-camera using spectral-cutting and band-pass filters. A total of eight images were taken which contain spectral information from 380-850 nm. The images were used to reconstruct spectral data cubes with a 5-nm resolution. The spectral data were then used to reconstruct spectral reflectance and colorimetric information. Referring to the physical model shown in Fig. 1, it may be inferred that the sensor response of an imaging device when an object is irradiated with visible and near infrared radiation is proportional to its spectral reflectance. The sensor response, characterized by the image pixels, can be mathematically expressed as a function of the object's spectral reflectance, camera sensitivity, light source spectral radiance and system error. This is shown in Eq.1:

$$\mathbf{p} = \int \mathbf{C}(\lambda)L(\lambda)r(\lambda)d\lambda + \mathbf{e} \tag{1}$$

$\mathbf{p}$ is an M $\times$ 1 sensor response vector from the M channel sensor, $\mathbf{C}(\lambda)$ is an M $\times$ 1 vector of spectral sensitivity of the sensor, $L(\lambda)$ is the spectral radiance of the illumination, $r(\lambda)$ is the spectral reflectance of the object, and $\mathbf{e}$ is an M $\times$ 1 additive noise vector. For mathematical convenience, Eq.1 can also be expressed in vector form as follows:

$$\mathbf{p} = \mathbf{CLr} + \mathbf{e} \tag{2}$$

where $\mathbf{C}$ is an M $\times$ N matrix of spectral sensitivity of the sensor, $\mathbf{L}$ is an N $\times$ N diagonal matrix of spectral radiance of the light source, and $\mathbf{r}$ is an N $\times$ 1 spectral reflectance vector of the target. In this study, an indirect method of solving the vector relationship between the sensor response and spectral reflectance is implemented. The technique is based on Moore-Penrose pseudoinverse. The vector relationship is solved without the prior knowledge of the spectral characteristics of the system by using a learning sample. The learning sample can be used to estimate a conversion matrix to approximate the camera and light source spectral characteristics without having to worry about systemic changes. This makes the method device independent.

Since the samples characterized in this study are Japanese pigments, a specially designed and selected palette of Japanese organic and inorganic mineral pigments was used as the learning sample. The learning sample is composed of 173 pigments. They represent a wide variety of pigments including natural and artificial; organic and inorganic; ancient and modern; and a broad spectrum of colors with distinct spectral sensitivities at the infrared region. These learning samples are used to estimate the spectral reflectance. Going back to Eq. 2, it can be rewritten as,

$$\mathbf{p} = H\mathbf{r} \tag{3}$$

where H represents the camera and light source spectral characteristics and $\mathbf{e}$ is omitted for simplicity. H in this case represents an M x N matrix with M being the number of spectral channels and N as the number of spectral interval covering the desired spectral range. The pseudoinverse model is a modification of the Wiener estimation by regression analysis [14]. In this model, a matrix W is derived by minimizing $\|R - WP\|$ from a known spectral reflectance of a learning sample, R, and the corresponding pixel values, P, captured at a certain spectral band. The matrix W is given by Eq.4:

$$W = RP^{+} = RP^{t}(PP^{t})^{-1} \tag{4}$$

Where P^+ represents the pseudoinverse matrix of P. By multiplying the derived matrix W to the pixel value of the target image, $\mathbf{p}$, the spectral reflectance $\hat{\mathbf{r}}$ can be estimated using Eq.5:

$$\hat{\mathbf{r}} = W\mathbf{p} \qquad (5)$$

The size of the matrices used in Eq.4 and Eq.5 is a function of the number of learning sample k, number of multispectral bands M and number of spectral reflectances N. In this study, the value of M and N depends on the spectral range and number of filters used. The number of filters used is $M=8$ while N is either 95 for the 5-nm interval spectral reconstruction between 380-850 nm. The images were taken at 600 dpi (~42 μm/pixel). Since the images have high spatial and spectral resolution, the ROI for spectral reflectance reconstruction is reliable up to pixel level. This enables spectral measurement at spatial resolutions which are not possible with conventional spectrometers. The effect of the ROI size is investigated by reconstructing the spectral reflectance of the discolored Japanese pigments.

2.2   Pigment Discoloration and Characterization

In this study, a method for investigating pigment discoloration and degradation mesoscopically is described. This was achieved by taking an accurate recording of discoloration as it happens *in situ* using high resolution multispectral imaging and spectral reflectance reconstruction. There are two groups of pigments selected as test cases. All pigments are in powder form. The first group is composed of copper-based pigments such as malachite and azurite. The second group includes iron-based pigments specifically hematite and ochre. Whenever possible, both natural and artificial pigments were used. All but ochre has an artificial pigment corresponding to the natural pigment. A total of seven pigments were subjected to extreme temperature.

The pigments were heated at 300°C in air for 36 hours. Sampling was done for the first hour of heating every 10 minutes. At this interval, the pigments were taken out of the heating chamber, scanned multispectrally then returned to the chamber for additional heating. Extra care was observed when taking the pigments in and out of the chamber to minimize the disturbance. This was done to preserve the initial discoloration sites which occur at random. After one hour, the sampling was halted until the pigments underwent a 36-hour heating at extreme temperature. At this point, the pigments would have had enough time to decompose completely. The recorded multispectral images where then used for spectral reflectance measurement with pin-point accuracy.

The analytical imaging results provides a lot of useful information on the degradation mechanism of the pigments. Through the analysis performed in this study, it was possible to observe degradation and discoloration associated with structural changes, reflectance and absorbance patterns.

3   Results and Discussion

Spectral reflectance is the plot of the reflectance of a material as a function of wavelength. In optics and photometry, reflectance is the fraction of the incident radiation that is reflected by a surface. It is a directional property of materials. Similar to other properties which can be characterized by advanced analytical techniques (e.g. X-ray analysis), the response from visible light and near infrared irradiation is characteristic of the material and can provide useful insight on its properties. In this study, spectral reflectance measurements were performed on discolored and degraded Japanese pigments by analytical imaging. This was achieved by acquiring high-resolution multispectral images of the pigments using a flat-bed scanner. The method of reconstructing spectral and colorimetric information is described in the pervious section. The scanning resolution was 42μm/pixel. Since the images were taken at high resolution it has good spatial resolution. This enables spectral reflectance measurement at mesoscopic levels. What is significant about this is that conventional spectrometers require a big sampling area, normally about few millimeters. This ROI is acceptable for investigating bulk samples with homogeneous spectral distribution but this is not usually the case. Some of these spectrometers may also require contact with the sample to minimize ambient light interference. This can become problematic when investigating cultural heritage which requires non-invasive analysis.

ROI is not only an issue connected to the sampling area but it is also related to the amount of reflection from the background. For thick and homogenous sample this is not a problem since the re-reflection is less likely but for thin samples this is a serious concern. The background reflection is proportional to the size of the ROI. Since the usual method takes the average of big sampling area, a lot of background re-reflection is also recorded. This is demonstrated by Fig. 1. In this figure, the spectral reflectance of the pigment were measured for eight different square ROI with 1pxl, 2pxls, 4pxls, 8pxls, 16pxls, 32pxls, 64pxls and 128pxls corresponding to dimensions depicted in the figure. It can be seen from the figure that the reflectance is not homogeneous where white spots on the images corresponding to specular reflection are visible. The figure shows the strong correlation of background reflection to ROI.

The strong background reflection from big ROI spectral reflectance measurement is acceptable in some cases as long as this is carefully observed. Since measurements are usually done using a fixed ROI, it is possible to subtract the background effectively. However the issue with big ROI is not only because of this but mainly because of its limitation in size. Big ROI is not a problem if the area of interest is bigger than the sampling area. However, there are cases that it is the other way around. For example, in the discoloration and degradation experiment performed in this study, it was observed that pigment discoloration initiates at seemingly random spots. Although in theory these events are not really random. This initiation at certain spots may be analogous to how mechanical defect, like cracks propagate. Cracks are initiated and propagate from regions of high stress concentration. Similarly, the pigment's initial discoloration spots are region with high chemical reaction sites. These sites require less time and push for chemical reaction to begin. Since the pigments were being heated at a fast rate, the pigment particles will degrade at different rates. This phenomenon is depicted by Fig.2. This behavior may also be attributed to the form of the pigments used as samples. The pigments were prepared as powders. Since there was no binding media holding the particles together, the surface to volume ratio is magnified significantly at the micron or submicron level as compared to bulk samples [21]. This then raises a question whether studying the discoloration and degradation in powder form is a good idea since pigments are applied with a binding media when

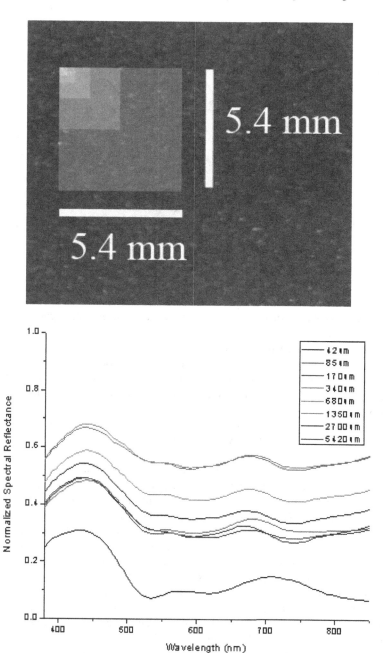

Fig. 1. Pictogram of the sampling area for measurement with the corresponding spectral reflectance. The graph shows the effect of ROI to the background re-reflection.

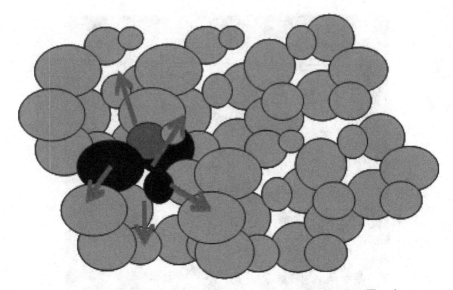

Fig. 2. Schematic diagram depicting how pigments degrade and discolor. The sites seem to appear at random but are actually associated to the surface energies of the pigments.

used in cultural heritage pieces. Although this is true, the mechanism for pigment degradation would still be the same. It will begin at favorable spots and not happen instantaneously through out the entire object. The binding media would affect the rate of degradation since it holds agglomerates of powder which could behave as bulk samples instead of particles. The discoloration and degradation of painted pigments were reported elsewhere [3]. In this study, the focus was given to how discoloration sites are initiated and the scale at which it happens.

The size of the initial discoloration site is in order of sub-mm to few millimeters. Measurement of the spectral reflectance can be a problem. This is where a mesoscopic spectral reflectance measurement is advantageous. Since these sites are very small, they are very easy to miss and not very visible with the naked eye. The problem with conventional spectral measurement is that it normally does not have a high-resolution display of where the measurements are being taken. This entails that the measurements were taken as-detected or by blind-sampling. Using the high-resolution recording of the pigments sample, it is very easy to pan through the entire surface and zoom in to specific area with great details. As a test case, Fig.3 shows the discoloration of natural azurite taken at 10-minute interval. It was observed (circled in red) that discoloration site started to appear after 10minutes of exposure. After 20 minutes, more sites started to appear and continued to appear until the pigments were completely transformed after 36 hours of heating. A similar observation was seen for natural malachite pigments. However, in the case of artificial azurite and malachite pigments, there were no visible signs of degradation. This would be discussed in detail in the succeeding section.

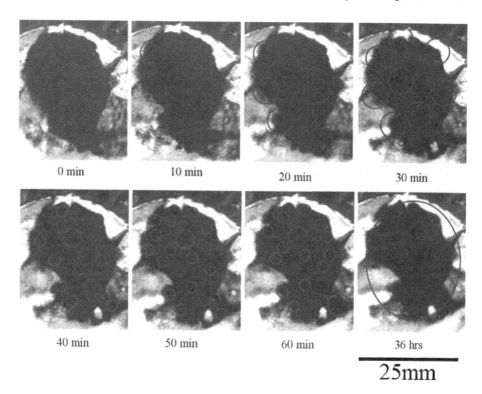

Fig. 3. Discoloration and degradation pattern of natural azurite pigments. It was observed that the discoloration sites seemed to appear sporadically.

Fig.4 shows another type of spectral measurements. In this case, three spots were selected the spots were measured using two different ROI size. The first one is 42µm and the other one is 2.7mm. P1 and P3 are points with visible discoloration while the color in P2 remained unchanged after 20 minutes. The size of the discoloration sites at P1 and P3 is about 1mm. Since the second ROI is bigger than the desired sampling area, the measurement includes area which are does not exhibit visible discoloration yet. The effect of ROI to the accuracy of the measurement is shown in Fig.5. Using the small ROI it was possible to distinguish between discolored and not discolored pigments. Unfortunately, this is still a physical limitation of normal spectrometers. However this highlights the advantage of using analytical imaging. With this method, it is not only possible to measure mesoscopically but the measurements need not be taken blindly. The accuracy of the spectral reflectance reconstruction is reported elsewhere [22].

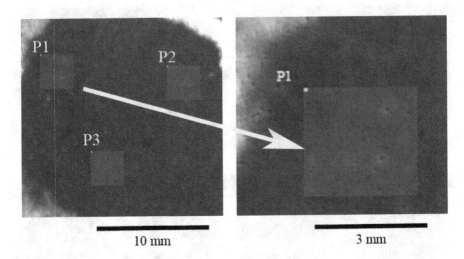

Fig. 4. Spectral reflectance measurement at different spots on the pigment after 20 minutes of exposure to high temperature

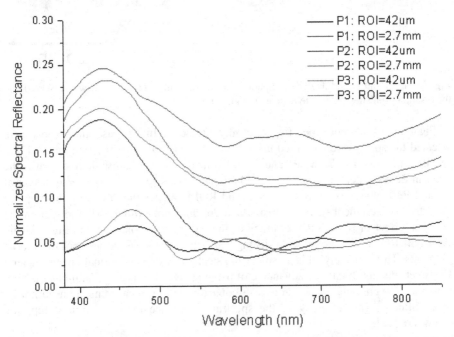

Fig. 5. Spectral reflectance at three different points measured at two ROI. It was not possible to distinguish the spectral reflectance of discolored pigments using the big ROI.

Finally, Fig.6 shows another advantage of using small ROI for spectral reflectance measurement. The figure shows the spectral reflectance of heated artificial azurite. Visually, there was no distinguishable change in color but the spectral measurement at

42μm reveals otherwise (Fig.8a). This suggests that it is not often reliable to depend on visual signs as indicator for degradation since the human vision is sensitive to a limited spectrum of visible radiation. Fig.8b seems to support this observation as characterized by overlapping spectral reflectance. These measurements were performed at big ROI (~2.7mm). However, XAFS and XANES measurements agree with the pattern observed at small ROI measurements. More discussion is reserved for the next section. In addition, as pointed out previously, high background reflection is observed with big ROI.

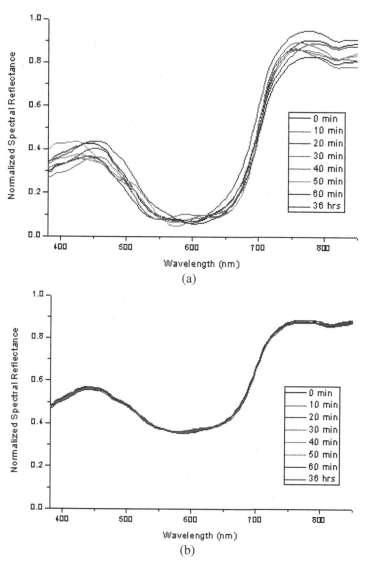

Fig. 6. Spectral reflectance measurement of degraded artificial azurite at (a) 42μm ROI and (b) 2.7mm ROI

4   Conclusion

This study presented a method for investigating the discoloration and degradation mechanism of traditional Japanese paintings. The technique is based on analytical imaging through spectral reflectance reconstruction from multispectral images. The data processing technique used a mathematical model based on the Moore-Penrose pseudoinverse. The images were taken at high resolutions (~42μm/pixel) which means that it has high spatial resolution, good color reproduction and accurate spectral reconstruction. The spectral measurements could be done remotely and noninvasively which satisfies an important requirement of cultural heritage investigation. Due to the high spatial resolution of the images, the spectral measurements can be done at mesoscopic scale. This proved to be useful in understanding the discoloration and degradation patterns of selected Japanese mineral pigments. The technique provided great flexibility in the ROI size which is not usually available with conventional spectrometers. The results have shown that the ROI size is highly correlated with the background reflection which is important in detecting small changes in spectral reflectance. In addition, it is crucial that the ROI of the measurement is smaller than the size of the object. In the case of the initiation site of pigment discoloration this usually is in the sub-mm or mesoscopic scale. Accurate spectral reflectance measurements were done using mesoscopic ROI from multispectral images. It was also possible to detect small changes in the spectra which are not observed from big ROI. Overall, the results have shown that high resolution multispectral scanning has great potential for the noninvasive investigation of cultural heritage.

References

1. Lehmann, E.H., Vontobel, P., Deschler-Erd, E., Soares, M.: Non-invasive studies of objects from cultural heritage. Nucl. Instr. and Meth. A **542**, 68–75 (2005)
2. Balas, C., Papadakis, V., Papadakis, N., Papadakis, A., Vazgiouraki, E., Themelis, G.: A novel hyper-spectral imaging apparatus for the non-destructive analsyis of objects of artistic and historic values. J. Cult. Herit. **4**, 330–337 (2003)
3. Toque, J.A., Sakatoku, Y., Anders, J., Murayama, Y., Ide-Ektessabi, A.: Analytical imaging of cultural heritage by synchrotron radiation and visible light-near infrared spectroscopy. In: Proc. of the International Joint Conference on Computer Vision, Imaging and Computer Graphic (2009)
4. Toque, Jay Arre, Komori, Masateru, Murayama, Yusuke, Ide-Ektessabi, Ari: Analytical imaging of traditional japanese paintings using multispectral images. In: Ranchordas, AlpeshKumar, Pereira, J.M., Araújo, Hélder J., Tavares, Joào Manuel R.S. (eds.) VISIGRAPP 2009. CCIS, vol. 68, pp. 119–132. Springer, Heidelberg (2010)
5. Nakai, I., Terada, Y., Shindo, Y., Utaka, T.: X-ray Spectrometry **34**, 46–51 (2005)
6. Tantrakarn, K., Kato, N., Hokura, A.: X-ray Spectrometry **38**, 121–127 (2009)
7. Toque, J.A., Nishimura, R., Ide-Ektessabi, A.: Analysis of cultural heritage by synchrotron radiation and visible light-near infrared spectroscopy. Photon Factory Activity Report 2007, #25 Part B, 255 (2008)
8. Toque, J.A., Ide-Ektessabi, A.: Characterization of mineral pigments used in traditional japanese paintings. In: Proceedings of the 27th Samahang Pisika ng Pilipinas Physics Congress, Tagaytay, Philippines, SPP-2009:025 (2009)

9. Duran, A., Castaing, J., Walter, P.: X-ray diffraction studies of Pompeian wall painting using synchrotron radiation and dedicated laboratory made systems. Appl. Phys. A **99**, 333–340 (2010)
10. Kockelmann, W.: Radiation in art and archeometry. Elsevier Science Science B.V. (2000)
11. Chene, G., Garnir, H.P., Marchal, A., Mathis, F., Strivay, D.: Improved energy resolution of a cyclotron beam RBS measurements. Nucl. Instr. and Meth. B **266**, 2110–2112 (2008)
12. Anglos, D., Georgiou, S., Fotakis, C.: Lasers in the analysis of cultural heritage materials. J. Nano Res. **8**, 27–60 (2009)
13. Navdenabeele, P., Edwards, H.G.M., Moens, L.: A decade of raman spectroscopy in art and archaeology. Chemical Reviews **3**, 675–686 (2007)
14. Toque, J.A., Ide-Ektessabi: Investigation of degradation mechanism and discoloration of traditional Japanese pigments by multispectral imaging. In: Proc. of SPIE, vol. 7869, 78690E (2011)
15. Murakami, Y., Obi, T., Yamaguchi, M., Ohyama, N., Komiya, Y.: Opt. Commun. **188**, 47–54
16. Shen, H.L., Xin, J.H., Shao, S.J.: (2007) Opt. Express **15**, 5531–5536 (2001)
17. López-Álvarez, M.A., Hernández-Andrés, J., Valero, E.M., Romero, J.: J. Opt. Soc. Am. A **24**, 942–956 (2007)
18. Shimano, N.: Opt. Eng. **45**, 013201 (2006)
19. Ntziachistos, V.: Going deeper than microscopy: the optical imaging frontier in biology. Nature Methods **7**, 603–614 (2010)
20. Razansky, D., Vinegoni, C., Ntziachristos, V.: Mesoscopic imaging of fluorescent proteins using multispectral optoacoustic tomography (MSOT). In: Proc. of SPIE, vol. 7717, 77170D (2009)
21. Toque, J.A., Herliansyah, M.K., Hamdi, M., Ide-Ektessabi, A., Wildan, M.W.: The effect of sample preparation and calcinations temperature on the production of hydroxyapatite from bovine bone powders. In: Biomed 2006. IFMBE Proceedings, vol. 15, pp. 152–155 (2007)
22. Sakatoku, Y., Toque, J.A., Ide-Ektessabi, A.: Reconstruction of hyperspectral images based on regression analysis: optimum regression model and channel selection. In: Proceefings of IMAGAPP 2009, pp. 50–54 (2009)

Data Fusion of Objects Using Techniques Such as Laser Scanning, Structured Light and Photogrammetry for Cultural Heritage Applications

Citlalli Gámez Serna[1]([⊠]), Ruven Pillay[2], and Alain Trémeau[1]

[1] Hubert Curien Laboratory, Building F, 18 Rue Professeur Benoît Lauras,
42000 St-Etienne, France
citlalli.gamez@gmail.com
[2] C2RMF, Palais du Louvre - Porte des Lions, 14 Quai Francois Mitterrand,
75001 Paris, France

Abstract. In this paper we present a semi-automatic 2D-3D local registration pipeline capable of coloring 3D models obtained from 3D scanners by using uncalibrated images. The proposed pipeline exploits the Structure from Motion (SfM) technique in order to reconstruct a sparse representation of the 3D object and obtain the camera parameters from image feature matches. We then coarsely register the reconstructed 3D model to the scanned one through the Scale Iterative Closest Point (SICP) algorithm. SICP provides the global scale, rotation and translation parameters, using minimal manual user intervention. In the final processing stage, a local registration refinement algorithm optimizes the color projection of the aligned photos on the 3D object removing the blurring/ghosting artefacts introduced due to small inaccuracies during the registration. The proposed pipeline is capable of handling real world cases with a range of characteristics from objects with low level geometric features to complex ones.

Keywords: Cultural heritage · 3D reconstruction · 2D-3D registration · Local error

1 Introduction

Digitization of cultural heritage objects has gained great attention around the world due to the importance and awareness of what they represent for each culture. Researchers have been trying to achieve the same goal: capturing a 3D digital representation together with its color information to be able to pass them down safely to future generations.

The recovery and generation of the 3D digital representation requires high geometric accuracy, availability of all details and photo realism [1]. Any single 3D imaging technique is unable to fulfill all of these requirements and the only way to solve this problem is through the fusion of multiple techniques.

© Springer International Publishing Switzerland 2015
A. Trémeau et al. (Eds.): CCIW 2015, LNCS 9016, pp. 208–224, 2015.
DOI: 10.1007/978-3-319-15979-9_20

There have been a number of recent studies which have tried to map auto-matically, semi-automatically or manually a photo-realistic appearance onto a 3D model. Some of these have used only photogrammetry [2],[3], which provides poor geometric precision. However for cultural heritage applications, especially for conservation, a high density of the 3D point cloud is needed. In order to satisfy the demanding needs of cultural heritage, the combination of both photogram-metry and range scans [4–6] have been considered. These approaches generally start by computing an image-to-geometry registration, followed by an integra-tion strategy. The first one generally seeks to find the calibration parameters of the set of images, while the second tries to select the best color for each of the images.

There has been research focusing on improving the alignment in all the images [7–9] (global registration). However, the visual results show significant blurring and ghosting artefacts. Others have proved that a perfect global registration is not possible because the two geometries come from different devices and conse-quently the only solution available is to consider a local registration refinement [10–12].

This paper proposes a solution for a full end-to-end pipeline in order to process data from different acquisition techniques to generate both a realistic and accurate visual representation of the object. Our solution recovers the 3D dimension from 2D images to align the 3D recovered object with a second more geometrically accurate scan. The input 2D images are enhanced to improve the feature detection by the Structure from Motion algorithm (SfM) which provides the position and orientation of each image together with a sparse 3D point cloud. The idea behind the 3D reconstruction is to perform the alignment in 3 dimen-sions through the Scale Iterative Closes Point (SICP) algorithm obtaining the transformation parameters to be applied in the extrinsic ones of the cameras. Even though, the alignment is performed minimizing the distance between both 3D models, it is approximate for different reasons (sparseness, noise) and a local registration refinement is needed. In the last stage of our pipeline, color projec-tion, an algorithm to correct the local color error displacement is performed. Our local correction algorithm works in an image space finding the correct matches for each point in the 3D model.

2   Related Work

The main related issues taken into account in our pipeline can be divided into 3 major fields: (1) 2D/3D registration, (2) color projection, and (3) registration refinement process. The important related work in these fields is outlined below.

2.1   2D/3D Registration

Image to Geometry registration consists of registering the images with the 3D model defining all the parameters of the virtual camera (intrinsic and extrinsic) whose position and orientation gives an optimal inverse projection of the image onto the 3D model.

Numerous techniques exist and a number of different ways try to solve this problem. The methods can be classified into (i) manual, (ii) automatic or semi-automatic depending mainly on matches or features. In the (i) manual methods the registration is performed manually selecting correspondences between each image and the 3D geometry. This technique is often used for medical applications [13]. Others instead, have used features in order to automate the process, but finding consistent correspondences is a very complex problem. Due to the different appearance of photographs and geometric models, (ii) automatic methods are limited to some specific models and information. For example, line features are mostly used for urban environments [7],[14]; and silhouette information is used when the contour of the objects is visible in the images and the 3D model projected onto an image plane [15–17].

Nevertheless there are 3D scanners which provide also reflectance images and the registration is performed in a 2D space [18],[19]. On the other hand, some authors perform their registration in a 3D space reconstructing the 3D object from the 2D images and aligning both 3D objects [5],[9],[20]. This procedure is carried out in two steps: (1) 3D reconstruction and (2) point cloud alignment. Through the widely used Structure from Motion technique (SfM), a 3D reconstruction and intrinsic and extrinsic camera parameters are recovered without making any assumptions about the images in the scene. The registration is usually performed by selecting correspondences [9] that minimize the distances between a set of points.

Our work is based on SfM approach and the use of the SICP algorithm [21] to register both point clouds with the only constraint being to locate them relatively close to each other.

2.2 Color Projection

Once the images are registered onto the 3D model, the next step is to exploit the photo-realistic information (color, texture) obtained by an optical sensor, together with the geometric details (dense point cloud) obtained by some type of 3D scanner (laser scanner, structured light). The aim is to construct a virtual realistic representation of the object.

As a point in the 3D model projects onto different images and images may possess some artefacts (highlights, shadows, aberrations) or small calibration errors, the selection of the correct color for each point is a critical problem. In order to deal with this task, research has been based on different solutions, each one with its own pros and cons.

Orthogonal View. In [16],[22], the authors assign the best image to each portion of the geometry. This assignment relies on the angle between the viewing ray and the surface normal. As the color of a group of 3D points comes from one image, seams are produced when adjacent groups are mapped with different images and also artefacts such as differences in brightness and specularities are visible. Even though some research has dealt with the seams by smoothing the transitions [16], important and critical detail can be lost.

Weighting Scheme. In these kind of approaches [4],[9],[23], an specific weight is assigned to each image or to each pixel in the images according to different quality metrics. The metrics vary between authors considering visible points, borders or silhouettes, depth [9],[23] or the distance to the edge of the scan [4]. All these methods, in comparison with orthogonal view, are able to eliminate the artefacts previously mentioned but instead introduce blurring/ghosting when the calibration of the images is not sufficiently accurate.

Illumination Estimation. Alternatively, approaches such as [24] attempt to make an estimation of the lighting environment. This approach is able to remove possible illumination artefacts presented in the images (shadows/highlights). Unfortunately, in real scenarios it is difficult to accurately recover the position and contribution of all the light sources in the scene. Furthermore they will complicate the photo acquisition step and processing phases, leaving apart this kind of approaches.

Due to the evaluation criteria used and advantages provided by all of these approaches, a weighting procedure was selected as the best option for our work. We used the approach by Callieri et al. [23] because of its robustness, availability and the good results obtained with it from our data set.

2.3   Registration Refinement

Since the data comes from 2 different devices and the geometry and camera calibration is imprecise after the 2D/3D registration; blurring or ghosting artefacts appear once the color projection is performed. In order to remove them, a global or local refinement is necessary.

Global Refinement. Some approaches try to correct the small inaccuracies in a global manner [7–9],[16] by computing a new registration of the camera parameters according to the dense 3D model obtained with the scanner. The goal is to distribute the alignment error among all the images to minimize the inaccuracies and improve the quality of the final color of the model. Unfortunately as the registration is mostly based on features, an exact alignment will not be possible due to image distortions or low geometric features. Nevertheless even if the global alignment refinement finds the best approximate solution, the matches will not be exactly the same. As a consequence blurry details (ghosting effects) will appear after the color projection [10], especially when the color details are in areas with low geometric features. The only straightforward solution to correct these small inaccuracies, is to perform a local refinement.

Local Refinement. A number of studies have been carried out based on local refinements which locally analyze the characteristics of each point and try to find the best correspondence in the image series [10–12]. Finding these correspondences locally has been addressed in the literature by using optical flow. Some studies have computed dense optical flow [10],[11] but the results depend on the image resolution and the amount of mismatch (displacement) together with the computational power available. On the other hand, others instead of working in the image space, have tried to optimize the 3D geometry in order to deform textures more effectively [12]. As our 3D geometry cannot be modified, these kind of approaches are not feasible for our purpose.

Computing dense optical flow in our datasets was impossible due to relatively high resolution of the images, e.g. 4008×5344 pixels compared to the 1024×768 pixels used in the literature in [11]. For this reason we decided to use sparse optical flow to compute the color for each point in the 3D geometry limiting the number of images to the best three, evaluated according to the quality metrics of Callieri et al. [23].

3 Data Fusion

Our goal is to fuse the information provided by the two different devices (3D scanner and 2D camera) in order to recreate a high resolution realistic digital visualization with both very accurate geometric and visual detail. The procedure to achieve this result needs to take into account various problems which will be solved in essentially four main stages (see figure 1): (1) Image preprocessing, (2) Camera calibration through Structure from Motion, (3) Cloud registration to align the images to the geometry, and (4) Color projection which involves the most correct images to project the color onto the 3D geometry. The whole process is designed to consider as input a set of uncalibrated images and a dense 3D point cloud or a 3D triangulated mesh. By uncalibrated images we refer to images in which the intrinsic and extrinsic camera parameters are unknown.

3.1 Stage 0: Image Preprocessing

Even though a number of studies have used a set of uncalibrated images to perform camera calibration and 3D reconstruction through some Structure from Motion algorithm [5],[9],[20],[27], very few have considered a preprocessing step [27].

This stage is performed in order to improve the camera calibration procedure (Stage 1) and consequently obtain more accurate camera parameters together with a better 3D representation.

Three preprocessing steps were considered. The first two had already been applied by the C2RMF to their data sets and the introduction of a third preprocessing step also enabled an improvement for the next stage.

1. Color calibration. Performed to accurately record the colorimetric appearance of the object in the set of color images and to eliminate mis-matches

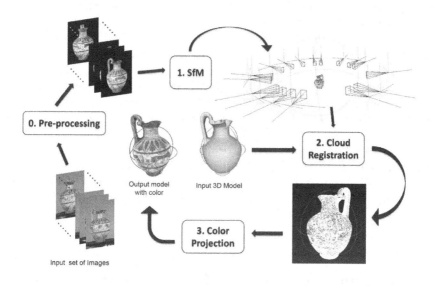

Fig. 1. General overview of the pipeline

caused by varying lighting conditions. In order to calibrate, a color chart is used during the image acquisition to determine a color transformation between the captured values and the reference color target.

2. Background subtraction. As a SfM procedure is based on feature matching, features will be detected in the foreground as well as in the background. In order to avoid the reconstruction of unwanted points (outliers) and have a clean 3D object, the background was removed manually. There are many segmentation techniques available in the literature [25] but in order to be precise the manual method was considered by the C2RMF.

3. Image enhancement. Through histogram equalization, we enhance the image contrast in order to find a larger number of features and generate more 3D points in the next stage. The original principle applies to gray-scale images, but we used it in color, changing from RGB to the HSV color space and equalizing the Value (V) channel in order to avoid hue and saturation changes [26]. This step is very useful especially when the object lacks texture details. The same idea was exploited in [27] with a Wallis filter.

3.2   Stage 1. Camera Calibration and 3D Reconstruction

The second stage of our pipeline consists of a self-calibration procedure. It is assumed that the same camera, which is unknown, is used throughout the sequence and that the intrinsic camera parameters are constant. The task consists of (i) detecting feature points in each image, (ii) matching feature points between image pairs, and (iii) running an iterative robust SfM algorithm to recover the camera parameters and a 3D structure of the object.

For each image, SIFT keypoints are detected [28] to find the corresponding matches using approximate nearest neighbors (ANN) kd-tree package from Arya et al. [29] and the RANSAC algorithm [30] to remove outliers. Then a Structure from Motion (SfM) algorithm [31],[32] is used to reconstruct a sparse 3D geometry of the object and obtain the intrinsic (i.e. focal length, principal point and distortion coefficients) and extrinsic (i.e. rotation and translation) camera parameters.

In order to achieve a more geometrically complete surface of the 3D object, Clustering Views from Multi-view Stereo (CMVS) [33] and Patch-based Multi-view Stereo (PMVS) [34] tools are used. This aims to increase the density of the 3D geometry and be able to obtain a more precise parameter estimation during the cloud registration (stage 2).

3.3 Stage 2. Cloud Registration

After the 3D geometry obtained with the SfM algorithm and from the 3D scanner, a 3D-3D registration process is performed. As both points clouds possess different scales and reference frames, we will need to find the affine transformation that determines the scale (s), rotation (r) and translation (t) parameters which align better both 3D geometries.

Usually a 3D-3D registration refers to the alignment between multiple point clouds scanned with the same device. Algorithms like Iterative Closest Point (ICP) [35] and 4 Point Congruent Set [36] evaluate the similarity and minimize the distance between the 3D point clouds considering only the rotation and translation parameters. But when a scale factor is involved it can be solve separately or together from the registration procedure.

Calculating a bounding box for both 3D geometries and applying the ratio found between them seems to solve the scale problem, but if some outliers are present in one of the geometries the result will not be correct. Therefore Zhu et al. [21], extended the Iterative Closest Point algorithm to consider also the scale transformation (SICP), introducing a bidirectional distance measurement into the least squared problem. This algorithm works as follows: (i) define a target (fixed) and source (transforming) point clouds, which will be the scanned and reconstructed point clouds respectively in order to bring the camera parameters from the image space to the real object space; and (ii) perform iteratively the distance error minimization using the root mean square error (RMSE), until the best solution is found. The output is a set of 3D points aligned to the object coordinate system (real scale) by means of a 3×3 rotational matrix, 3×1 scale matrix and vector indicating the translation in X, Y and Z axis.

3.4   Stage 3. Color Projection

Color projection is the last and the core of our proposed pipeline. The aim is to project accurate color information onto the dense 3D model to create a continuous visual representation from the photographic image set.

Selecting the best color is not an easy task; first because a single point in the 3D geometry is visible in multiple images and those may present differences in illumination. Secondly small errors in the camera parameters cause small misalignments between the images, and in consequence, a point which projects onto a specific location in one image plane will project onto a slightly different area in another one. This can result in different colors for each 3D point projected from several 2D images.

In order to address this problem, some research based the color selection on the most orthogonal image for a certain part of the 3D geometry [16],[22] generating artefacts like highlights, shadows and visible seams.

Others project all images onto the 3D mesh and assign some weight to each image, as, for example, in [4],[9],[23], which remove artefacts that the orthogonal view is not capable of removing, but this can produce some ghosting artefacts when the alignment is not perfect.

In order to deal with less artefacts, we consider the approach based on Callieri et al. [23], which weights all the pixels in the images according to geometric, topological and colorimetric criteria.

The general procedure to perform the color projection in our pipeline takes into account two steps: (1) a color selection considering weights assigned according to the quality of each pixel, and (2) a local error correction in the image space in order to produce sharp results.

Weighted Blending Function. Through the approach by Callieri et al. [23] it is possible to compute the weights for each 3D point in the number of images they are visible. The three metrics are based on: angle, depth and borders. For each of these metrics, a mask is created which has the same resolution as the original image. The aim is, therefore, to create a unique mask combining the three masks through multiplication. The result is a weighting mask for each image that represents a per-pixel quality (see an example in figure 2).

Once the weights are defined for each image, and knowing the camera parameters obtained in Stage 1, it is possible to perform a perspective projection from the 3D world onto an image plane. This projection allows us to know the color information for each 3D point in the geometry. The final color for each point is a weighted mean obtained by multiplying the RGB values from the pixels with their respective weights.

Local Error Correction. The results obtained projecting the color information with the quality metrics of Callieri et al. [23] into the 3D geometry, generated blurring/ghosting effects in some parts of the mesh. These problems appear due to small inaccuracies introduced in the image-to-geometry registration [10].

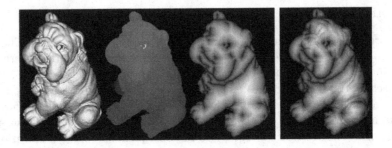

Fig. 2. Example of weighting masks [23]. From left to right: Angle mask, Depth mask, Border mask. Right-most, the combination of the previous three masks. For illustration purposes the contrast for the depth and border mask have been increased.

Research such as that by [10–12],[37] have considered these kind of artefacts; but their origin, is explained by Dellepiane et al. [10] in figure 3 .

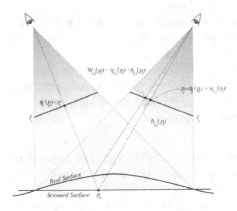

Fig. 3. Graphic representation of the local displacement defined by Dellepiane et al. [10] where p_o is the original point located in the scanned surface geometry; $\phi_i(p_o)$ represents the projection from the 3D world int a 2D image plane; $\psi_{i,j}(p_i)$ is the relation between corresponding points on different images; $\Delta_{i,j}(p_i)$ is the necessary displacement required to find the correct matches; and $W_{i,j}(p_i)$ is the warping function necessary to find the correspondent point in the second image plane.

The simplest way to correct these inaccuracies which generate the blurring artefacts, consists of finding for each 3D point, the local displacement in the best 3 image planes where it is visible. This local error estimation algorithm, based on [10], is performed through a template matching algorithm shown in figure 4.

The reason for considering only the best three images for each point, instead of all where it is visible, is to speed up the process in the final color calculation. Instead of computing *(n-1)p* evaluations, we reduce them to *(3-1)p* where n is the number of images and p the points. Dellepiane et al. [10] affirmed that three images are enough to correct illumination artefacts.

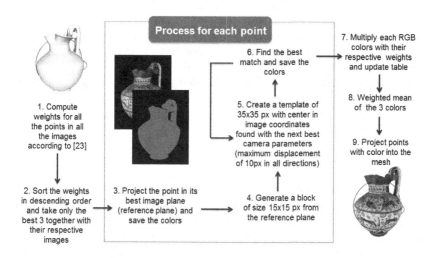

Fig. 4. Illustration of the local error estimation procedure

The size of the block and template was defined according to some experimental evaluation performed on the highest resolution dataset (FZ36147). Normally if the cloud registration step in Stage 2 is accurate enough, the different 3D points projected in the image plane will not be so far from each other. For this reason the same parameters can be applied to lower resolution images, but they cannot be considered for even higher ones. The most straightforward solution is to tune the parameters depending on the image resolution and the 3D cloud registration output.

Considering the parameters defined, the matching procedure is done on a pixel-by-pixel basis in a Luminance-Chrominance color space. The conversion of the RGB values into YCbCr color space was performed directly with the built-in Matlab function 'rbg2ycbcr' and the similarity measurement, mean square error (MSE,) was defined considering also changes in brightness for each block by subtracting the average value in each channel. Through this subtraction we account for big changes in illumination between images. The notation is the following:

$$MSE = \frac{1}{N^2} \sum_{i=0}^{N-1} \sum_{j=0}^{N-1} ((S_{ij} - \overline{S}) - (T_{i,j} - \overline{T}))^2 \qquad (1)$$

where N is the total number of pixels in each block, S is the block in the source/reference image, T is the block inside the template of the target image,

$\overline{S}$ and $\overline{T}$ are the mean values of their respective channels. At the end the error with the minimum value is considered as the best match.

$$Error = \frac{MSE_Y + MSE_{Cb} + MSE_{Cr}}{3} \tag{2}$$

In the case where there is more than one block matching the same criterion, a comparison of the colors from the center points will decide which block in the template is the closest to the block from the reference image.

When the three RGB color values are found for each point, we proceed with the multiplication of them with their respective weights to average the results and assign final color values to each point in the 3D geometry.

4   Experimental Results

In this section we present experiments performed on real data from the C2RMF. 3D Scans from objects from the Department of Roman and Greek Antiquities at the Louvre museum were considered in order to assess the performance of the proposed pipeline. The data had been captured at different times using different equipment. Each object had data from a structured light scanner and a set of color images used for photogrammetry.

The 2 data sets (FZ36147 and FZ36152) contain information with different qualities and sizes. A small description of the datasets used, is listed below together with a brief explanation of the criteria used for a visual quality evaluation.

- **Dataset FZ36147.** This Greek vase, an Oenocho from around 610BC, contains 1,926,625 3D points (pts) and 35 high resolution images (4008×5344 pixels). The images were acquired under an uncalibrated setup, but our method was capable to remove the lighting artifacts and preserve details in its decorations. For the final evaluation of our proposed local error estimation algorithm implemented as part of the color projection procedure (stage 3), three small patches selected manually from the 3D geometry were extracted. Each patch was carefully selected according to visual details where misregistration of the camera parameters led to blurring artifacts.
- **Dataset FZ36152.** This Greek vase, an Oenocho from between 600-625BC, is represented by a 3D model which contains 1,637,375 points and 17 images of resolution 2152×3232 pixels. With this dataset, the registration in the second stage of our pipeline, was not accurate enough to avoid blurring effects appearing in the whole 3D geometry. The local error correction in our method, brings sharp results in the three patches extracted in the same way as in the previous dataset.

Due to the fact that the images of the datasets are uncalibrated (no ground truth is available) only qualitative, meaning visually, evaluations were performed, as found also in the state of the art [10], [20].

The reason for performing the evaluation only in small patches, refers to the high density of points each 3D geometry contains and the programming language used for the implementation (CPU programming).

Our algorithm, implemented in stage 3, corrects the small errors in the projected image planes, converging to good results regardless the initial rough alignment obtained during stage 2. Figure 5 shows the results of the color projection once the small errors are corrected. The quality of the appearance in the new projections (down red squares) is improved, removing the unpleasant blurring artefacts. Table 1 shows a summary of the characteristics of the datasets used, together with the patches evaluated and their corresponding computational time.

Table 1. Overview of tests performed with our Local error estimation algorithm

Dataset	3D model size	N. of images (Resolution)	Patch	S. Patch	Computational Time
FZ36147	1,926,625 pts	35 (4008×5344)	Up	4049 pts	2 hrs 30 min
			Middle	4834 pts	3 hrs 3 min
			Down	3956 pts	6 hrs 40 min
FZ36152	1,637,375 pts	17 (2152×3232)	Up	4750 pts	3 hrs 10 min
			Middle	4903 pts	2 hrs 46 min
			Down	6208 pts	3 hrs 8 min

The time required to perform the local error estimations, depends on the amount of 3D points the geometry has, and on the displacement found for every projected point in the 2D image plane. If the density increases, the computational time will be higher.

Discussion. A visible comparison with the state of the art [10] is presented in figure 6. Dellepiane et al. also evaluated their method with one dataset from the Louvre museum, but it possess different resolution characteristics. The implementation in [10] is based on dense optical flow and GPU programming, for which really high resolution images are a disadvantage. The maximum resolution tested by Dellepiane et al. [10] was 3000×1996 (5,988,000 pixels) which took around 5 hours in 6 images. In our dataset FZ36147, its resolution is 4008×5344 and contains 35 images. The pixels needed to be evaluated with our dataset in [10] will be 21,418,152 which is at least 5.57 times more than in their dataset with maximum resolution, and 6 times more the number of images. Only with extremely powerful processing capable of handling such computations can their approach be applied, otherwise their method is not a feasible solution with our data set.

In general the state of the art methods [11], [10] are based on dense optical flow which is the main reason there is no possible comparison with our datasets.

Even though our implementation has proven to be robust and reliable, some limitations still remain. The main one relates to the programming language for the acceleration of the computational time (from CPU to GPU programming).

Fig. 5. Final color projection in datasets from left to right FZ36147 and FZ36152. In the first row some of the original images are illustrated; second to fourth represents the 3 patches used for the direct color projection with Callieri et al. approach [23] and the local error correction results for each of them (down red squares).

(a) Rendering of the colored model without and with the flow correction by Dellepiane et al. [10]

(b) Rendering of the colored model (dataset FZ36152) without and with our local error correction algorithm

Fig. 6. Final color projection comparison with the State of the Art

Also, in the evaluations performed, the maximum local displacement found was not large (10 pixels); but for other cases (e.g. images with higher resolution), the displacement can be bigger and in consequence, the parameters for the template matching algorithm in Stage 3, have to be adjusted.

There are also some limitations related to lighting artefacts. Factors like high-lights/shadows may complicate the estimation of the local error displacement, and inclusive mislead the motion to totally wrong values. Nevertheless , these drawbacks are shared with every method based on optical flow calculations.

5   Conclusion

We have proposed a semi-automatic 2D-3D registration pipeline capable to provide extremely accurate realistic results from a set of 2D uncalibrated images and a 3D object acquired through laser scanning.

The main advantage of our pipeline is the generality, since no assumption is made about the geometric characteristics or shape of the object. Our pipeline is capable of handling registration with any kind of object, since the algorithm used is a brute force (SICP) which evaluates every single point and finds the best position. The only requirements needed are a set of 2D images containing sufficient overlapping information to be able to use the Structure from Motion (SfM) technique in stage 1; and a user intervention during stage 2 to locate the dense point cloud, coming from the scanner, closer to the one obtained by SfM, in order to provide the input that the Scale Iterative Closest Point (SICP) algorithm needs to converge. This user intervention during the second stage in our pipeline is what makes our approach semi-automatic.

In conclusion, our main contribution is the local error correction algorithm in stage 3 which proved to be:

1. Robust: it works with low and high resolution images, as it considers only the interest points (projected 3D points into the image plane) for the matching. Not even the state of the art [10], [11] is capable of dealing with as high resolution images as our algorithm does.
2. Accurate: it finds the best possible matching for the small error displacements considering luminance and chrominance channels. Through the best match, it removes the unpleasant blurring artefacts and produces sharp results.
3. Photo-realistic: with the point cloud generated by SFM [31],[32] and the registration algorithm SICP [21], the color information from the 2D images is projected onto the 3D object transferring the photo-realistic appearance.

An interesting direction for future research would be to define a criterion with a respective threshold to identify the possible borders where the sharp results start to blur (in the cases where only some parts of the 3D object are visible with ghosting effects). This identification has to be based on depth differences between the 2 registered point clouds, and probably a segmentation according to depth may help to optimized our proposed local error estimation algorithm.

Acknowledgments. Special thanks to Centre de Recherche et de Restauration des Musees de France (C2RMF) for the data provided to evaluate the pipeline. Thanks to J.H. Zhu, N.N. Zheng, Z.J. Yuan, S.Y. Du and L. Ma for sharing their SICP code implementation in Matlab.

References

1. El-Hakim, S., Beraldin, J. A.: Detailed 3D reconstruction of monuments using multiple techniques. In: Proceedings of the International Workshop on Scanning for Cultural Heritage Recording-Complementing or Replacing Photogrammetry, pp. 58–64 (2002)
2. Pollefeys, M., Koch, R., Vergauwen, M., Van Gool, L.: Automated reconstruction of 3D scenes from sequences of images. ISPRS Journal of Photogrammetry and Remote Sensing 55(4), 251–267 (2000)
3. Fitzgibbon, A.W., Zisserman, A.: Automatic camera recovery for closed or open image sequences. In: Burkhardt, H.-J., Neumann, B. (eds.) ECCV 1998. LNCS, vol. 1406, pp. 311–326. Springer, Heidelberg (1998)

4. Bernardini, F., Martin, I.M., Rushmeier, H.: High-quality texture reconstruction from multiple scans. IEEE Transactions on Visualization and Computer Graphics **7**(4), 318–332 (2001)

5. Liu, L., Stamos, I., Yu, G., Wolberg, G., Zokai, S.: Multiview geometry for texture mapping 2d images onto 3d range data. In: 2006 IEEE Computer Society Conference Computer Vision and Pattern Recognition, vol. 2, pp. 2293–2300. IEEE (2006)

6. Dellepiane, M., Callieri, M., Ponchio, F., Scopigno, R.: Mapping highly detailed colour information on extremely dense 3D models: the case of david's restoration. In: Computer Graphics Forum, vol. 27(8), pp. 2178–2187. Blackwell Publishing Ltd. (2008)

7. Liu, L., Stamos, I.: Automatic 3D to 2D registration for the photorealistic rendering of urban scenes. In: IEEE Computer Society Conference on Computer Vision and Pattern Recognition, CVPR 2005, vol. 2, pp. 137–143. IEEE (2005)

8. Dellepiane, M., Scopigno, R.: Global refinement of image-to-geometry registration for color projection on 3D models. In: Digital Heritage International Congress, pp. 39–46. The Eurographics Association (2013)

9. Li, Y., Low, K. L.: Automatic registration of color images to 3d geometry. In: Proceedings of the 2009 Computer Graphics International Conference, pp. 21–28. ACM (2009)

10. Dellepiane, M., Marroquim, R., Callieri, M., Cignoni, P., Scopigno, R.: Flow-based local optimization for image-to-geometry projection. IEEE Transactions on Visualization and Computer Graphics **18**(3), 463–474 (2012)

11. Eisemann, M., De Decker, B., Magnor, M., Bekaert, P., De Aguiar, E., Ahmed, N., Sellent, A.: Floating textures. In: Computer Graphics Forum, vol. 27(2), pp. 409–418. Blackwell Publishing Ltd. (2008)

12. Takai, T., Hilton, A., Matsuyama, T.: Harmonised texture mapping. In: Proc. of 3DPVT (2010)

13. Liu, A., Bullitt, E., Pizer, S. M.: 3D/2D registration using tubular anatomical structures as a basis. In: Proc. Medical Image Computing and Computer-Assisted Intervention, pp. 952–963 (1998)

14. Musialski, P., Wonka, P., Aliaga, D.G., Wimmer, M., Gool, L., Purgathofer, W.: A survey of urban reconstruction. Computer Graphics Forum **32**(6), 146–177 (2013)

15. Ip, H.H., Yin, L.: Constructing a 3D individualized head model from two orthogonal views. The Visual Computer **12**(5), 254–266 (1996)

16. Lensch, H., Heidrich, W., Seidel, H. P.: Automated texture registration and stitching for real world models. In: Proceedings of the Eighth Pacific Conference on Computer Graphics and Applications, pp. 317–452. IEEE (2000)

17. Lensch, H., Heidrich, W., Seidel, H.P.: A silhouette-based algorithm for texture registration and stitching. Graphical Models **63**(4), 245–262 (2001)

18. Ikeuchi, K., Oishi, T., Takamatsu, J., Sagawa, R., Nakazawa, A., Kurazume, R., Okamoto, Y.: The great buddha project: Digitally archiving, restoring, and analyzing cultural heritage objects. International Journal of Computer Vision **75**(1), 189–208 (2007)

19. Kurazume, R., Nishino, K., Zhang, Z., Ikeuchi, K.: Simultaneous 2D images and 3D geometric model registration for texture mapping utilizing reflectance attribute. In: Proc. Fifth ACCV, pp. 99–106 (2002)

20. Corsini, M., Dellepiane, M., Ganovelli, F., Gherardi, R., Fusiello, A., Scopigno, R.: Fully automatic registration of image sets on approximate geometry. International Journal Of Computer Vision **102**(1–3), 91–111 (2013)

21. Zhu, J.H., Zheng, N.N., Yuan, Z.J., Du, S.Y., Ma, L.: Robust scaling iterative closest point algorithm with bidirectional distance measurement. Electronics Letters 46(24), 1604–1605 (2010)

22. Callieri, M., Cignoni, P., Scopigno, R.: Reconstructing Textured Meshes from Multiple Range RGB Maps. In: VMV, pp. 419–426 (2002)

23. Callieri, M., Cignoni, P., Corsini, M., Scopigno, R.: Masked photo blending: Mapping dense photographic data set on high-resolution sampled 3D models. Computers & Graphics 32(4), 464–473 (2008)

24. Dellepiane, M., Callieri, M., Corsini, M., Cignoni, P., Scopigno, R.: Improved color acquisition and mapping on 3d models via flash-based photography. Journal on Computing and Cultural Heritage (JOCCH) 2(4), 9 (2010)

25. Pal, N.R., Pal, S.K.: A review on image segmentation techniques. Pattern Recognition 26(9), 1277–1294 (1993)

26. Naik, S.K., Murthy, C.A.: Hue-preserving color image enhancement without gamut problem. IEEE Transactions on Image Processing 12(2), 1591–1598 (2003)

27. Gallo, A., Muzzupappa, M., Bruno, F.: 3D reconstruction of small sized objects from a sequence of multi-focused images. Journal of Cultural Heritage 15(2), 173–182 (2014)

28. Lowe, D.G.: Distinctive image features from scale-invariant keypoints. International Journal of Computer Vision 60(2), 91–110 (2004)

29. Arya, S., Mount, D.M., Netanyahu, N.S., Silverman, R., Wu, A.Y.: An optimal algorithm for approximate nearest neighbor searching fixed dimensions. Journal of the ACM (JACM) 45(6), 891–923 (1998)

30. Fischler, M.A., Bolles, R.C.: Random sample consensus: a paradigm for model fitting with applications to image analysis and automated cartography. Communications of the ACM 24(6), 381–395 (1981)

31. Snavely, N., Seitz, S.M., Szeliski, R.: Photo tourism: exploring photo collections in 3D. ACM Transactions on Graphics (TOG) 25(3), 835–846 (2006)

32. Snavely, N., Seitz, S.M., Szeliski, R.: Modeling the world from internet photo collections. International Journal of Computer Vision 80(2), 189–210 (2008)

33. Furukawa, Y., Curless, B., Seitz, S. M., Szeliski, R.: Towards internet-scale multiview stereo. In: 2010 IEEE Conference Computer Vision and Pattern Recognition (CVPR), pp. 1434–1441). IEEE (2010)

34. Furukawa, Y., Ponce, J.: Accurate, dense, and robust multiview stereopsis. IEEE Transactions on Pattern Analysis and Machine Intelligence 32(8), 1362–1376 (2010)

35. Zhang, Z.: Iterative point matching for registration of free-form curves (1992)

36. Aiger, D., Mitra, N. J., Cohen-Or, D.: 4-points congruent sets for robust pairwise surface registration. ACM Transactions on Graphics (TOG) 27(3), 85 (2008)

37. Pighin, F., Hecker, J., Lischinski, D., Szeliski, R., Salesin, D.H.: Synthesizing realistic facial expressions from photographs. In: ACM SIGGRAPH 2006 Courses, p. 19. ACM (2006)

Accuracy in Colour Reproduction: Using a ColorChecker Chart to Assess the Usefulness and Comparability of Data Acquired with Two Hyper-Spectral Systems

Tatiana Vitorino[1(✉)], Andrea Casini[1], Costanza Cucci[1], Ana Gebejes[2],
Jouni Hiltunen[2], Markku Hauta-Kasari[2], Marcello Picollo[1], Lorenzo Stefani[1]

[1] Istituto di Fisica Applicata "Nello Carrara" - Consiglio Nazionale delle
Ricerche (IFAC-CNR), Florence, Italy
`tatianamfv@gmail.com`,
`{a.casini,c.cucci,m.picollo,l.stefani}@ifac.cnr.it`
[2] Institute of Photonics, University of Eastern Finland, Joensuu, Finland
`{ana.gebejes,jouni.hiltunen,markku.hauta-kasari}@uef.fi`

Abstract. Hyper-spectral imaging has been applied as an *in situ* technique for the study and accurate digital documentation of coloured artworks. Providing spectral and colorimetric characterisation across the entire surface of an object, it can be used to identify the coloured materials, measure colour changes, and document it with high fidelity. However, depending on the system used, data accuracy and reliability may vary. In this work, developed within the Round Robin Test being carried out by COSCH Working Group 1, an X-Rite® ColorChecker Classic chart was analysed with two push-broom hyper-spectral systems developed by different groups (IFAC-CNR and IP-UEF), in the 400-1000 nm range, and the data obtained were compared. This comparison allowed to assess the accuracy of colour reproduction processes performed by the two systems. The results obtained are satisfactory in terms of spectral and colorimetric accuracy for some colours, but show differences at both ends of the visible range.

Keywords: Hyper-spectral imaging · Spectral and spatial resolution · Accuracy · Colour reproduction · ColorChecker · CIELAB colorimetric values · COSCH

1 Introduction

We are not only inheriting cultural heritage from our ancestors, but we are also borrowing it from our children. Starting from this premise, curators and conservators realise that the study and documentation of the artworks that constitute our cultural heritage is important to preserve them and to increase accessibility and possibilities for our and for future generations [1]. For either of these purposes - study and documentation -, accuracy and high quality are very important features concerning the data that is acquired and kept [2]. These records have to be true and accurate representations that show the required information, without anything added to or taken away from the original artwork [3]. This is particularly important when coloured materials are concerned.

© Springer International Publishing Switzerland 2015
A. Trémeau et al. (Eds.): CCIW 2015, LNCS 9016, pp. 225–235, 2015.
DOI: 10.1007/978-3-319-15979-9_21

Colour is an essential language of cultural heritage that often needs more decoding than what was originally intended by the artist. Coloured materials are generally prone to changes, leading to alterations in the artworks visual appearance and, consequently the objects are interpreted differently from the artists' intention. Often conservators need to go beyond what is seen, and to successfully conserve the artworks, they need to identify and document colours with as much accuracy as possible.

The study of colour in artworks using *in situ* spectral imaging techniques, therefore avoiding that colour measurement is restricted to a limited number of points on the surface of the object, is of great importance [4,5]. These techniques provide a highly accurate way to measure colour across the entire surface of the object, and may indeed be crucial to guarantee a high-quality colorimetric reproduction [2], [5]. They allow to acquire the objects' spectral reflectance, which is a physical quantity characteristic of the material [6,7]. In other words, for each spatial pixel (picture element), a reflectance spectrum is acquired in a determined spectral region. This is obtained by recording a collection of reflectographic images of the same area at almost contiguous spectral bands (hundreds in the case of hyper-spectral systems). From the acquired data-set it is therefore possible to extract the spectral reflectance of each pixel, which has several advantages such as: the possibility to reconstruct it in the CIE colour space with any choice of illuminant and of the colour matching functions; the possibility to monitor the conservation state of the object since a change in the spectral reflectance evidences the alterations of the material; and the possibility to reliably identify and discriminate the coloured materials used by the artists [6,7,8,9,10].

In the context of the promotion of research, development and application of spectral imaging techniques towards the study and documentation of cultural heritage, COSCH[1] Working Group 1 (WG1) aims to identify and explore important characteristics of different spectral imaging systems and understand how they influence data accuracy and information reliability with respect to the various types of studied artworks [11]. As a matter of fact, several different types of devices have been developed to implement spectral imaging techniques for applications in cultural heritage [12]. These devices are commonly categorised according to the portion of the file-cube (the complete dataset formed by the three dimensions - two spatial and one spectral - over which data is collected) that is acquired in a single detector readout [13]. They can consist in cameras equipped with filtering systems for the optical selection of the wavelengths, or they can be constituted by scanners equipped with dispersive systems for the selection of the spectral bands (such as push-broom spectrometers), or they can also be based on snap-shot imaging systems, which collect the entire 3D file-cube in a single integration period without scanning [4], [13]. However, in practical terms, for the same object the acquired information can be significantly influenced by the method of data collection, the system used, and any other parameters influencing the general experimental setup. As such, WG1 is performing a Round Robin Test (RRT) with four objects of distinct characteristics, to explore different spectral imaging systems, identify the impact of each instrumentation on the results obtained, and ensure the usefulness, accuracy and comparability of the data. Colour being such an

---

[1] COST Action TD120: Colour and Space in Cultural Heritage (COSCH, www.cosch.info).

important issue, one of the objects that integrates the RRT is a ColorChecker reference chart.

ColorChecker charts are used as a colour reference, and are very important when colour image processing is concerned [6], [14]. Constituted by several standard coloured patches, these charts allow to assess the accuracy of the colour reproduction processes of the systems used, to guarantee that the information obtained is valuable and represents the true colours of the object that has to be studied and documented [3], [5], [15].

This contribution presents the comparison between data acquired from the Color-Checker chart used in the RRT with two hyper-spectral devices from different research groups that are part of the COSCH WG1 RRT: the "Nello Carrara" Institute of Applied Physics of the National Research Council (IFAC-CNR), in Florence, Italy; and the Institute of Photonics - University of Eastern Finland (IP-UEF), in Joensuu, Finland. Both groups measured the ColorChecker in their own laboratory with push-broom hyper-spectral systems that collect data with a 2D array detector at all wavelengths simultaneously for one spatial line of the object so that only one spatial dimension needs to be scanned to fill out the file-cube [13]. However, even though both systems are based on the same working principle, they were designed and optimised in different ways depending on the purpose of analysis of each group (for example, if they are seeking for high spatial or spectral resolution, or high colour accuracy). For this contribution, the data acquired with IFAC-CNR and IP-UEF systems were first used to confirm the homogeneity of the ColorChecker coloured patches. Afterwards, both set of data were compared with respect to the spectral reflectance curves, and, finally, colorimetric CIELAB values were calculated for a standard illuminant (D65) and observer (10°) and also compared.

2   Experimental Design

2.1   X-Rite® ColorChecker Classic

The X-Rite® ColorChecker Classic target is a matt chart with dimensions 279.4 mm x 215.9 mm. It has twenty-four coloured square patches, each with 40 mm of side, displayed in a 4 by 6 array, that include the representation of true colours of natural matter (such as skin, foliage and sky), additive and subtractive primary colours, various steps of grey, and black and white [15,16].

2.2   Methodology

The X-Rite® ColorChecker was analysed by the two different groups using their own push-broom hyper-spectral system. In each case, the working conditions and technical parameters were not predetermined, since the point was that each group used the setup commonly used in their laboratories. However, for treatment of the hyper-spectral file-cube (that contains both spatial and spectral information, and can easily reach several tens of megabytes), the participants were asked to follow a few guidelines.

The reflectance spectrum of ten selected coloured patches (Blue Sky 03, Foliage 04, Orange 07, Purple 10, Blue 13, Green 14, Red 15, Yellow 16, Magenta 17, Cyan 18) were extracted from centred squares with 35 mm of side, to represent the average of each patch. Reflectance spectra were also extracted from five different small areas (squares with 1 mm of side) of each patch (in the middle and in the four corners), to see if the colour within each coloured patch is uniform. Reflectance data were extracted as well from centred squares with 8 mm of side in order to resemble the common area of analysis of a contact colorimeter. The spectra extracted from each coloured patch were then used to calculate the colorimetric values of the same areas, using the CIELAB system with the CIE illuminant D65 (natural daylight) and the CIE 1964 standard observer (10°). From the L*, a* and b* coordinates, the colour-difference parameter, ΔE, was also calculated using the CIEDE2000 formula [17].

2.3   Apparatus

IFAC-CNR's hyper-spectral imaging spectroscopic measurements were carried out in the 400-960 nm range with the hyper-spectral scanner designed and assembled at IFAC-CNR. The system is based on a prism-grating-prism line-spectrograph ImSpector^{TM} V10E (SpecIm Ltd), with a 30 μm slit, which is connected to a high sensitivity CCD camera (Hamamatsu ORCA-ERG). The line-segment analysed is focused on the entrance slit of the spectrograph by means of a telecentric lens (Opto-Engineering Srl), which performs a parallel projection of the points falling within its working distance (3 cm deep at 23 cm from the lens), thus avoiding perspective displacements when the imaged points lie on a not perfectly planar surface. Illumination of the line-segment is made by two Schott-Fostec fibre-optic line-lights equipped with focusing lenses that are fixed to the scan-head and symmetrically project their beams at 45° angles with respect to the normal direction at the imaged surface (0°/2x45° observation/illumination geometry). Light is supplied by a QTH-lamp. The mechanical system can scan a maximum area of about 1 x 1 m^2, with 20 vertical line-scan stripes. The spatial sampling rate guarantees a spatial sampling of ~ 11 points/mm (~ 279 ppi) and resolution better than 2 lines/mm at 50% of contrast reduction. The system's spectral sampling is about ~ 1.2 nm and resolution is ~ 2.5 nm at half maximum. The scan is carried out in the "free-run" mode: the vertical movement runs freely at a constant speed of 1.5 mm/sec, while the acquisition of the camera images proceeds independently at a constant rate of 15 frames/sec. [18,19,20]

IP-UEF's hyper-spectral imaging spectroscopic measurements were carried with IP-UEF line scanning based spectral imaging system that uses a SpecIm VNIR camera (with a sCMOS detector) working in the 400-1000 nm range. The system consists of moving the camera and illumination unit together while the sample lies over a table with adjustable height. Illumination is carried out by QTH lamps on both sides of the camera, with a 0°/2x45° observation/illumination geometry. 240 spectral bands were recorded with a 2.8 nm nominal spectral resolution. The spatial resolution used is of 0.2 mm. 1032 spatial pixels were recorded with every line leading to about 0.23 mm resolution in spatial direction. Reflectance data were extracted in the 400-1000 nm range, with a 5 nm step. Colour calculations were performed in the 400-780 range, also with a 5 nm step. [21]

3   Results and Discussion

With respect to handing and organisation of data, the guide-lines provided to each group were of high significance since they allowed to compare information extracted from areas of the same size (considering size in millimetres, and not in pixels) and with approximate positions. Moreover, since each group has its own software to handle data, it was also important to prepare the information in a way easily accessible for the two research groups.

Both hyper-spectral systems provided high-quality RGB images of the ColorChecker (Fig. 1). To discuss the results obtained, in terms of spectral and colorimetric data, five coloured patches are presented: Blue 13, Green 14, Red 15, Yellow 16 and Magenta 17 (patches are numbered from left to right, and from up to bottom in the ColorChecker chart).

Fig. 1. RGB colour images of the X-Rite® ColorChecker chart reconstructed from the hyperspectral file-cube from IFAC-CNR (left) and IP-UEF (right)

To check the uniformity of the colours in the chart, the comparison between reflectance spectra extracted from 1 mm x 1 mm areas at different places of each coloured patch showed that, although not completely homogenous, there is a satisfactory degree of uniformity within the respective patch (Fig. 2). Not only that, spectra from such a small area present fairly good resolution. This was observed for both hyperspectral systems. When comparing the data obtained with the different systems, spectra are similar with the exception of the lower and higher wavelengths that show differences in intensity (*ca.* 0.08 in reflectance factor) and shape.

The colorimetric values are also in agreement between the different areas of each patch, apart from some small variations of 1-2 units in the L*, a* and b* coordinates that can be observed and which indicate that colours are not totally homogenous. On the other hand, when comparing the colorimetric values between the two hyperspectral systems, L* and a* values are similar but significant differences are observed for the b* coordinate (Table 1). In fact, for the blue colour, an average b* value of -41.8 was obtained with IFAC-CNR's system, while an average b* value of -46.8 was obtained with IP-UEF's system. A similar difference was observed with the red colour that presents average b* values of 26.5 and 19.0, respectively.

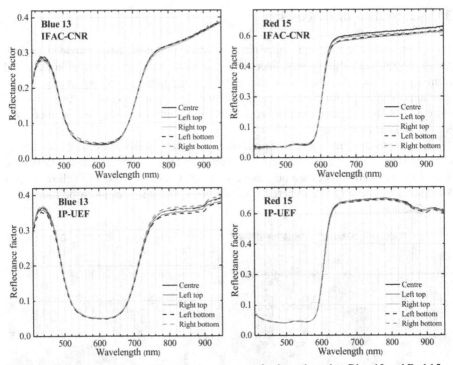

Fig. 2. Reflectance spectra from 1 mm x 1 mm areas of coloured patches Blue 13 and Red 15 from the X-Rite® ColorChecker chart extracted from the hyper-spectral file-cube from IFAC-CNR and IP-UEF

Within the same coloured patch, reflectance spectra extracted from areas of different size are the same. As a matter of fact, the spectral resolution of spectra extracted from areas of 8 mm x 8 mm and 1 mm x 1mm (high spatial resolution) was proved to be as good as that of spectra extracted from the average areas of 35 mm x 35 mm, showing that there is a good compromise between spectral and spatial resolution for both systems (Figs. 3 and 4). However, the increase of spatial resolution to 1 pixel had an obvious influence in the spectral resolution, particularly in the case of IFAC-CNR's system, for which spectra present more noise probably due to the higher rate of spectral acquisition step and spatial resolution (than that of IP-UEF system). When comparing between systems, as was already noticed, spectra are identical with the exception of differences in intensity (*ca.* 0.07 in reflectance factor for the magenta colour, and 0.04 for the green and yellow colours) and shape observed at the lower and higher wavelengths.

Table 1. Colour coordinates from 1 mm x 1 mm areas of patches Blue 13 and Red 15 from the X-Rite® ColorChecker chart extracted from the hyper-spectral file-cube from IFAC-CNR and IP-UEF

	Blue 13			Red 15		
	L*	a*	b*	L*	a*	b*
IFAC-CNR	32,3	12,3	-42,4	41,9	42,5	26,1
	32,4	11,6	-41,4	42,8	42,2	28,1
	32,7	11,7	-41,7	42,3	42,0	24,8
	33,7	10,6	-40,9	43,0	42,0	27,8
IP-UEF	36,4	12,6	-46,5	43,8	44,4	18,5
	37,0	12,6	-47,0	43,9	44,1	18,3
	36,1	12,7	-46,3	43,8	44,8	19,4
	36,7	12,8	-47,2	43,8	44,7	19,4

Regarding the colorimetric values, they are also constant within the same coloured patch (only some small variations of 1-2 units in the L*, a* and b* coordinates can be observed), regardless of the area size (Table 2). However, when comparing the L*, a* and b* values from both systems, again the most notable difference is observed for the b* coordinate and especially for the magenta colour (together with the blue and red ones, already discussed). Indeed, considering the 35 mm x 35 mm area, for the magenta colour, a b* value of -13.9 was obtained with IFAC-CNR's system, while a b* value of -20.2 was obtained with IP-UEF's system. It is possible to conclude that the colours presenting bigger differences for the b* coordinate are the magenta, bluish and reddish ones (ΔE 3.7, 3.8 and 5.1, respectively), which are at both ends of the visible range, where the reflectance spectra also present variations. On the other hand, colours as green and yellow present a higher similarity between the values obtained with the different systems, with only variations of 2-3 units in the L*, a* and b* coordinates (ΔE 3.3 and 2.5, respectively).

Table 2. Colour coordinates of patches Green 14, Yellow 16 and Magenta 17 from the X-Rite® ColorChecker chart extracted from the hyper-spectral file-cube from IFAC-CNR and IP-UEF

	Size of square side	Green 14			Yellow 16			Magenta 17		
		L*	a*	b*	L*	a*	b*	L*	a*	b*
IFAC-CNR	35 mm	55,5	-35,5	32,4	80,5	4,0	78,4	52,6	44,2	-13,9
	8 mm	55,7	-35,9	32,6	80,7	4,0	79,0	52,6	44,4	-14,0
	1 mm	55,6	-35,8	32,6	80,6	4,1	78,7	52,6	44,5	-14,1
	1 px	55,5	-36,1	33,6	80,7	3,7	81,6	52,4	44,0	-12,2
IP-UEF	35 mm	59,1	-33,2	30,3	82,6	6,9	75,8	54,6	45,1	-20,2
	8 mm	59,1	-33,3	30,3	82,7	6,8	75,6	54,7	45,1	-20,3
	1 mm	59,0	-33,3	30,2	82,5	6,9	75,3	54,6	45,0	-20,3
	1 px	59,1	-33,2	30,1	82,5	6,9	75,6	54,7	44,9	-20,0

The differences observed at the lower and higher wavelengths can be due to the different ways in which each system was designed, as well as to their sensitivities and distinct technical features. The optical module of IFAC-CNR's scanner has been optimised to reduce internal stray-light through the use of additional optical filters. Thus, the spectral variations observed near the 400 nm end are very likely due to differences in the method used to compensate for the internal stray-light. Moreover, at the higher wavelengths of the spectrographs small errors can arise when blue targets are measured due to the insufficient rejection of the SpecIm filter that blocks the second order visible spectrum. However, for a better understating of these differences, further work is needed, which goes beyond the scope of the present contribution.

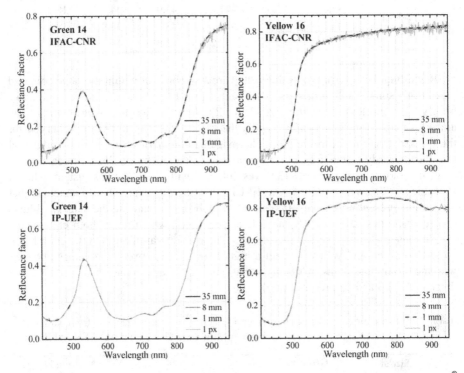

Fig. 3. Reflectance spectra from coloured patches Green 14 and Yellow 16 from the X-Rite® ColorChecker chart extracted from the hyper-spectral file-cube from IFAC-CNR and IP-UEF (data in millimetres correspond to the size of side of the squares of analysis)

In general, the results obtained indicate that the colorimetric data acquired with the two hyper-spectral systems have to be carefully used, and they should be always reported together with the specification of the instrumentation and experimental setup used, mostly if it will be necessary to compare results from both systems and for the same objects. On the other hand, the differences obtained between the two colour reproduction processes can be relevant to provide information about the way the human observer would see colour in pictures imaged by each system. Considering that magenta, blue and red colours show the most significant differences, if colours such as green, orange and yellow, which show small unnoticeable changes, are imaged with each system they should look like the same to the human eye. In this case, both hyper-spectral systems would be equally useful to image an artwork.

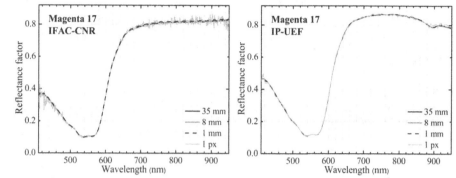

Fig. 4. Reflectance spectra from coloured patch Magenta 17 from the X-Rite® ColorChecker chart extracted from the hyper-spectral file-cube from IFAC-CNR and IP-UEF (data in millimetres correspond to the size of side of the squares of analysis)

4   Conclusions and Future Research

This paper presents the preliminary results obtained from the comparison of data from an X-Rite® ColorChecker chart acquired with different hyper-spectral systems developed by two different groups that are participating in the COSCH WG1 Round Robin Test. Both systems showed very good spectral and spatial resolution, being able to acquire information from areas as small as 1 mm x 1 mm and obtain spectra of high quality. Moreover, the spectral results from the different systems were in agreement, with the exception of information at the lower and higher wavelengths that show some variations. Consequently, colorimetric values can be comparable for colours such as green and yellow, but are not so accurate for the magenta, bluish and reddish hues that present more significant differences with respect to the b* coordinate. In order to further understand these differences and which system, or if both, is reproducing colour in a more accurate way, after the Round Robin Test is finished, the results obtained from the different participants will be all compared and further analysed. Future calculations should be performed as well, to provide numerical results for the comparison between the spectral shapes obtained with the two systems, to assess which range of wavelengths is the most comparable or different. Also, this approach to the use of an X-Rite® ColorChecker chart as a form of evaluating colour accuracy of hyper-spectral systems revealed that each coloured patch is not completely homogenous. In fact, data extracted from sub-areas in different places within the same patch showed small variations. This is an important aspect to take into consideration whenever the ColorChecker chart is used to assess the accuracy of a system's colour reproduction process.

Acknowledgements. Part of this work was supported by the European Cooperation in Science and Technology, COST Action TD120: Colour and Space in Cultural Heritage (COSCH, www.cosch.info). Tatiana Vitorino is sincerely grateful to the COST Action TD1201 Management Committee for approving the short-term mission COST-STSM-ECOST-STSM-TD1201-310814-048809, and to Vanessa Otero and Cristina Montagner for essential support.

References

1. Bianchi, C.: Making online monuments more accessible through interface design. In: MacDonald, L. (ed.) Digital Heritage – Applying Digital Imaging to Cultural Heritage, pp. 445–466. Butterworth-Heinemann (2006)
2. Saunders, D.: High-quality Imaging at the National Gallery: Origins, Implementation and Applications. Computers and the Humanities **31**, 153–167 (1998)
3. Beckett, N. et al.: Imaging historical architectural sites for conservation. In: MacDonald, L. (ed.) Digital Heritage – Applying Digital Imaging to Cultural Heritage, pp. 377–410. Butterworth-Heinemann (2006)
4. Cucci, C. et al.: A hyper-spectral scanner for high quality image spectroscopy: Digital documentation and spectroscopic characterization of polychrome surfaces. In: ART 2011 - 10th International Conference on Non-destructive Investigations and Microanalysis for the Diagnostics and Conservation of Cultural and Environmental Heritage (2011)
5. Martinez, K. et al.: Ten years of art imaging research. In: Proceedings of the IEEE, vol. 90(1), pp. 28–41 (2002)
6. Antonioli, G. et al.: Spectrophotometric scanner for imaging of paintings and other works of art. In: Proceedings of CGIV 2004, pp. 219–224 (2004)
7. Liang, H.: Advances in Multispectral and Hyperspectral Imaging for Archaeology and Art Conservation. Applied Physics A **106**, 309–323 (2012)
8. Colantoni, P.: Analysis of multispectral images of paintings. In: 14th European Signal Processing Conference (EUSIPCO 2006), Florence, Italy (2006)
9. Burns, P.D., et al.: Error Propagation Analysis in Color Measurement and Imaging. Color Research and Application **22**(4), 280–289 (1997)
10. Kubik, M.: Hyperspectral imaging: A new technique for the non-invasive study of artworks. In: Creagh, D., Bradley, D. (eds.) Physical Techniques in the Study of Art, Archaeology and Cultural Heritage, pp. 199–259. Elsevier (2007)
11. Boochs, F. et al.: Towards optimal spectral and spatial documentation of cultural heritage. COSCH – An interdisciplinary action in the cost framework. In: International Archives of the Photogrammetry, Remote Sensing and Spatial Information Sciences, vol. XL-5/W2, pp. 109–113 (2013)
12. Fischer, C., Kakoulli, I.: Multispectral and hyperspectral imaging technologies in conservation: current research and potential applications. Reviews in Conservation **7**, 3–16 (2006)
13. Hagen, N. et al.: Snapshot Advantage: A Review of the Light Collection Improvement for Parallel High-dimensional Measurement Systems. Optical Engineering **51**(11), 111702. 1–111702.7 (2012)
14. Berns, R.S.: The Science of Digitizing Paintings for Color-Accurate Image Archives: A Review. Journal of Imaging Science and Technology **45**(4), 305–325 (2001)
15. McCamy, C.S., et al.: A Color-Rendition Chart. Journal of Applied Photographic Engineering **2**(3), 95–99 (1976)

16. ColorChecker Classic for Image Reproduction - X-Rite. http://xritephoto.com/ph_product_overview.aspx?ID=1192
17. Sharma, G., et al.: The CIEDE2000 Color-Difference Formula: Implementation Notes, Supplementary Test Data, and Mathematical Observations. Color Research and Application **30**(1), 21–30 (2005)
18. Cucci, C. et al.: Open issues in hyperspectral imaging for diagnostics on paintings: when high spectral and spatial resolution turns into data redundancy. In: Salimbeni, R., Pezzati, L. (eds.) Proc. of SPIE, vol. 8084, O3A: Optics for Arts, Architecture, and Archaeology III, 739106, pp. 80848.1–80848.10 (2011)
19. Cucci, C. et al.: Extending hyper-spectral imaging from vis to nir spectral regions: a novel scanner for the in-depth analysis of polychrome surfaces. In: Pezzati, L., Targowski, P. (eds.) Proc. of SPIE, vol. 8790, O3A: Optics for Arts, Architecture, and Archaeology IV, pp. 879009-1– 879009-9 (2013)
20. Vitorino, T., Casini, A., Cucci, C., Melo, M.J., Picollo, M., Stefani, L.: Hyper-spectral acquisition on historically accurate reconstructions of red organic lakes. In: Elmoataz, A., Lezoray, O., Nouboud, F., Mammass, D. (eds.) ICISP 2014. LNCS, vol. 8509, pp. 257–264. Springer, Heidelberg (2014)
21. Hirvonen, T., et al.: A Wide Spectral Range Reflectance and Luminescence Imaging System. Sensors **13**, 14500–14510 (2013)

Estimating the Colors of Paintings

Sérgio M.C. Nascimento[1(✉)], João M.M. Linhares[1], Catarina A.R. João[1],
Kinjiro Amano[2], Cristina Montagner[3], Maria J. Melo[3], and Marcia Vilarigues[3]

[1] Centre of Physics, Campus de Gualtar, University of Minho,
4710-057 Braga, Portugal
{smcn,jlinhares}@fisica.uminho.pt, car.joao89@gmail.com
[2] School of Electrical and Electronic Engineering, University of Manchester,
Manchester M13 9PL, UK
kinjiro.amano@manchester.ac.uk
[3] Department of Conservation and Restauration, Faculdade de Ciências e
Tecnologia, Universidade Nova de Lisboa, Caparica, Portugal
moncri@hotmail.it, mjm@dq.fct.unl.pt, mgv@fct.unl.pt

Abstract. Observers can adjust the spectrum of illumination on paintings for optimal viewing experience. But can they adjust the colors of paintings for the best visual impression? In an experiment carried out on a calibrated color monitor images of four abstract paintings obtained from hyperspectral data were shown to observers that were unfamiliar with the paintings. The color volume of the images could be manipulated by rotating the volume around the axis through the average (a^*, b^*) point for each painting in CIELAB color space. The task of the observers was to adjust the angle of rotation to produce the best subjective impression from the paintings. It was found that the distribution of angles selected for data pooled across paintings and observers could be described by a Gaussian function centered at $10°$, i.e. very close to the original colors of the paintings. This result suggest that painters are able to predict well what compositions of colors observers prefer.

Keywords: Colors of paintings · Color vision · Art visualization · Color rendering · Aesthetics

1 Introduction

The visual impression from paintings and other artworks is dramatically influenced by the energy and color of the illumination. It has been shown empirically that an ideal illumination spectrum can be spectrally tuned for each painting [1-4]. Although a light source with a correlated color temperature close to that of skylight appears to be suited for most of the paintings [3] it is still unclear what determines observers' preferences. These results are relevant for museums to optimize their art displays but also for virtual displaying of artworks.

What chromatic composition would be obtained if instead of spectrally tuning the illumination observers tune the colors of the paintings by some global transformation? How close that composition would be to the original one produced by the artist?

A. Trémeau et al. (Eds.): CCIW 2015, LNCS 9016, pp. 236–242, 2015.
DOI: 10.1007/978-3-319-15979-9_22

The aim of this work was to investigate which composition of colors selected from a large set of possibilities observers prefer for each artwork. Abstract paintings were digitalized by hyperspectral imaging and their spectral reflectance estimated for each pixel. The transformation of colors selected was a rotation of the color volume. Thus, the original colors of the paintings could be changed by rotating the corresponding color volume around the axis defined by the average color in CIELAB color space. In an experiment on a calibrated color monitor observers that were unfamiliar with the paintings adjusted the rotation angle to obtain the preferred composition. Results indicate that they select a composition very close to the original one.

2   Methods

2.1   Paintings

Four paintings from Amadeo de Souza-Cardoso (1887-1918) were selected for testing. Images of the paintings are shown in Figure 1. The paintings belong to the collection of Centro de Arte Moderna da Fundação Calouste Gulbenkian, Lisboa, Portugal. These paintings were selected because they are of abstract nature and chromatically rich (see Figure 1).

2.2   Stimulus

The paintings were digitalized at the museum with a hyperspectral imaging system. Detailed description of the system and methodology is given elsewhere [2]. Only the essential information is repeated here. The digitalization was from 400 to 720 nm at 10 nm intervals using a fast-tunable liquid-crystal filter (Varispec, model VS-VIS2-10-HC-35-SQ, Cambridge Research & Instrumentation, Inc.,Massachusetts) and a low-noise digital camera (Hamamatsu, mod. C4742-95-12ER, Hamamatsu Photonics K. K., Japan), with a spatial resolution of 1344 × 1024 pixels and 12 bit intensity. The spectral reflectance of each pixel of the paintings was estimated from a gray reference surface present close to the painting at the time of image acquisition. Illuminant spatial non-uniformities and angular variations in the system transmittance were compensated using measurements of a uniform surface imaged in the same location and under the same illuminating conditions as the paintings.

Stimuli were images of the paintings transformed by a variable chromatic rotation around an axis in the in CIELAB color space. First, the painting was simulated illuminated by D_{65} and the corresponding coordinates of each pixel in CIELAB space were computed. Figure 2 shows for illustrative purposes the tridimensional representation of the top right painting shown in Figure 1. The chromatic center of this volume was then computed and an axis parallel to the L* dimension through this point adopted as the axis of the chromatic rotation. In the experiment the observer could adjust the angle of rotation by actuating on a joy-pad. The rotational step could be selected by the observers to be 1° or 6°.

The paintings were presented on the computer screen with an average luminance of 20 cd/m^2. The viewing distance was 1 m and the paintings subtended on the screen a visual angle of about 10° ×10°.

Fig. 1. Images of the four paintings tested. They are from Amadeo de Souza-Cardoso (1887-1918) and belong to the collection of Centro de Arte Moderna da Fundação Calouste Gulbenkian, Lisboa, Portugal. The stimuli for the experiments were images of the paintings derived from hyperspectral imaging data collected at the museum.

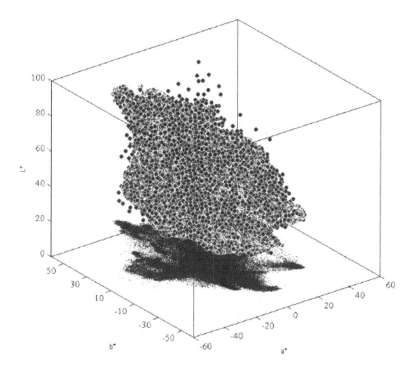

Fig. 2. Representation of the CIELAB color volume of the top right painting shown in Figure 1. In the experiment the observers could vary the angle of rotation of the color volume around the axis through the average ($a*$, $b*$) in CIELAB space and view the corresponding image on the screen.

2.3   Apparatus

The images were displayed on a CRT monitor (GDM-F520, Sony Corp., Japan) controlled by a video board (ViSaGe Visual Stimulus Generator; Cambridge Research Systems, Rochester, Kent, UK) in 24-bits-per-pixel true-color mode. The monitor was calibrated in color and luminance with a telespectroradiometer (PR-650 SpectraScan Colorimeter; Photo Research, Chatsworth, CA). The stimuli were displayed with half of the original spatial resolution and a frequency of 80 Hz.

2.4   Procedure

In the beginning of each trial a painting selected at random from the set of four was presented with its colors rotated in CIELAB color space by angle selected at random in the range +180° - -180°. The task of the observer was to adjust the angle of the chromatic rotation such that the painting produced the best subjective impression. For the adjustment the observers used a joy-pad. No indication was given to the observers about the effect of the adjustment, they just perceive a change of the colors of the paintings. There was no time limit for each trial. Experiments were carried out in a darkened room. In each session each painting was tested 3 times in a random order. Each observer performed a total of 3 sessions.

2.5 Observers

There were 7 normal observers all unaware of the purpose of the experiment and without previous knowledge of the paintings to be tested. They also did not have any formal artistic education. Each had normal or corrected-to-normal acuity. Their color
vision was teste with Rayleigh anomaloscope (Oculus Heidelberg Multi Color), Cambridge Colour Test[5], Ishihara plates and the Color Assessment and Diagnosis
Test[6]. The experiments were performed in accordance with the tenets of the Decla-
ration of Helsinki, and informed consent was obtained from all observers.

3 Results

Figure 3 shows the histogram of the responses for two of the paintings tested with
data pooled across observers. The histogram on the left corresponds to the painting
represented on the bottom right of Figure 1 and the histogram on the right to the
painting represented on the top left of the same figure. Figure 4 shows the histogram
of the responses of observers with data pooled across observers and paintings. The
horizontal axis represents the angular rotation of the adjustments in degree. The vertical axis represents the number of times each angle was selected as producing the
best subjective impression. Bin size is 20°. In Figure 4 the solid line represents a
Gaussian fit to the data with a maximum at 10° and FWHW of 80°.

The data shows that observers have a clear common preference which is very close
(within about 10°) to the original composition. As they were unfamiliar with the
paintings and did not have any formal artistic education, the selection of colors may
be determined by some fundamental property of the visual system.

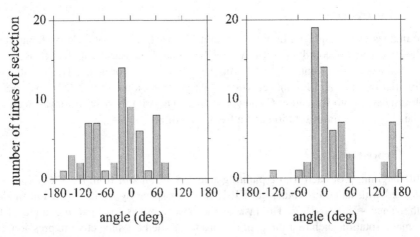

Fig. 3. Histogram of observers' responses based on data pooled across observers for two of the
paintings tested. The histogram on the left corresponds to the painting represented on the bottom
right of Figure 1 and the histogram on the right to the painting represented on the top left of Figure
1. The horizontal axis represents angular rotation and the vertical axis represents the number of
times each angle was selected as producing the best visual impression. Bin size is 20°.

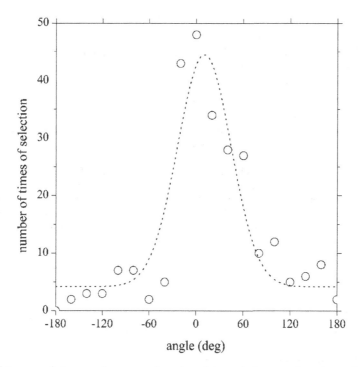

Fig. 4. Histogram of observers' responses based on data pooled across observers and paintings. The horizontal axis represents angular rotation and the vertical axis represents the number of times each angle was selected as producing the best visual impression. Bin size is 20°. The solid line represents a Gaussian fit to the data with a maximum at 10° and FWHW of 80°.

4   Discussion and Conclusions

In the psychophysical experiment described here observers adjusted the chromatic composition of unfamiliar abstract paintings to obtain the best subjective visual impression. The results show that they clearly prefer a chromatic composition very close to the original.

The chromatic transformation selected to manipulate the colors of the paintings was a rotation of the color volume around the axis through the average color of the paintings. Although other kinds of global chromatic transformations could have been selected this choice is convenient as it is simple to implement, provides a continuous change of each color, avoids gamut problems like those posed by volume expansion-compression and does not produce spatial artifacts like those posed by permuting the colors of the palette.

What information are observers using to select a specific chromatic composition for each painting that is unfamiliar? They could be using memory color based on realistic elements of the paintings. The representations of real elements, e.g. windows, guitar, face, among others, is so distorted in these painting that it is unlikely they can be seen as chromatic references.

Several studies have been exploring quantitatively the relationships between artworks and the visual system [7] and, in particular, to what extent they reproduce properties of natural scenes [8]. The properties of the paintings tested here do not have evident similarities with natural scenes thus it is unlikely they underlie observers' choices. In any case, the findings reported here suggest that some fundamental property of vision is intuitively known by painters.

Acknowledgements. This work was supported by the Centro de Física of Minho University, by FEDER through the COMPETE Program and by the Portuguese Foundation for Science and Technology (FCT) in the framework of the projects PTDC/MHC-PCN/4731/2012 and PTDC/EAT-EAT/113612/2009, by and the COST-Action TD1201, Colour and Space in Cultural Heritage (COSCH) through Short Term Scientific Missions (STSM): "Hyperspectral imaging on historical manuscripts and natural scenes" (COST-STSM-TD1201- 010813-032699, 2013). Cristina Montagner was supported by the grant SFRH/BD/66488/2009. The authors are grateful to all team members of CAM - Centro de Arte Moderna da Fundação Gulbenkian for their collaboration, in particular to director Isabel Carlos and curator Ana Vasconcelos e Melo.

References

1. Pinto, P.D., Linhares, J.M., Carvalhal, J.A., Nascimento, S.M.: Psychophysical estimation of the best illumination for appreciation of Renaissance paintings. Vis Neurosci **23**, 669–674 (2006)
2. Pinto, P.D., Linhares, J.M.M., Nascimento, S.M.C.: Correlated color temperature preferred by observers for illumination of artistic paintings. Journal of the Optical Society of America A-Optics Image Science and Vision **25**, 623–630 (2008)
3. Nascimento, S.M.C., Masuda, O.: Best lighting for visual appreciation of artistic paintings-experiments with real paintings and real illumination. Journal of the Optical Society of America A-Optics Image Science and Vision **31**, A214–A219 (2014)
4. Liu, A., Tuzikas, A., Zukauskas, A., Vaicekauskas, R., Vitta, P., Shur, M.: Cultural Preferences to Color Quality of Illumination of Different Artwork Objects Revealed by a Color Rendition Engine. Photonics Journal, IEEE **5**, 6801010–6801010 (2013)
5. Regan, B.C., Reffin, J.P., Mollon, J.D.: Luminance Noise and the Rapid-Determination of Discrimination Ellipses in Color Deficiency. Vision Research **34**, 1279–1299 (1994)
6. Rodriguez-Carmona, M.: Variability of Chromatic Sensitivity: fundamental studies and clinical applications. vol. PhD. City University London (2006)
7. Graham, D.J., Redies, C.: Statistical regularities in art: Relations with visual coding and perception. Vision Research **50**, 1503–1509 (2010)
8. Graham, D.J., Field, D.J.: Statistical regularities of art images and natural scenes: Spectra, sparseness and nonlinearities. Spatial Vision **21**, 149–164 (2008)

Author Index

Printed in the United States
By Bookmasters